Pro Android Games

Vladimir Silva

Apress®

Pro Android Games

ISBN-13 (pbk): 978-1-4302-2647-5

ISBN-13 (electronic): 978-1-4302-2648-2

Printed and bound in the United States of America 9 8 7 6 5 4 3 2 1

President and Publisher: Paul Manning
Lead Editor: Steve Anglin, Douglas Pundick
Technical Reviewer: Kunal Mittal and Vikram Goyal
Editorial Board: Clay Andres, Steve Anglin, Mark Beckner, Ewan Buckingham, Gary Cornell, Jonathan Gennick, Jonathan Hassell, Michelle Lowman, Matthew Moodie, Duncan Parkes, Jeffrey Pepper, Frank Pohlmann, Douglas Pundick, Ben Renow-Clarke, Dominic Shakeshaft, Matt Wade, Tom Welsh
Coordinating Editor: Fran Parnell
Copy Editors: Heather Lang and Marilyn Smith
Formatter: Nancy Wright
Compositor: LaurelTech
Indexer: BIM Indexing and Proofreading Services
Artist: April Milne
Cover Designer: Anna Ishchenko

Distributed to the book trade worldwide by Springer-Verlag New York, Inc., 233 Spring Street, 6th Floor, New York, NY 10013. Phone 1-800-SPRINGER, fax 201-348-4505, e-mail orders-ny@springer-sbm.com, or visit http://www.springeronline.com.

For information on translations, please e-mail info@apress.com, or visit http://www.apress.com.

Apress and friends of ED books may be purchased in bulk for academic, corporate, or promotional use. eBook versions and licenses are also available for most titles. For more information, reference our Special Bulk Sales–eBook Licensing web page at http://www.apress.com/info/bulksales.

The source code for this book is available to readers at http://www.apress.com. You will need to answer questions pertaining to this book in order to successfully download the code.

Contents at a Glance

Contents

About the Author

■ **Vladimir Silva** holds a master's degree in computer science from Middle Tennessee State University. He worked for four years for IBM as a research engineer, where he acquired extensive experience in distributed and grid computing research. Vladimir is a highly technical, focus-based individual and team player. He belongs to two National Honor Societies and has published many computer science articles for IBM. He is the author of *Grid Computing for Developers* (Charles River Media, 2005) and *Practical Eclipse RCP Projects* (Apress, February 2009).

About the Technical Reviewer

 **Kunal Mittal** serves as executive director of technology at Sony Pictures Entertainment, where he is responsible for the SOA and Identity Management programs. He provides a centralized engineering service to different lines of business and consults on the open-source technologies, content management, collaboration, and mobile strategies.

Kunal is an entrepreneur who helps startups define their technology strategy, product roadmap and development plans. With strong relations with several development partners worldwide, he is able to help startups and even large companies to build appropriate development partnerships. He generally works in an advisor or consulting CTO capacity, and serves actively in the project management and technical architect functions.

He has authored and edited several books and articles on J2EE, cloud computing, and mobile technologies. He holds a master's degree in software engineering and is an instrument-rated private pilot.

Introduction

Pro Android Games will help you to create the best games for the Android platform. There are plenty of books out there that tackle this subject, but only this book gives you a unique perspective by showing you how easy it is to bring native PC games to the platform with minimum effort. This is done using real-world examples and source code on each chapter. Keep in mind that, before you dig into this book, you will need a solid foundation in Java and ANSI C. I have made a great effort to explain the most complicated concepts as clearly and as simply as possible with a combination of graphics and sample code. The source code provided for each chapter will help you understand the concepts in detail and make the most of your time as a mobile game developer.

What Software Will You Need?

To make the most of this book, you will need the following tools:

A Windows or Linux PC with a Java SDK Properly Installed

I guess this is kind of obvious, as most development for Android is done in Java. Note that I mentioned a Java SDK, not JRE. The SDK is required because of the JNI header files and command line tools used throughout the latter chapters.

Eclipse IDE and Android SDK Properly Installed

Eclipse is the de facto IDE for Android development. I have used Eclipse Galileo to create the workspace for the book; nevertheless, Eclipse Ganymede should work as well.

Need a Development IDE?

Even though Eclipse Galileo has been used to create the code workspace, you can use your favorite IDE. Of course, that will require a bit of extra setup. You can get Eclipse Galileo from

http://www.eclipse.org/.

For instructions on how to set up the Android SDK with other IDEs, such as IntelliJ or a basic editor, see http://developer.android.com/guide/developing/other-ide.html.

Android SDK properly installed means two things:

1. You must install the Android SDK plug-ins for Eclipse:

    a. From the IDE main menu click Help Install New Software.

    b. Click the Add button to add a new Site and enter:

        • A name: Android SDK

        • A location: https://dl-ssl.google.com/android/eclipse/. Click OK.

    c. Select the Android SK from the Available Software dialog and follow the easy installation instructions from the wizard.

2. You must install the Android SDK: It can be downloaded from the Android site above. Keep in mind that Eclipse must be told about the location of the Android SDK. From the main IDE menu click Window Preferences. On the left navigation menu select Android and enter the SDK location (see Figure 1). I have used SDK 1.5 because that was the latest available by the time of this writing; however, the code in this book has been tested with SDK 1.6 and 2.0 (see the SDK compatibility section for details).

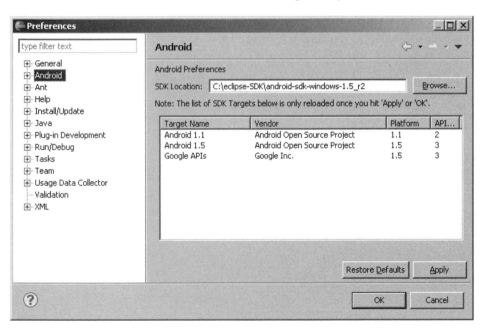

Figure 1. *Android SDK configuration dialog in Eclipse Galileo*

GNU C Compiler for ARM Processors

A GNU C compiler is required for the hybrid games in the book. These games combine Java code with a native core library, hence the need for a C compiler that targets the mobile ARM processor. The compiler used in this book and detailed in Chapter 1 is the Code Sourcery GNU G++ Toolkit. You are not bound, however, to use this compiler; as a matter of fact, you can use any C compiler capable of generating ARM code, including the Android Native Development Kit (NDK).

Chapter Source

This is an optional tool but it will help you greatly to understand the concepts as you move along. I have made my best effort to describe each chapter as simply as possible. Nevertheless, some of the games (especially Wolf 3D and Doom) have very large core engines written in C (100K lines for Doom), which are poorly commented and very hard to understand. All in all you will see how easily these great languages (Java and C) can be combined with minimal effort. Get the companion source for the book from the publisher at http://www.apress.com. It was built using Eclipse Galileo.

What Makes This Book Unique?

I think it is important for the reader to understand my goal with this manuscript and what I believe sets this book apart. Even though Java is the primary development language for Android, Google has realized the need for hybrid Java/C development if Android is to succeed as a gaming platform, so much so that they released the Native Development Kit (NDK). Google is realizing the need to support C development to catch up with the overwhelming number of native games written for other mobile platforms like the iPhone. PC games have been around for decades (mostly written in C), and by using a simple ARM C compiler, you could potentially bring thousands of PC games to the Android Platform. This is what makes this book unique. Why translate 100k lines of painfully complicated code from C to Java if you can just combine both languages in an elegant manner with significant savings on time and money? My book will help you to do just that. This is my goal and what makes this book stand out. In the other hand, this book also includes chapters of pure Java games in a well-balanced layout to satisfy both the Java purist and the C lover in you.

Android SDK Compatibility

As a developer you may ask yourself about the SDK compatibility of the code in this book. This is an important question as new versions of the Android SDK come out frequently. By the time of this writing, Google released the Android SDK version 2.0. The code in this chapter has been tested with the following versions of the Android SDK:

- SDK version 2.0
- SDK version 1.6
- SDK version 1.5
- SDK version 1.0

The bottom line is that the code in this book will run in any version of the SDK from 2.0 to 1.0, and that was my intention all along.

SDK Changes for Version 1.6

Virtually nothing has changed from versions 1.5 to 1.6 of the platform when it comes to game development. For a detailed list of API changes in version 1.6, see

http://developer.android.com/sdk/RELEASENOTES.html.

This book has a well-balanced layout of pure Java and hybrid games, divided as follows:

Chapter 1

This chapter provides the first step to set up a Linux system for hybrid game compilation, including fetching the Android source, extracting device system libraries, setting up a custom compilation toolchain, custom compilation scripts, plus details on setting up the Eclipse IDE for use throughout the rest of the book.

Chapter 2

In this chapter you will learn how to combine Java and C code in an elegant manner by building a simple Java application on top of a native library. You will learn exciting concepts about the Java Native Interface (JNI) and the API used to combine Java and C in a single unit, including how to load native libraries, how to use the native keyword, how to generate the JNI headers, plus all about method signatures, Java arrays vs. C arrays, invoking Java methods, compiling and packing the product, and more.

Chapter 3

This chapter is the first in a series to explore pure Java gaming with a real-world game dubbed Space Blaster. The goal of this game is to maneuver (using your finger tips or the keyboard) a space ship through a field of meteors. This chapter will teach you how to build custom XML-based linear layout, how to use an abstract class and timer tasks to simulate a simple game loop, how to invalidate views within a non-UI thread, how to load sprites and sounds from the project resources, plus drawing techniques such as sprite animations, drawing simple objects, and setting style and color using the Paint object.

Chapter 4

Pure Java games continue in Chapter 4 with the arcade classic Asteroids. This chapter will teach you all about drawing polygon sprites on the Android canvas. This is a somewhat difficult technique due to the lack of polygon support in the Android API. The chapter relies on the high portability of the Java language to bring polygon code from the J2SE API into the Android API to ultimately create Asteroids. As you may have noticed, this is a mostly Polygon-based game. Other interesting topics include game life cycle steps, initialization, draw, and update physics, responding to key and touch events, plus testing on the device emulator.

Chapter 5

This chapter deals with 3D graphics with OpenGL. It presents a neat trick I stumbled on by coincidence that allows for mixing OpenGL API calls in both Java and C. This concept is illustrated by using the 3D cubes sample provided by Google to demonstrate OpenGL in pure Java and hybrid modes. This trick could open a new frontier of 3D development for Android with the potential to bring a large number of 3D PC games to the platform with enormous savings in development costs and time.

Chapter 6

This is the first chapter in a series of two, which are my personal favorites of this book. Here it brings the godfather of all PC 3D shooters to the Android platform—Wolfenstein 3D. Who would have thought that a PC game like this one could be brought to an Android mobile device with minimal effort? This chapter demonstrates how Java and C can coexist harmoniously and includes topics such as the basic game architecture (showing how the Java and C components fit together), resource handlers for sound, music, key and touch events, how to use JNI to cascade graphics information, video buffers, and sound/music requests back to Java, plus compilation and testing.

Chapter 7

Chapter 7 takes things to the next level with the ground-breaking game for the PC—Doom. Doom is arguably the greatest 3D game ever created and opened new frontiers in 3D graphics. The ultimate goal of this chapter is not to describe the game itself, but to show you how easy it is to bring a complex PC game like Doom to the Android platform. The proof? Doom is 100+K lines of C code and brought to Android with less than 200 lines of extra JNI API calls, plus the Java code required to build the mobile UI. This chapter shows that you don't have to translate 100K lines of C into Java but simply marry these two powerful languages in an elegant application. Consider the potential savings in development time and costs! This chapter is a must-read.

CHAPTER 1

■ ■ ■

Welcome to Android Gaming

Welcome to the world of *Android Games*! The goal of this book is to help you build the best games for the platform. As you work your way through the chapters, you will learn how to create two kinds of games: pure Java, and perhaps most interestingly, hybrid games that combine the elegant design of Java with the raw power of C for maximum performance. The ability to combine both Java and C in this way is what makes the games in this book unique, as Google does not support this kind of development. But you may ask, "Why even bother with hybrid games?" After all, Java provides all the APIs you need to build any kind of game. This is certainly true. However, there are thousands of games out there written in C that can be brought to Android by compiling the C core and wrapping a Java graphical user interface (GUI) using the Java Native Interface (JNI). In this book, you'll learn how to bring to the platform two of the great 3D shooter games for the PC: Wolfenstein 3D and Doom.

The bottom line? My goal is to bring to you the latest documented and undocumented secrets to building games for Android. Furthermore, if your plan is to port a PC game, this book will provide you with invaluable expertise to do so. But before we get started, there are some things you need to know to get the most from this book.

What Skills Do You Need?

In this book, I am targeting seasoned game developers, not only in Java, but also in C. This makes sense, as performance is critical in game development. Java provides elegant object-oriented capabilities, but only C gives you the power boost that game development needs. This is the best of both worlds in the palm of your hand. This book assumes you are familiar with Android, as well as Linux and shell scripting.

A Solid Foundation of Android

This book assumes that you already know the basics of Android development. For example, you need to know what activities, views, and layouts are. Consider the following fragment. If you understand what it does just by looking at it, then you are in good shape.

```
public class MainActivity extends Activity
{
    public void onCreate(Bundle savedInstanceState) {
        super.onCreate(savedInstanceState);
        setContentView(R.layout.main);
```

```
    }
}
```

This fragment defines the main activity or class that controls the life cycle of the application. The onCreate method will be called once when the application starts, and its job is to set the content layout or GUI for the application.

You should also have a basic understanding of how GUIs are created using XML. Look at the next fragment. Can you tell what it does?

```xml
<?xml version="1.0" encoding="utf-8"?>
<RelativeLayout
    xmlns:android="http://schemas.android.com/apk/res/android"
    android:layout_width="fill_parent"
    android:layout_height="fill_parent">

<ImageView android:id="@+id/doom_iv"
    android:layout_width="fill_parent"
    android:layout_height="fill_parent"
    android:background="@drawable/doom"
    android:focusableInTouchMode="true" android:focusable="true"/>

 <ImageButton android:id="@+id/btn_upleft"
        android:layout_width="wrap_content"
        android:layout_height="wrap_content"
        android:layout_alignParentBottom="true"
        android:layout_alignParentLeft="true"
        android:src="@drawable/img1" />
</RelativeLayout>
```

This code defines a relative layout. In a relative layout, widgets are placed relative to each other (sometimes overlapping). In this case, there is an image view that fills the entire screen. This image will display as the background the file called doom.png stored in the res/drawable folder of the project, and receive key and touch events. In the lower left of the screen, overlapping the image view, an image button with the ID btn_upleft will be displayed.

Need an Android Tutorial?

There are a lot of concepts related to Android development, and it is impossible to remember every detail about activities, views, and layouts. A handy place to access this information quickly is the Android tutorial:

http://developer.android.com/

The ultimate guide for Android developers—the latest releases, downloads, SDK Quick Start, version notes, native development tools, and previous releases—can be found here:

http://developer.android.com/sdk/1.6_r1/index.html

Throughout this book (especially in the chapters dealing with native code), I make extensive use of the Android Software Development Kit (SDK) command tools (for system administrator tasks). Thus, you should have a clear understanding of these tools, especially the Android Debug Bridge (adb). You should know how to do the following:

- Create an Android Virtual Device (AVD). An AVD encapsulates settings for a specific device configuration, such as firmware version and SD card path. Creating an AVD is really simple and can be done from the integrated development environment (IDE) by using the AVD Manager (accessed by clicking the black phone icon in the toolbar).

- Create an SD card file. Some of the games in later chapters have big files (5MB or more). To save space, the code stores all game files in the device SD card, and you should know how to create one. For example, to create a 100MB SD card file called sdcard.iso in your home directory, use this command:

```
$ mksdcard 100M $HOME/sdcard.iso
```

- Connect to the emulator. You need to do this for miscellaneous system administration, such as library extraction. To open a shell to the device, use this command:

```
$ adb shell
```

- Upload and pull files from the emulator. These tasks are helpful for storing and extracting game files to and from the device. Use these commands:

```
$ adb push <LOCAL_FILE> <DEVICE_FILE>
$ adb pull <DEVICE_FILE> <LOCAL_FILE>
```

■ **Note** Make sure the SDK_HOME/tools directory is added to your system PATH variable before running the commands to create an SD card file, connect to the emulator, or upload and pull files.

A Basic Knowledge of Linux and Shell Scripting

For the chapters dealing with the hybrid games, you will do the work within Ubuntu Linux, so dust off all those old Unix skills.

You should know the basic shell commands, such as those for listing files, installing software components (this can be tricky, depending on your Linux distribution), and basic system administration.

There are a few very simple shell scripts in this book. A basic knowledge of the bash shell is always helpful.

■ **Tip** If you need a refresher on your Linux and shell scripting, check out the following tutorial by Ashley J.S Mills: http://supportweb.cs.bham.ac.uk/documentation/tutorials/docsystem/build/tutorials/unixscripting/unixscripting.html.

What Software Tools Do You Need?

This chapter kicks things off by explaining how to set up your environment to compile hybrid (C/Java) games. This includes the development IDE (Eclipse) and the Android SDK, which are the tools required to build any basic Android application. This information is critical if you wish to learn how to combine the elegant object-oriented features of Java with the raw power of C for maximum performance, and it is required when we build Doom and Wolfenstein 3D in later chapters.

The following software is assumed to be already installed on your desktop:

- *VMware Player or Workstation*: This is required to run a Linux virtual machine (VM). VMware is available for free from the VMware download site (http://www.vmware.com/products/player/).

- *Ubuntu Linux VMware appliance*: This is the actual Linux operating system (OS), where all development will take place. If you don't have it, appliances are available for download for free from the VMware Virtual Appliance Marketplace (http://www.vmware.com/appliances/). Note that the appliance can be quite large (600+MB).

- *Eclipse*: This is the development IDE used to create your projects. Version 3.3 (Europa), 3.4 (Ganymende), or 3.5 (Galileo) will do.

- *Android SDK, properly configured*: At the time of this writing, the latest version of the SDK is 1.6. You'll use the Android Debug Bridge to connect to the device. Unzip the SDK to your favorite folder. Make sure you add the command-line tools to the PATH of your system. Edit the file .bashrc in your home directory, and modify the PATH environment variable: PATH=[PATH_TO_SDK]/tools:$PATH. Now you should be able to start and connect to the emulator from the command line. For a simple test, open a terminal and type adb. You should see the tool's help text on your screen.

- *Java JDK 5.0 or later*: This is required to run Eclipse and the Android SDK itself.

We'll begin by setting up the Ubuntu VM with the required software. Log in, and let's get started.

Setting Up Your Machine

To set up for building Android games, you need to install three software components on your Linux desktop:

- *Android source*: This contains the entire Android source code, plus C/C++/JNI header files used to build custom shared libraries.

- *Android native libraries*: These include things like the C runtime, math, XML, sound, and other libraries.

- *GNU C/C++ Toolchain for ARM processors*: This toolchain provides a C/C++ compiler and linker required to build native libraries, plus other useful tools, such as debuggers and profilers to aid in the debugging process.

You will also write two custom shell scripts that will save you a lot of headaches in the process of compiling a hybrid game.

Getting the Android Source

To store the source, Google uses a software versioning tool dubbed Gittool (available from http://git-scm.com/). Depending on your Ubuntu version, you may need to install some required packages to use it. To make sure everything is present, open a console and type the following command (all on one line):

```
$ sudo apt-get install git-core gnupg
  sun-java5-jdk flex bison gperf
  libsdl-dev libesd0-dev libwxgtk2.6-dev
  build-essential zip curl libncurses5-dev zlib1g-dev
```

This command will install the required packages to run Git. It requires system administrator (sysadmin) access.

■ **Tip** For more details on setting the Android source, see the Android Open Source Project at http://source.android.com/download.

You also need to install and configure a tool called repo, which is provided by Google to facilitate working with Git. Create a folder called bin in your home directory and download repo:

```
$ cd ~
$ mkdir bin
$ curl http://android.git.kernel.org/repo >~/bin/repo
$ chmod a+x ~/bin/repo
```

Add the bin folder to your search path with the following command:

```
$ export PATH=$HOME/bin:$PATH
```

Add this command to the file $HOME/.bashrc if you want to make it available every time you log in to your system.

Next, create a folder called mydroid in your home directory to store the source, and then change to it:

```
$ mkdir mydroid
$ cd mydroid
```

Finally, download the code:

```
$ repo init -u git://android.git.kernel.org/platform/manifest.git
$ repo sync
```

■ **Tip** The `repo init` command will download the master branch. To download other branches, use `repo init -u git://android.git.kernel.org/platform/manifest.git -b [BRANCH_NAME]`.

Now fetch some coffee, sit down, and wait. Depending on your network speed, the download can take up to one hour.

Once the source download completes, the folder tree should look as shown in Figure 1-1. The most important folder is called `bionic`. Bionic is the C library that supports the ARM and x86 instruction sets, and it is meant to run on an Android device. Bionic is part BSD and part Linux—its source code is a mix of BSD C library with custom Linux-specific bits used to deal with threads, processes, signals, and other things. This folder will provide most of the C header files used to build your shared libraries.

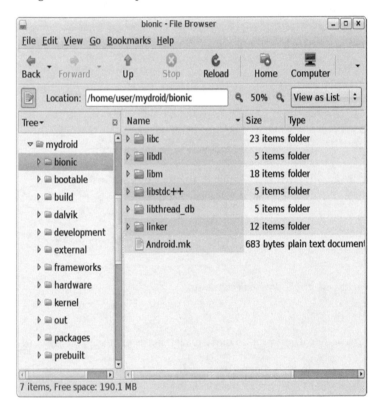

Figure 1-1. *Android source tree*

Extracting Native Android Libraries

The header libraries from the previous section provide the required files to compile the code. However, you also need the system image shared libraries for the linking process; that is, you need the *.so files stored in /system/lib in your device. For example, using the emulator shell, you can take a look at device file systems and some of the system libraries. Using the Android Debug Bridge (adb), connect to the device, and then run the df command to inspect the device file systems, as shown in the next fragment:

```
user@ubuntu:~$ adb shell
# df
```

```
/dev: 47284K total, OK used, 47284K available (block size 4096)
/sqlite_stmt_journals: 4096K total, OK used, 4096K available (block size 4096)
/system: 65536K total, 43496K used, 22040K available (block size 4096)
/data: 65536K total, 43004K used, 22532K available (block size 4096)
/cache: 65536K total, 1156K used, 64380K available (block size 4096)
/sdcard: 40309K total, 34114K used, 6195K available (block size 512)
```

```
# ls -l /system/lib
```

```
-rw-r--r-- root     root        9076 2008-11-20 00:10 libdl.so
-rw-r--r-- root     root      227480 2008-11-20 00:10 libc.so
-rw-r--r-- root     root       13368 2008-11-20 00:10 libthread_db.so
-rw-r--r-- root     root        9220 2008-11-20 00:10 libstdc++.so
-rw-r--r-- root     root      140244 2008-11-20 00:10 libm.so
-rw-r--r-- root     root       79192 2008-11-20 00:10 libz.so
-rw-r--r-- root     root       92572 2008-11-20 00:10 libexpat.so
-rw-r--r-- root     root      767020 2008-11-20 00:10 libcrypto.so
-rw-r--r-- root     root      155760 2008-11-20 00:10 libssl.so
[Other files...]
```

The df command displays information about the device file systems. From there, you can inspect the libraries stored in the device /system/lib folder. The ls command shows the most important libraries: C runtime (libc.so), Math runtime (libm.so), Gzip (libz.so), XML (libexpat.so), and others. These are the files you need to extract to the local system for the linking step. To extract them, you can create a simple script and use the emulator tool adb pull command to pull a file from the device to the local file system.

First, create a folder in your home directory to store these libraries:

```
$ mkdir -p $HOME/tmp/android/system/lib
$ cd $HOME/tmp/android/system/lib
```

Next, create a simple script to fetch the files from the device to the $HOME/tmp/android/system/lib folder. The bash script in Listing 1-1 loops through the library names and pulls the file from the device /system/lib folder to the local file system current directory.

Listing 1-1. *Script to Fetch Device Libraries from /system/lib into the Local File System*

```
#!/bin/bash

# Device libraries for Emulator 1.5+
# These are located in/system/lib
libs="browsertestplugin.so libEGL.so libFFTEm.so
 libGLESv1_CM.so libaes.so libagl.so libandroid_runtime.so
 libandroid_servers.so libaudioflinger.so libc.so libc_debug.so
 libcameraservice.so libcorecg.so libcrypto.so
 libctest.so libcutils.so libdl.so libdrm1.so
 libdrm1_jni.so libdvm.so libemoji.so
 libexif.so libexpat.so libhardware.so libhardware_legacy.so
 libicudata.so libicui18n.so libicuuc.so libjni_latinime.so
 libjni_pinyinime.so liblog.so libm.so libmedia.so libmedia_jni.so
 libmediaplayerservice.so libnativehelper.so libnetutils.so
 libopencoreauthor.so libopencorecommon.so libopencoredownload.so
 libopencoredownloadreg.so libopencoremp4.so libopencoremp4reg.so
 libopencorenet_support.so libopencoreplayer.so libopencorertsp.so
 libopencorertspreg.so libpagemap.so libpixelflinger.so
 libpvasf.so libpvasfreg.so libreference-ril.so libril.so libsgl.so
 libskiagl.so libsonivox.so libsoundpool.so libsqlite.so
 libsrec_jni.so libssl.so libstdc++.so libsurfaceflinger.so
 libsystem_server.so libthread_db.so libui.so
 libutils.so libvorbisidec.so libwbxml.so libwbxml_jni.so
 libwebcore.so libwpa_client.so libxml2wbxml.so libz.so"

# Loop thru lib names
for lib in $libs
do
          # Pull the library into the local file system
          adb pull /system/lib/$lib ./
done
```

Installing the GNU Toolchain for ARM Processors

So far, so good. You have the Android source and the libraries for the device. The final software you need is a C compiler. This tool provides the C library, binary utilities, preprocessor, compiler, debugger, profiler, and linker required to build software for the ARM hardware used by the Android device. You will use the toolchain provided by the Sourcery G++ Lite Edition for ARM (http://www.codesourcery.com/sgpp/lite/arm/portal/subscription?@template=lite).

   You have two choices:

- Download the easy installer (see Figure 1-2).

- Get the tool in tar format and simply unzip it in your system. (I prefer to do it this way, as it is much faster).

   If you choose to install from the tarball, you can unzip the archive on your desktop using the following command:

```
$ cd $HOME/Desktop
$ tar zxvf arm-2008q3-72-arm-none-linux-gnueabi.tar.gz
```

Either way you choose to install the toolchain, you must add the bin folder to your system path so the toolchain can be invoked from the console. Add the following text to your $HOME/.bashrc file:

```
ARM_HOME=$HOME/Desktop/arm-2008q3
export PATH=$PATH:$ARM_HOME/bin
```

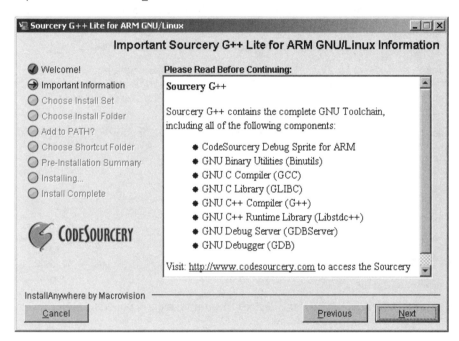

Figure 1-2. *Sourcery G++ Lite installer*

Now you should have the toolchain ready for use. Perform a quick test by typing the following:

```
user@ubuntu:~$ arm-none-linux-gnueabi-gcc --version
```

```
arm-none-linux-gnueabi-gcc (Sourcery G++ Lite 2008q3-72) 4.3.2
Copyright (C) 2008 Free Software Foundation, Inc.
This is free software; see the source for copying conditions.
There is NO warranty; not even for MERCHANTABILITY or FITNESS FOR A PARTICULAR PURPOSE.
```

Let's take a quick look at some of the most useful commands provided by the toolchain:

- arm-none-linux-gnueabi-gcc: This is the C compiler and is equivalent to the Linux gcc command. Most of the options are very close to those provided by its Linux counterpart.

- arm-none-linux-gnueabi-g++: This is the C++ compiler, which wraps the gcc command with extra options for C++.

- arm-none-linux-gnueabi-ld: This is the linker used to build a final binary, either as a monolithic file (statically) or as a shared library (dynamically).

- arm-none-linux-gnueabi-objdump: This displays information about binary files.

- arm-none-linux-gnueabi-strip: This removes symbols and sections from binary files, including symbol and relocation information, debugging symbols and sections, nonglobal symbols, and others. This can help to reduce the size of the final executable.

For example, arm-none-linux-gnueabi-objdump is a very useful tool for peeking into your binaries. It shows you information such as the following:

- Archive header information

- Contents of the overall file header

- Assembler contents of executable sections

- Intermix source code with disassembly

- Contents of the dynamic symbol table

- Relocation entries in the file

So, to display symbol table information about the device C runtime (libc.so) pulled from the device into $HOME/tmp/android/system/lib, use this command:

```
$ arm-none-linux-gnueabi-objdump -T ~/tmp/android/system/lib/libc.so
```

```
DYNAMIC SYMBOL TABLE:
00008560 l    d  .text 00000000 .text
0002c638 l    d  .rodata   00000000 .rodata
00032264 l    d  .ARM.extab 00000000 .ARM.extab
00035004 l    d  .data.rel.ro 00000000 .data.rel.ro
00035e58 l    d  .data 00000000 .data
000370e4 l    d  .bss 00000000 .bss
000195ec g    DF .text    00000034 getwchar
0000d134 g    DF .text 00000000 longjmp
...
```

A command like this can help you detect symbols used by your program but missing from the device standard libraries.

As you can see, the toolchain mirrors the GNU GCC toolchain. In fact, the only noticeable difference is that all the commands start with the prefix arm-none-linux-gnueabi.

With the toolchain in place, the last piece is a set of custom scripts to invoke the preceding commands.

Writing Custom Compilation Scripts

Why do you need a set of custom compilation scripts? Because they will make the original Linux compilation process as painless and transparent as possible when moving from the x86 to the ARM platform. Ideally, you shouldn't need to change anything in the original Makefile to compile code for ARM. However, as you'll see, this step can be incredibly painful, even for the seasoned C/C++ Linux developer.

This section presents two custom compilation scripts:

- agcc: This is a bash script meant to replace the GNU GCC compiler and wrap all dependencies for an Android device.

- ald: This is a bash script used in the linking process to create a final executable.

These scripts are critical and must be fully understood. But before we look at them, let's take a look at the x86 compilation process and how it differs for an ARM device.

The Traditional Linux Compilation Process

In the traditional x86 Linux compilation process, a developer has a set of C/C++ programs and a Makefile to build a final executable. The basic skeleton of a Makefile looks like this:

```
# Makefile Skeleton

# Object files
OBJS = file1.o file2.o....

# Header files
INC = -Ifolder1 -Ifolder2 ...

# Libraries and paths (used when linking)
LIB = -lc -lm -Lpath1 -Lpath2 ...

# Main target
all: $(OBJS)
        @echo Linking..
        gcc -o myapp $(OBJ) $(LIB)

# Compile C files
%o:%.c
        @echo Compiling $<...
        gcc -c $<  $(INC)
```

The values OBJS, INC, and LIB (for objects, includes/headers, and libraries, respectively) are called *variables*. The all and %o entries are called *targets*. Variables have a value separated by an equal sign (=).

Targets have dependencies separated by a colon (:). Below each target is a list of commands, preceded by a tab character.

To compile the application, type the command $ make. This will trigger the execution of the main target all (this is a built-in name). The target is followed by a colon, then a series of dependencies—in this case, all: $(OBJ). Thus, when the main target kicks in, it will trigger the execution of the $(OBJ) dependencies, which define the application object files. These object files will, in turn, start the compilation process, defined by the target %o:%c, which essentially says, "process all .c files whenever an .o dependency is found." So. when a .c source file is read from the current directory, the following will be displayed in the console:

```
Compiling file1.c ...
gcc -c file1.c -Ifolder1 -Ifolder2 ...

Compiling file2c ...
gcc -c file2c -Ifolder1 -Ifolder2 ...
```

Note the following lines in the Makefile:

```
@echo Compiling $<...
gcc -c $<  $(INC)
```

The instruction @echo tells GNU make to display a message to the console, and the value $< is a built-in variable that tells make to use the second argument from the target %o:%c as an argument to the command (in this case, a .c file read from the file system). Note that the % character is equivalent to the DOS * character, thus %.c means "all .c files in the current directory," The next line, gcc -c $< $(INC), will expand to gcc -c file1.c -Ifolder1 -Ifolder2 ....

The process will continue for all object files defined in the variable OBJ. Execution will then resume for the all target (provided there are no errors in the compilation process) with the linking step, and with the following line displayed on the console:

```
Linking...
```

The line gcc -o myapp $(OBJ) $(LIB) will be expanded as follows:

```
gcc -o myapp file1.o file2.o ... -lc -lm -Lpath1 -Lpath2
```

This will produce the final binary myapp, which can then be run from the console.

This works fine for a x86 PC system. However, it will not work in an Android device for several reasons. One is that the GCC produces binary files for an x86 architecture; desktop binaries will not run in an ARM processor. (This could be easily fixed by replacing gcc with arm-none-linux-gnueabi-gcc.)

Another problem is that commands such as arm-none-linux-gnueabi-gcc -c file1.c -Ifolder1 -Ifolder2 ... will compile the source code using standard header files (for the C runtime and others) bundled with the toolchain. Depending on the version you are using, this could cause undesired side effects, such as missing symbols at linkage time. For example, the following error is thrown when trying to compile a file from the 3D game Doom for ARM:

```
arm-none-linux-gnueabi-gcc -Werror -Dstricmp=strcasecmp
-msoft-float -mcpu=arm9
```

```
-g -Wall -DX11 -fpic -o sys_linux.o -c
/home/user/workspace/Android.Quake/native/Doom/sys_linux.c

cc1: warnings being treated as errors
/home/user/workspace/Android.Quake.Preview/native/Quake/sys_linux.c:
In function 'floating_point_exception_handler':
/home/user/workspace/Android.Quake.Preview/native/Quake/sys_linux.c:350:
error: implicit declaration of function 'sysv_signal'
```

This error is thrown because of a difference in the naming convention of the C system call signal (used to bind a user-defined function to an OS signal) between the toolchain (which implements the system call as signal), and the Android implementation (sysv_signal).

Regarding missing symbols, if you build a shared library, the compiler will not choke when there are missing subroutines or variables within your code. This will ultimately cause the library not to load once the program starts. I found this difficult to deal with, as the tools to work with native code are cumbersome and difficult to use, especially for the newcomer. I have used a simple solution, which is to build a mini main program to invoke the shared library, as demonstrated in Chapter 2.

An Android Compilation Script

Listing 1-2 shows the bash script to aid in Android compilation, called agcc.

Listing 1-2. *Compilation Helper Script (agcc)*

```
#!/bin/bash
##########################################
# Android Compilation helper script
# Uses the CodeSourcery G++ Toolchain for ARM
##########################################

##########################################
# Root folder where files are installed
# Update this to match your system
##########################################
HOME=/home/user

# JVM location. Set to your location
JAVA_HOME=/usr/lib/jvm/java-6-sun

# Device system image
SYS_ROOT=$HOME/tmp/android/system

# Android source code
SYS_DEV=$HOME/mydroid

# Code Sourcery Toolchain location
TOOLCHAIN_ROOT=$HOME/Desktop/android/arm-2008q3
```

```
##############################################
# Include locations
# No need to change this
##############################################
BASE=$SYS_DEV/frameworks/base

# C - Runtime
LIBC=$SYS_DEV/bionic/libc

# Math library
LIBM=${SYS_DEV}/bionic/libm

# Location of some required GCC compiler libraries
TC=${SYS_DEV}/prebuilt/linux-x86/toolchain/arm-eabi-4.3.1/lib/gcc/arm-eabi/4.3.1

# Kernel headers
KERNEL=${SYS_DEV}/kernel

# GNU GZIP
LIBZ=${SYS_DEV}/external/zlib

# XML Expat parser
EXPAT=${SYS_DEV}/external/expat/lib

# Includes
AND_INC="-I$JAVA_HOME/include"
AND_INC+=" -I${JAVA_HOME}/include/linux"
AND_INC+=" -I${LIBC}/include "
AND_INC+=" -I${LIBC}/arch-arm/include"
AND_INC+=" -I${LIBC}/kernel/arch-arm/include "
AND_INC+=" -I${LIBM}/include"
AND_INC+=" -I${BASE}/include"
AND_INC+=" -I${TC}/include"
AND_INC+=" -I${KERNEL}/include"
AND_INC+=" -I${KERNEL}/arch/arm/include -I${KERNEL}/arch/arm/mach-ebsa110/include"
AND_INC+=" -I${SYS_DEV}/system/core/include"
AND_INC+=" -I${LIBZ}"
AND_INC+=" -I${EXPAT}"

##############################################
# Toolchain compiler command
##############################################
CROSS=arm-none-linux-gnueabi-
GCC=${CROSS}gcc

# Uncomment for debugging
# echo ${GCC} -nostdinc $AND_INC  $@

# Go!
${GCC} -nostdinc ${AND_INC} "$@"
```

The agcc script defines a series of variables that can be adjusted to match your system (if you choose to install the G++ toolchain and Android source in different locations):

- HOME: This is the root location where all the software components reside (in this case, /user/home). This variable is used within other variables.

- JAVA_HOME: This is the location of the Java SDK. You need a Java SDK for building the hybrid games that mix Java and C code, which talk to each other using JNI. From the SDK, you'll use JNI header files and JNI libraries.

- SYS_ROOT: This is the location of the device's system libraries extracted from the device in the previous section. The default value is $HOME/tmp/android/system.

- SYS_DEV: This is the location of the Android source you downloaded earlier. From this code, you will use header files and shared libraries. The default value is $HOME/mydroid.

- TOOLCHAIN_ROOT: This is the location where the CodeSourcery toolchain is installed ($HOME/Desktop/android/arm-2008q3 in this case).

Next, the script defines the locations of the basic libraries used in the compilation step. The following are the most important:

- *C runtime (LIBC)*: This is the location of the C runtime header files, located under $SYS_DEV/bionic/libc.

- *Math library (LIBM)*: This is a commonly used library. It contains system functions such as pow, trigonometric functions, and others. It is located under ${SYS_DEV}/bionic/libm.

- *Kernel headers (KERNEL)*: Kernel headers are likely to be used by your games, especially high-performance 3D games. It is located under ${SYS_DEV}/kernel.

- *GNU Gzip (LIBZ)*: If your game manipulates zip files, you'll need this library. It is located under ${SYS_DEV}/external/zlib.

- *XML parser (EXPAT)*: Most of today's modern games use XML files to store game and configuration information. Thus, this library is required. By default, it is located under ${SYS_DEV}/external/expat/lib.

The following are other variables that are used to include extra compile-time dependencies:

```
BASE=$SYS_DEV/frameworks/base
TC=${SYS_DEV}/prebuilt/linux-x86/toolchain/arm-eabi-4.3.1/lib/gcc/arm-eabi/4.3.1
```

Next, the script defines the paths to the required header locations (with AND_INC) as a sequence of includes: -Ipath1, -Ipath2, and so on. And, finally, the critical step is to call the toolchain gcc command, as follows:

```
${GCC} -nostdinc ${AND_INC} "$@"
```

${GCC} will expand to arm-none-linux-gnueabi-gcc, ${AND_INC} will expand to the previously defined includes, and "$@" indicates that all arguments sent by the user should be passed along. Note the parameter -nostdinc. This is a critical argument that tells the compiler not to include the standard include files (that is, the header files bundled with the toolchain itself). You do not wish to use the toolchain's headers, but instead use the headers provided by the Android source, as you will be linking against Android's system libraries as well.

That takes care of the compilation step, but you also need to link against the device system libraries, which is the purpose of the next script.

An Android Linker Script

Listing 1-3 shows the Android linker helper script, called ald.

Listing 1-3. *Linker Helper Script (ald)*

```
#!/bin/bash

############################################
# Android Linker helper script
# Set these values to match your system
############################################
HOME=/home/user
JAVA_HOME=/usr/lib/jvm/java-6-sun

# System image location
SYS_ROOT=$HOME/tmp/android/system

# Toolchain location
TOOLCHAIN_ROOT=$HOME/Desktop/android/arm-2008q3

# Android Toolchain libgcc.a
LIBGCC=${SYS_DEV}/prebuilt/darwin-x86/toolchain/arm-eabi-4.2.1/lib/gcc/↵
arm-eabi/4.2.1/libgcc.a

# CodeSourcery libgcc.a
#LIBGCC=${TOOLCHAIN_ROOT}/lib/gcc/arm-none-linux-gnueabi/4.3.2/libgcc.a

# Linker libraries: C runtime, Math, and extra symbols
LIBRARIES="-lc -lm ${LIBGCC}"

# Library locations
LIB_PATHS="-rpath /system/lib \
 -rpath ${SYS_ROOT}/lib \
 -L${SYS_ROOT}/lib \
 -L${JAVA_HOME}/jre/lib/i386 -L."

# Linker flags
LD_FLAGS="--dynamic-linker=/system/bin/linker -nostdlib"

############################################
# Linker command
############################################
```

```
CROSS=arm-none-linux-gnueabi-
GCC=${CROSS}ld

# Uncomment for debugging
#echo "${GCC} $LD_FLAGS $LIB_PATHS $@ $LIBRARIES"

# Go!
${GCC} $LD_FLAGS $LIB_PATHS $@ $LIBRARIES
```

The ald script defines variables similar to those use used by the agcc script, which specify the location of the required software components, plus some extra linker variables:

- LIBRARIES: This variable defines the basic libraries against which the final binary should be linked. These are the C runtime (-lc), the Math library (-lm), and libgcc.a, which contains extra symbols required at link time. Note that the linker will expand -lc to the name libc.so when reading the library from the file system.

- LIB_PATHS: Besides the library names defined in the previous step, the linker needs to be able to find the libraries on the file system. Thus, you need to tell it where to look. The -Lpath1, -Lpath2, and so on tell the compiler where to look for libraries. Also, -rpath sets the runtime shared library search path. You need to define two runtime search paths:

  - -rpath /system/lib is the location of the runtime libraries in the device. It must be defined so the program will be able to run properly in the device itself.

  - -rpath ${SYS_ROOT}/lib is the location of the same libraries on the desktop system. It is required so the binary can compile properly.

- LD_FLAGS: This variable defines linker flags. Two flags are used by the script:

  - --dynamic-linker=/system/bin/linker sets a program to use as the dynamic linker. In this case, /system/bin/linker is the device.

  - -nostdlib tells the linker not to use the standard libraries (C runtime, Math library, and so on) defined by the toolchain, but instead use the libraries defined by the user at link time.

And, finally, the command ${GCC} $LD_FLAGS $LIB_PATHS $@ $LIBRARIES will expand to the following:

```
$ arm-none-linux-gnueabi-ld --dynamic-linker=/system/bin/linker
 -nostdlib -rpath /system/lib
 -rpath /user/home/tmp/android/system/lib
 -L/user/home/tmp/android/system /lib
 -L/usr/lib/jvm/java-6-sun/jre/lib/i386
 -L. [USER_ARGUMENTS] -lc -lm
 /user/home/Desktop/android/arm-2008q3/lib/gcc/
 arm-none-linux-gnueabi/4.3.2${LIBDIR}/libgcc.a
```

Note that $@ in the script will expand to all arguments sent by the user in the command line.

Testing the Scripts

Save the scripts in Listings 1-2 and 1-3 as agcc and ald in your $HOME/bin directory. Then issue the following commands to test them:

```
user@ubuntu:~$ agcc --version
```

```
arm-none-linux-gnueabi-gcc (Sourcery G++ Lite 2008q3-72) 4.3.2
Copyright (C) 2008 Free Software Foundation, Inc.
This is free software; see the source for copying conditions.  There is NO
warranty; not even for MERCHANTABILITY or FITNESS FOR A PARTICULAR PURPOSE.
```

```
user@ubuntu:~$ ald --version
```

```
arm-none-linux-gnueabi-ld: warning: library search path
"/usr/lib/jvm/java-6-sun/jre/lib/i386" is unsafe
for cross-compilation
GNU ld (Sourcery G++ Lite 2008q3-72) 2.18.50.20080215
Copyright 2007 Free Software Foundation, Inc.
This program is free software; you may redistribute it under the terms of
the GNU General Public License version 3 or (at your option) a later version.
This program has absolutely no warranty.
```

■ **Caution** Do not edit the scripts with your Windows host using Notepad or WordPad. That will insert invalid characters in the file and give strange results when you run the script. I made the mistake of doing just that, and wasted a lot of time when the compiler started giving some funky output.

Setting Up Your Development Environment

Now you are ready to get your IDE up and running with the Android development kit. Let's go through the installation of the latest available Android SDK (1.6 at the time of this writing; available from http://developer.android.com/sdk/index.html) over Eclipse 3.5 (Galileo, available from http://www.eclipse.org).

1. Start Eclipse Galileo and select Help ➤ Check for Updates, as shown in Figure 1-3.

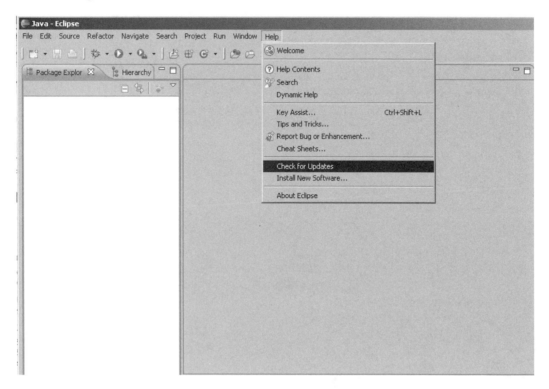

Figure 1-3. *Choosing Check for Updates from the Eclipse 3.5 (Galileo) workbench's Help menu*

2. In the Available Software window, shown in Figure 1-4, click the Add button to install new software.

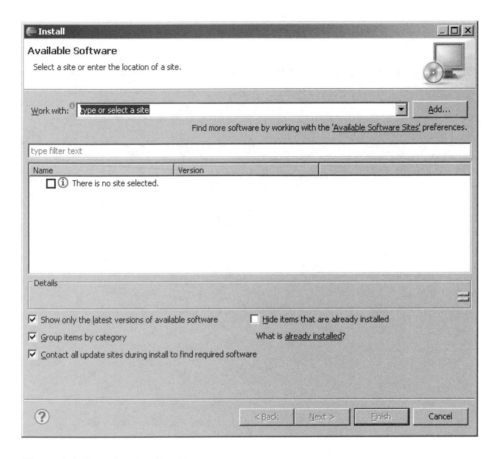

Figure 1-4. *Choosing to add software*

3. In the Add Site dialog box, enter **Android** for the name and `https://dl-ssl.` `google.com/android/eclipse` for the location, as shown in Figure 1-5.

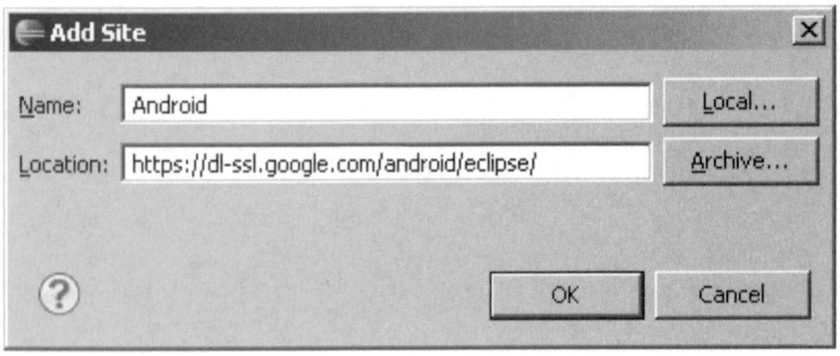

Figure 1-5. *Adding the Android site*

4. From the Available Software window (Figure 1-4), select the Android site you just added from the Work with combo box. If the name is not shown in the list, click the Available Software Sites preferences link, and then click Add to insert the site into the list (see Figure 1-6).

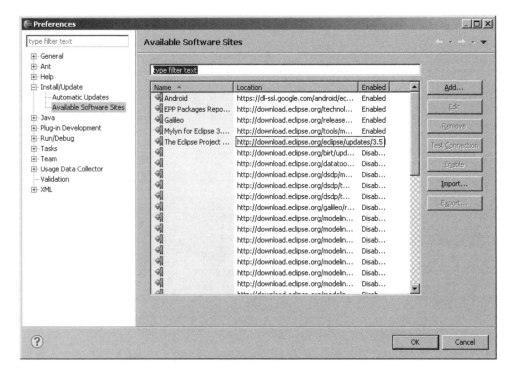

Figure 1-6. *The Available Software Sites Preferences window shows the recently added Android site.*

5. Check the Developer Tools check box in the details section, as shown in Figure 1-7, and then click Next.

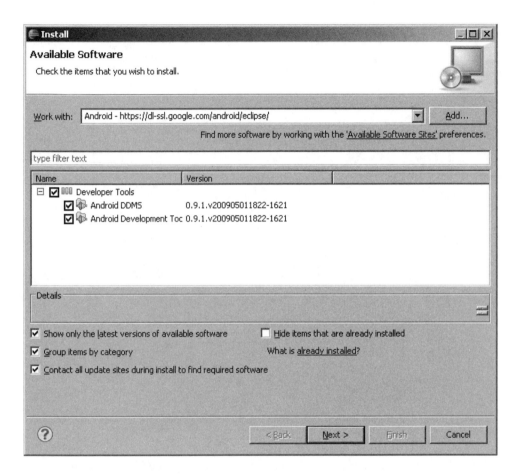

Figure 1-7. *Available Software window with the Android plug-in selected*

6. Follow the wizard installation instructions, accept the license agreement, as shown in Figure 1-8, and then complete the installation. At the end, the workbench should ask for a restart.

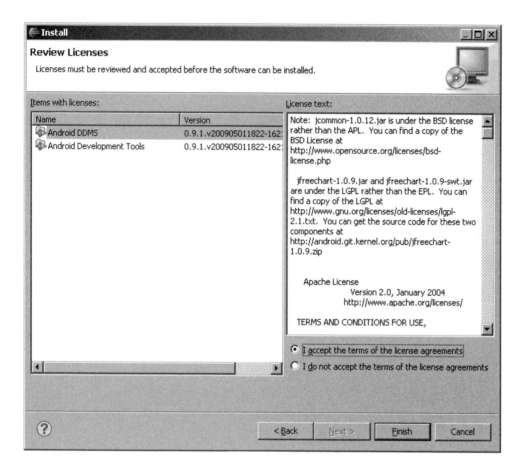

Figure 1-8. *Software license agreement from the installation wizard*

7. After the workbench restarts, select Window ➤ Preferences to open the workbench Preferences window, and select the Android option from the left navigation tree. In the Preferences section, set the location of your SDK, as shown in Figure 1-9. Make sure all the build targets are shown. Then click Apply

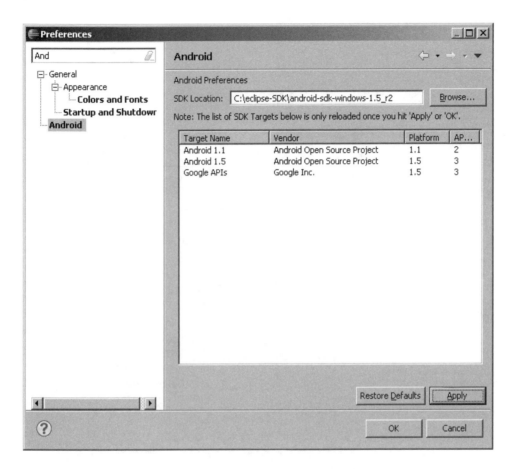

Figure 1-9. Workbench Preferences window showing Android options

8. Click OK, and then open the New Project wizard to make sure the Android plug-in has been successfully installed. If so, you should see a folder to create an Android project, as shown in Figure 1-10.

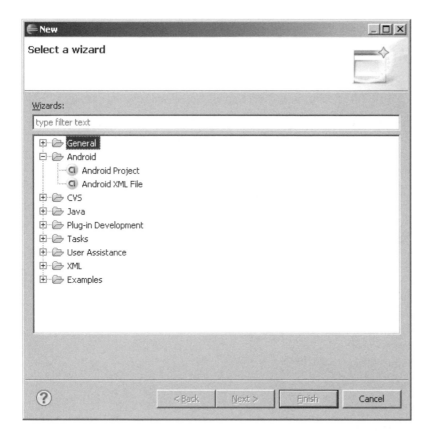

Figure 1-10. *New Project wizard showing the Android options after final configuration*

At this point, your environment should be configured and ready for development.

About the Android Native Development Kit

With version 1.5 of the SDK, Google has released a new tool called the Native Development Kit (NDK), available from http://developer.android.com/sdk/ndk/1.5_r1/index.html. According to Google, this is a companion tool to the SDK for building native portions of your code. It provides a set of system headers, such as the following:

- libc (C library) headers
- libm (math library) headers
- JNI interface headers

- `libz` (Zlib compression) headers

- `liblog` (Android logging) header

- Headers for C++ support

The NDK also includes cross-toolchains to generate native ARM binaries, documentation, and samples.

Unfortunately, Google claims that the NDK can be used only on devices running the Android 1.5 platform version or later, due to toolchain changes that make the native libraries incompatible with SDK versions 1.0 and 1.1. This makes the NDK hard to use for the goal of this book, which is to support all versions of the platform. However, the appendix will show you how to compile the examples in Chapters 6 and 7 with the NDK.

You Have Taken the First Step

Congratulations! You have taken the first step toward your mastery of Android game development. In this chapter, you learned how to set up your Linux system to compile hybrid games, which included the following tasks:

- Obtaining the Android source

- Extracting device system libraries for compilation

- Setting up the CodeSourcery G++ toolchain

- Writing custom compilation scripts

- Setting up your Eclipse IDE

This chapter provided the foundation to compile the 3D shooter games, Doom and Wolfenstein 3D, as well as the pure Java games. In the next chapter, you will learn how to write and compile a basic native program—a simple shared library—and call the shared library within a Java application.

■ ■ ■

## CHAPTER 2

Compiling Native Code in Android

In this chapter, we will explore the basics of a simple native program, also known as static binary, to be run in the device. You will also learn how to build a shared library (dynamic binary), and finally how to call that shared library within a simple Android project. Let's get started.

Your First Native Android App

You will need an Android project to host your native application, but before you create that, you must create an Android Virtual Device (AVD).

Creating an AVD

With version 1.5 of the SDK, Google introduced the concept of virtual devices (AVDs). An AVD is simply a set of configuration attributes applied to an emulator image that allows the developer to target a specific version of the SDK. The following are the basic versions of the SDK targeted by AVDs:

- *Android 1.1*: This target maps to the Android SDK version 1.1 R2.

- *Android 1.5:* This target maps to the Android SDK version 1.5 R2.

- *Android 1.6*: This target maps to the Android SDK versions 1.6 and 2.0.

- *Google APIs - 1.5 or 1.6*: This target must be used if you are building an application that uses Google APIs such as Maps and Search.

■ **Caution** In Android 1.5 and later, an AVD does not include the Google Maps API. Keep this in mind if you are building a maps-enabled app. Your map application will not start in an Android 1.5 AVD.

Let's create an AVD to target an SDK 1.5 for the sample application.

1.   In Eclipse Galileo, click the black phone icon on the Android toolbar (see Figure 2-1). This opens the Android Virtual Devices Manager dialog box.

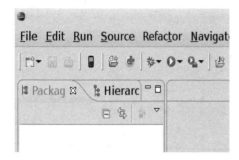

Figure 2-1. *Android toolbar within Eclipse*

2. In the dialog box, enter a name for the AVD (`droid1.5` in this example).

3. Select a target SDK (Android 1.5 in this example).

4. Optionally, enter an SD card absolute path (if you already have one), such as `/home/user/sdcard.iso`, or a size, such as 128MB. Figure 2-2 shows the Android Virtual Devices Manager dialog box for this example.

5. Click Create AVD.

■ **Tip** You should create an SD card for the AVD, and use it for the examples in later chapters to store large game files (for Doom and Wolfenstein 3D). Game files should not be saved in the device main file system, unless you want to run out of space after installing one game.

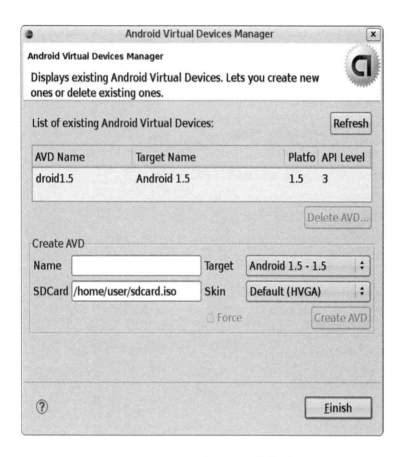

Figure 2-2. Android Virtual Device Manager dialog box settings for SDK 1.5

Note that in Android 1.6 and later, the GUI has changed a little, as shown in Figure 2-3. To create an AVD, click New to open the Create New AVD dialog box, enter a name, select a firmware target plus SD card size, and then click Create AVD.

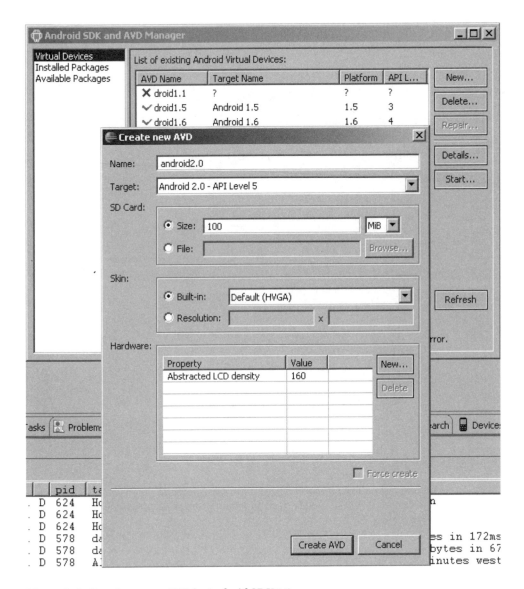

Figure 2-3. Creating a new AVD in Android SDK 1.6

Creating the Android Project

With the AVD in place, the next task is to create the project for this chapter, as follows:

1. Click the New Android Project icon on the main toolbar (see Figure 2-1). This opens the New Android Project dialog box.

2. In the dialog box, enter a project name (ch02.Project in this example).

3. Enter an application name (Chapter2 in this example).

4. Enter a package name (ch02.project in this example).

5. Enter an activity name (MainActivity in this example).

6. Specify a minimum SDK version (3 in this example). Figure 2-4 shows the completed New Android Project dialog box for this example.

7. Click Finish.

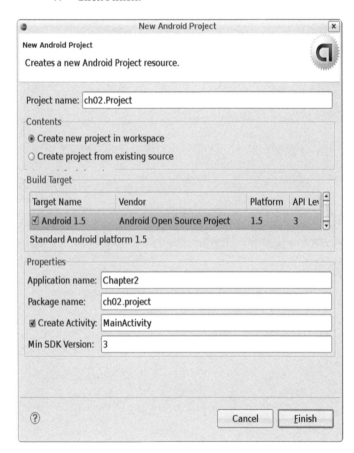

Figure 2-4. *New Android Project dialog box for this chapter's example*

Application Architecture

Let's consider what we wish to accomplish with this application:

- We want to create the basic Android application. When run in the emulator, the app will create a default view with the text "Hello Chapter2!".

- Within the project, we will create a native folder with files to accomplish the following:

  - Create a native library with a main subroutine that will be called from the Android main activity using JNI.

  - The main library subroutine will invoke a Java method (using JNI) within the Android project, sending a text message back to the Android Java layer.

- The library will be loaded at runtime within Java using a System.load(path).

Figure 2-5 shows the file system layout of the project.

■ **Tip** It would be helpful to import the project source (ch02.Project) into your workspace to go along with this chapter.

The following Java files describe the project:

- ch02.project.MainActivity.java: This file is created by the wizard and should already exist in the project.

- jni.Natives.java: This is a new file that contains native methods to be invoked within the native library and callbacks that the C library will perform within Java.

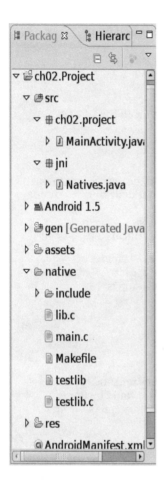

Figure 2-5. *Project layout*

You must create the following files within the native folder (see Figure 2-5):

- lib.c: This is the main library code. It contains all the necessary JNI system calls to cascade information back and forth between Android and C.

- testlib.c: This is a test program for the library. Its main function is to make sure there are no symbols missing from the native library.

- main.c: This is a static program used to demonstrate how to compile a static native program that can be run in the device.

- *Makefile*: This is the project's native build file. It has targets for the following:

  - Build the native library

  - Build the library test program

- Generate JNI header files required to cascade information back and forth between Java and C

- Build the static test program

- Deploy the files to the device for testing

Let's look at the files in more detail to understand what they do. We'll start with the Java layer.

Main Activity

The 8.70ch02.project.MainActivity.java file is created by the wizard, and it is the entry point to the phone application. Listing 2-1 shows the code for this file. There are some remarkable things to note about this file.

As you should know, when the application starts, the method onCreate(Bundle savedInstanceState) will be invoked by Android. This method performs three critical steps:

- It installs (simply copies) the native library (libch02.so) from the assets folder of the application package to the project's files folder (located in /data/data/ PACKAGE_NAME/files; the name of the package is ch02.project). This step is required before the library can be loaded by JNI.

- It loads the native library using System.load(path).

- Finally, it runs the main library sub by invoking the native method Natives.LibMain(String[] argv).

Native libraries cannot be loaded within the application package; thus, they must be copied somewhere in the file system before invoking System.load(). The obvious place would be the application's file folder (located in /data/data/Package_Name/files), but the library can be saved anywhere where permissions allow it.

■ **Caution** Shared libraries should not be saved on the SD card, as Android does not allow you to run executable code from the SD card. Developers that have large shared libraries might be tempted to do so to save some space. Save yourself some trouble and don't do it.

Note the way the library is installed:

```
writeToStream(
getAssets().open(LIB),
openFileOutput(LIB, 0)
);
```

The getAssets().open() method will open a stream from the package assets folder (where the library will be stored). The writeToStream method will then write the stream using openFileOutput(LIB, 0), which will open an output stream to the default application folder (/data/data/ch02.project/files). getAssets and openFileOutput are Android system calls, and LIB is the name of the shared library (libch02.so). The second argument to openFileOutput (zero) tells Android to assign private permissions to the file (that means it can be read by only the application itself).

Listing 2-1. *Main Activity for This Chapter's Example*

```
package ch02.project;

import java.io.IOException;
import java.io.InputStream;
import java.io.OutputStream;

import jni.Natives;

import android.app.Activity;
import android.os.Bundle;

public class MainActivity extends Activity {
    private static final String LIB = "libch02.so";
    private static final String LIB_PATH =
        "/data/data/ch02.project/files/" + LIB;

    /** Called when the activity is first created. */
    @Override
    public void onCreate(Bundle savedInstanceState) {
        super.onCreate(savedInstanceState);
        setContentView(R.layout.main);

        try {
            // Install lib
            System.out.println("Installing LIB: " + LIB);

            // Copy lib from assests folder to files folder:
            // /data/data/PKG_NAME/files
            writeToStream(getAssets().open(LIB), openFileOutput(LIB, 0));

            // Load Lib
            System.load(LIB_PATH);

            // Run it
            String[] argv = { "MyLib", "arg1", "arg2" };

            Natives.LibMain(argv);

        } catch (Exception e) {
            e.printStackTrace();
        }
    }

    /**
     * Write to a stream
     *
```

```
 * @param in
 * @param out
 * @throws IOException
 */
public static void writeToStream(InputStream in, OutputStream out)
        throws IOException {
    byte[] bytes = new byte[2048];

    for (int c = in.read(bytes); c != -1; c = in.read(bytes)) {
        out.write(bytes, 0, c);
    }
    in.close();
    out.close();
}
}
```

In Android 1.5 and later, native libraries can be stored within the project under a folder named libs/armeabi, then loaded using the system call System.loadLibrary(LIB_NAME). Thus, Listing 2-1 can be simplified by removing the library installation step:

```
public class MainActivity extends Activity
{
    private static final String LIB = "ch02";

    // Load library: Note that the prefix (lib) and the extension (.so) must be stripped.
    static {
        System.loadLibrary(LIB);
    }

    public void onCreate(Bundle savedInstanceState) {
        // ...
        Natives.LibMain(argv);
    }
}
```

Native Interface

The native interface is defined in the Java class jni.Natives.java. It has two important methods that deal with the C library (see Listing 2-2):

- static native int LibMain(String[] argv): This is the native library main subroutine. It will be called within the Android main activity. The method also takes a list of argument strings to be passed along. Notice the keyword native, which tells the Java compiler it is implemented natively.

- private static void OnMessage(String text, int level): This method is meant to be called from the C library, with a string message and integer value (level). This method will simply print the message to the console.

■ **Note** As you should know, with JNI, you can invoke subroutines both ways: from Java to C (using the `native` keyword) or from C to Java, as you'll see once we get to the native stuff.

Listing 2-2. Native Interface Class

```
package jni;

public class Natives
{

    /**
     * Native Main Loop
     *
     * @param argv
     * @return
     */
    public static native int LibMain(String[] argv);

    /**
     * This fires on messages from the C layer
     *
     * @param text
     */
    @SuppressWarnings("unused")
    private static void OnMessage(String text, int level) {
        System.out.println("OnMessage text:" + text + " level=" + level);
    }

}
```

Natives.LibMain requires a native implementation. On the other hand, OnMessage (which is invoked from C) simply prints the message to standard output. With this in mind, let's take a look at the native code.

Native Library

Here 11.330is where all the work should take place. We start with the implementation of the actual library lib.c (see Listing 2-3). This file lives in the native folder within the project folder.

■ **Note** Native libraries in Linux (also known as shared objects) are the equivalents of dynamic link libraries (DLLs) in Windows. By convention, shared objects are named as `lib<NAME><VERSION>.so`.

Listing 2-3. *Native Library Implementation*

```
#include <stdio.h>
#include <stdlib.h>

/* JNI Includes */
#include <jni.h>

#include "include/jni_Natives.h"

#define CB_CLASS "jni/Natives"

/**
 * OnMessage callback
 */
#define CB_CLASS_MSG_CB  "OnMessage"
#define CB_CLASS_MSG_SIG  "(Ljava/lang/String;I)V"

// prototypes

// Lib main Sub
int lib_main(int argc, char **argv) ;

// Used to get the len of a Java Array
const int getArrayLen(JNIEnv * env, jobjectArray jarray);

// printf str messages back to java
void jni_printf(char *format, ...);

// Global env ref (for callbacks)
static JavaVM *g_VM;

// Global Reference to the native Java class jni.Natives.java
static jclass jNativesCls;

/*
 * Class:     jni_Natives
 * Method:    LibMain
 * Signature: ([Ljava/lang/String;)V
 */
JNIEXPORT jint JNICALL Java_jni_Natives_LibMain
  (JNIEnv * env, jclass class, jobjectArray jargv)
{
    // Obtain a global ref to the caller jclass
    (*env)->GetJavaVM(env, &g_VM);

    // Extract char ** args from Java array
    jsize clen =  getArrayLen(env, jargv);

    char * args[(int)clen];
```

```
    int i;
    jstring jrow;
    for (i = 0; i < clen; i++)
    {
        // Get C string from Java String[i]
        jrow = (jstring)(*env)->GetObjectArrayElement(env, jargv, i);
        const char *row  = (*env)->GetStringUTFChars(env, jrow, 0);

        args[i] = malloc( strlen(row) + 1);
        strcpy (args[i], row);

        // Print args
        jni_printf("Main argv[%d]=%s", i, args[i]);

        // Free Java string jrow
        (*env)->ReleaseStringUTFChars(env, jrow, row);
    }

    /*
     * Load the jni.Natives class
     */
    jNativesCls = (*env)->FindClass(env, CB_CLASS);

    if ( jNativesCls == 0 ) {
        jni_printf("Unable to find class: %s", CB_CLASS);
        return -1;
    }

    // Invoke the Lib main sub. This will loop forever
    // Program args come from Java
    lib_main (clen, args);
    return 0;
}


/**
 * Send a string back to Java
 */
jmethodID mSendStr;

static void jni_send_str( const char * text, int level) {
    JNIEnv *env;

    if ( !g_VM) {
        printf("I_JNI-NOVM: %s\n", text);
        return;
    }

    (*g_VM)->AttachCurrentThread (g_VM, (void **) &env, NULL);

    // Load jni.Natives if missing
```

```
    if ( !jNativesCls ) {
        jNativesCls = (*env)->FindClass(env, CB_CLASS);

        if ( jNativesCls == 0 ) {
                printf("Unable to find class: %s", CB_CLASS);
                return;
        }
    }

    // Call jni.Natives.OnMessage(String, int)
    if (! mSendStr ) {
        // Get  aref to the static method: jni.Natives.OnMessage
        mSendStr = (*env)->GetStaticMethodID(env, jNativesCls
            , CB_CLASS_MSG_CB
            , CB_CLASS_MSG_SIG);
    }
    if (mSendStr) {
        // Call method
        (*env)->CallStaticVoidMethod(env, jNativesCls
                , mSendStr
                , (*env)->NewStringUTF(env, text)
                , (jint) level );
    }
    else {
        printf("Unable to find method: %s, signature: %s\n"
                , CB_CLASS_MSG_CB, CB_CLASS_MSG_SIG );
    }
}

/**
 * Printf into the Java layer
 * does a varargs printf into a temp buffer
 * and calls jni_sebd_str
 */
void jni_printf(char *format, ...)
{
    va_list         argptr;
    static char             string[1024];

    va_start (argptr, format);
    vsprintf (string, format,argptr);
    va_end (argptr);

    jni_send_str (string, 0);
}

/**
 * Get Java array length
 */
const int getArrayLen(JNIEnv * env, jobjectArray jarray)
{
```

```
    return (*env)->GetArrayLength(env, jarray);
}

/**
 * Library main sub
 */
int lib_main(int argc, char **argv)
{
    int i;

    jni_printf("Entering LIB MAIN");

    for ( i = 0 ; i < argc ; i++ ) {
        jni_printf("Lib Main argv[%d]=%s", i, argv[i]);
    }
    return 0;
}
```

Let's dissect this file to understand what it does. Any C/C++ program that plans to do JNI calls must include the header file:

```
#include <jni.h>
```

This header file has the prototypes for all the JNI system calls to be used by your library. It can be found in your system's Java home under JAVA_HOME/include, with extra Linux dependencies under JAVA_HOME/include/linux. At compile time, these paths must be included using -I$JAVA_HOME/include and -I$JAVA_HOME/include/linux in the Makefile (The agcc script you created in Chapter 1 will take care of all this).

Next, it includes the jni_Natives header file:

```
#include "include/jni_Natives.h"
```

This file contains the user-defined JNI prototypes for all native methods defined in the jni.Natives class. It is machine-generated and must not be edited by the user. The actual generation will be set up in the Makefile. To generate this file manually, the following command can be used:

```
javah -cp ../bin -d include jni.Natives
```

Here, javah is the Java Virtual Machine (JVM) command to generate native header files from Java classes, -cp defines the class path search path, -d include tells javah to save the file in the include folder (creating it if required), and jni.Natives is the Java class name from which you wish to extract the headers.

Next, the following constants are defined:

```
#define CB_CLASS "jni/Natives"
#define CB_CLASS_MSG_CB  "OnMessage"
#define CB_CLASS_MSG_SIG  "(Ljava/lang/String;I)V"
```

CB_CLASS is the name of the Java class that will be invoked within C (note that the period separating path names is replaced by /). CB_CLASS_MSG_CB is the name of the Java method (OnMessage) that will be invoked (see Listing 2-2). CB_CLASS_MSG_SIG is a critical constant that defines the Java signature of the OnMessage Java method. Let's take a closer look at this signature:

(Ljava/lang/String;I)V

A Java method signature has the format (ARGUMENTS)RETURN_TYPE, where the arguments can be encoded as follows:

I = Integer

B = Byte

S = Short

C = Char

LJava_Class; = For Java classes enclosed by : L and ;

In our case, the first argument is a Java string (Ljava/lang/String;), and the second is an integer (I). Note that all arguments are defined by a single character (except for classes that are enclosed by L;), and there are no separators between them. Finally, V is the return type defined as void.

■ **Caution** Method signatures are a major pain when coding in JNI. Any mistake in this string, and the library will not be able to find the method at runtime.

Next, the file defines the prototypes for the functions within the library:

- int lib_main(int argc, char **argv): This is the entry point to the library. It receives the number of arguments (argc) and a list of arguments (argv), similar to the standard C main() function.

- int getArrayLen(JNIEnv * env, jobjectArray jarray): This function is used to get the length of a Java array, which will be translated into a C array for use by the library.

- void jni_printf(char *format, ...): This function is used by the library to send a text message back to Java. Note that ... indicates that the function will receive a vector of arguments.

Finally, we need two global references:

```
static JavaVM *g_VM;
static jclass jNativesCls;
```

g_VM is a reference to the JVM, and it will be used make JNI system calls. jNativesCls is a reference to the jni.Natives Java class used to invoke the Java method OnMessage. Note that the static keyword tells the compiler that these variables should be visible only within code in lib.c.

Converting a Java Array to a C Array

Converting a Java string array to a C char array is a very useful tool to send arguments to a native library. As you can see from Listing 2-4, this can be a tricky situation. The following are the key steps:

- Get the size of the Java array, and for each element of the array:

  - Get the Java String[i] element using GetObjectArrayElement(JNIEnv * env, jobjectArray jarray, int pos).

  - Convert the retrieved element into a C string (char *) using GetStringUTFChars(JNIEnv * env, jstring jrow, 0).

- Allocate space for the C array using malloc(length of string + 1). Note that an extra space is allocated for the terminator character.

- Copy the characters using strcpy (char ** target , char * source).

- Release Java String[i] using ReleaseStringUTFChars(JNIEnv * env, jstring jrow, char * row).

Listing 2-4. Converting a Java String Array into a C Char Array

```
// Extract char ** args from Java array
jsize clen =  getArrayLen(env, jargv);

char * args[(int)clen];

int i;
jstring jrow;

// Loop thru Java array
for (i = 0; i < clen; i++)
{
    // Get String[i]
    jrow = (jstring)(*env)->GetObjectArrayElement(env, jargv, i);

    // Convert String[i] to char *
    const char *row  = (*env)->GetStringUTFChars(env, jrow, 0);

    // Allocate space
    args[i] = malloc( strlen(row) + 1);

    // Copy
    strcpy (args[i], row);

    // Free java string jrow
    (*env)->ReleaseStringUTFChars(env, jrow, row);
}
```

Getting the Size of a Java Array

To get the size of a Java array, use the JNI function (*env)->GetArrayLength(env, jobjectArray jarray), where env is a pointer to the JNI environment, and jarray is a reference to the Java array. For example, to get the size of the array jargs using environment env, use the following:

```
(*env)->GetArrayLength(env, jargs)
```

Invoking a Java Static Void Method

To invoke the static void jni.Natives.OnMessage method. you must perform the following steps:

    1.   Load the jni.Natives class with the following:

```
(*env)->FindClass(env, "jni/Natives")
```

    2.   Get the ID of the method to be invoked using a reference to the jni.Natives class, the name of the method (OnMessage), and the signature (Ljava/lang/String;I)V.

```
jmethodID mSendStr = (*env)->GetStaticMethodID(env
              , jNativesCls
              , "OnMessage"
              , "(Ljava/lang/String;I)V");
```

    3.   Call the static void method, passing the class, method ID, and the method arguments: a Java string and integer in this case.

```
(*env)->CallStaticVoidMethod(env, jNativesCls
            , mSendStr
            , (*env)->NewStringUTF(env, text)
            , (jint) level );
```

Defining a Variable-Arguments Function in C

The final piece of the puzzle is a function to perform the actual invocation of the Java method described in the previous section, as shown in Listing 2-5. This function is meant to be called anywhere within the library after jni.Natives.LibMain() is invoked. It is called jni_printf and works pretty much as printf does, using the very useful variable-arguments technique.

Listing 2-5. Sending a String to Java Using Variable Arguments

```
void jni_printf(char *format, ...)
{
    va_list        argptr;
    static char    string[1024];

    va_start (argptr, format);
    vsprintf (string, format, argptr);
    va_end (argptr);
```

```
        jni_send_str (string, 0);
}
```

va_list, va_start, and va_end are used to build an output string using a C string format and a sequence of arguments. This allows the developer to mimic a printf-style function for a specific need. Thus, for example, to print an arbitrary message to the Java console within the library, use the following command:

```
jni_printf("This is a message %d, %p, %x, %s", 10, somePointer, 0xFF, "Hello Java")
```

"This is a message %d, %p, %x, %s" is called a character format. The rest are variable arguments sent to the function. Also note that you should add the header #include <stdarg.h> to use variable arguments.

Compiling and Testing the Shared Library

We can now proceed to compile the native library. Listing 2-6 shows the Makefile for this purpose. This file defines the following targets:

- default (all): This target will build both the library and the test static binary a.out.

- lib: This target will build only the shared library.

- testlib: This target will build a simple program to test the library and make sure there are no missing symbols.

- jni: This target will generate the C header for the native Java class jni.Natives. The output will be stored in the include folder under the current directory.

- pushbin: This target will push the static test binary (a.out) to the device /data folder using the adb push command.

- pushlib: This target will push the library and the test program to the device /data folder.

■ **Caution** Commands within a target of a Makefile must use the tab separator, which has been replaced by spaces in Listing 2-6. Do not copy and paste this listing into a Makefile, as it will not run properly. Instead, refer to the source code for the chapter.

Listing 2-6. *Makefile for This Chapter's Example*

```
####################################
# Makefile
####################################
```

```
# Compiler and loader
CC = agcc
LD = ald

# Flags
CFLAGS  = -Werror
MACROS  =
INCLUDES =

# Static objects
OBJ = main.o

# Shared library ob
LIBOBJ = lib.o

# Test shared lib
TESTLIBOBJ = testlib.o

# Default make target
all: testlib $(OBJ)
    @echo
    @echo "Linking..."
    $(LD) -static -o a.out $(OBJ)

# Build lib
lib: $(LIBOBJ)
    @echo
    @echo "Linking Shared library..."
    $(LD) -shared -o libch02.so $(LIBOBJ)
    @echo
    @echo "Copying Shared library to assets folder"
    cp libch02.so ../assets

# Build test program for lib
testlib: lib $(TESTLIBOBJ)
    @echo
    @echo "Linking Test for Shared library"
    $(LD) -o testlib $(TESTLIBOBJ) -L. -lch02

# Build JNI Headers (for lib)
jni:
    @echo "Creating JNI C headers..."
    javah -jni -classpath ../bin -d include jni.Natives

# Compile
.c.o:
    @echo
    @echo "Compiling $<..."
    $(CC) -c $(FLAGS) $(MACROS) $(INCLUDES)  $<
```

```
# Cleanup
clean:
    rm *.o

#
# Push binary into device
#
pushbin:
    adb push a.out /data

# Push lib & test program to the device
pushlib:
    adb push testlib /data
    adb push libch02.so /data
```

Type make lib to compile the library (see Listing 2-7). Note that the Makefile uses the agcc and ald scripts created in the previous chapter. Other interesting aspects of the process include the following:

- CFLAGS=-Werror: This tells the compiler to abort whenever there is a warning in the compilation process. This can be a powerful debugging tool to find programming errors within your code.

- javah -jni -classpath ../bin -d include jni.Natives: This creates the C header file for the native methods in the jni.Natives class. Output is saved in the include folder.

- adb push FILENAME DEVICE_DEST: This is the Android SDK command to upload a file to a specific location in the device.

Listing 2-7. *Makefile Output*

```
user@ubuntu:~/ ch02.Project/native$ make lib
```

```
Compiling lib.c...
agcc -c     lib.c

Linking Shared library...
ald -shared -o libch02.so lib.o
arm-none-linux-gnueabi-ld: warning: library search path "/usr/lib/jvm/java-6-
sun/jre/lib/i386" is unsafe for cross-compilation

Copying Shared library to assets folder
cp libch02.so ../assets

Compiling testlib.c...
agcc -c     testlib.c

Linking Test for Shared library
ald -o testlib testlib.o -L. -lch02
```

```
arm-none-linux-gnueabi-ld: warning: library search path "/usr/lib/jvm/java-6-
sun/jre/lib/i386" is unsafe for cross-compilation
arm-none-linux-gnueabi-ld: warning: cannot find entry symbol _start; defaulting to 00008340
```

Notice the warnings in Listing 2-7:

```
Library search path "/usr/lib/jvm/java-6-sun/jre/lib/i386" is unsafe for cross-compilation.
```

Here, the compiler is letting you know that the local system Java JNI libraries in this folder are not safe (which makes sense, since you are compiling for a different architecture). However, you do need to link against JNI, thus you have no choice.

```
Cannot find entry symbol start; defaulting to 00008340
```

This indicates that the loader cannot find an entry point for the library test program. By default, it will call the first function in the file—main(int argc, char **argv) in this case.

■ **Note** Google does not provide support for JNI, or native development for that matter, as it wishes to push development in Java. I think this is a mistake, as there is a lot of native code that can be ported into the device (such as games). Sadly, native development has been neglected, although new tools such as the Native Development Kit (NDK), described in Chapter 1, are trying to fix the problem.

Troubleshooting Missing Symbols

Before you run the project, you should make sure there are no missing symbols in the native library. This can be a tricky process, as the successful compilation of a shared library will not tell you about missing symbols. Even worse, if symbols are missing, and you try to run the program, the library will fail to load at runtime, leaving you with the headache of figuring out what went wrong.

An easy solution is to write a simple C program that will invoke the library (see Listing 2-8). Then, when linked, the compiler will tell you about missing symbols, which can then be fixed. This program can be also useful in testing the library from the command line before testing from the application itself.

Listing 2-8. *Simple Test Program for the Library*

```
#include <stdio.h>

extern int lib_main(int argc, char **argv);

//void _start(int argc, char **argv)
int main(int argc, char **argv)
{
    int i;
    printf("Argc=%d Argv=%p\n", argc, argv);
```

```
for ( i = 0 ; i < argc ; i++ ) {
    printf("Main argv[%d]=%s\n", i, argv[i]);
}

printf("Starting Lib main sub\n");
lib_main(argc, argv) ;

exit (0);
}
```

Compile the program with make testlib, or manually using the helper scripts, as follows:

```
agcc -c     testlib.c
ald -o testlib testlib.o -L. -lch02
```

Note that you must link with -L. -lch02, which tells the compiler to link against libch02.so and search for the library in the current folder.

Now, start your emulator and let's test the library.

Testing the Dynamic Library on the Device

To test the library, upload the files to the device using make pushlib, which expands to the following commands:

```
adb push libcg02.so /data
adb push testlib /data
```

Then log in to the device, change to the /data folder, and execute the test program:

```
$ adb shell
# cd /data
# chmod 777 lib * test*
# ./testlib
```

```
bionic/linker/linker.c:1581| ERROR:   833 could not load 'libch02.so'
bionic/linker/linker.c:1641| ERROR: failed to link ./testlib
bionic/linker/linker.c:1741| ERROR: CANNOT LINK EXECUTABLE './testlib'
```

Here, you have run the program in the version 1.5 of the emulator. As you see, the library fails to load. The next section provides tips to figure out what is going on. If you try this process in the SDK version 1.0 R2, it will work.

Note that this doesn't mean the library will fail to load from the Java app. It simply tells you there is a problem with the native linker /system/bin/linker.

Debugging with strace

For some reason, the native test program for the library runs in version 1.0 R2 of the SDK, but fails to load in 1.5 R2. The output gives a clue: the file `bionic/linker/linker.c:1581` fails to load the library. There is a simple Linux tool called `strace` that can help in this situation.

The `strace` tool runs the specified command until it exits. It intercepts and records the system calls that are called by a process and the signals that are received by a process. The name of each system call, its arguments, and its return value are printed. This is a useful diagnostic and debugging tool for solving problems with programs for which the source is not readily available. You will find that a great deal can be learned about a system and its system calls by tracing even ordinary programs.

The book source provides an Android version of `strace`. (`strace` is now a built into versions 1.5 and later of the Android SDK.) Let's push it and see what is going on, as shown in Listing 2-9.

Listing 2-9. *strace Tool Output*

```
$ adb push strace /data
$ adb shell
# cd /data

# ./strace ./testlib
```

```
execve("./testlib", ["./testlib"], [/* 10 vars */]) = 0
getpid()                                = 835
gettid()                                = 835
sigaction(SIGILL, {0xb0001a99, [], SA_RESTART}, {SIG_DFL}, 0) = 0
sigaction(SIGABRT, {0xb0001a99, [], SA_RESTART}, {SIG_DFL}, 0) = 0
sigaction(SIGBUS, {0xb0001a99, [], SA_RESTART}, {SIG_DFL}, 0) = 0
stat64("/system/lib/libch02.so", 0xbef9ea58) = -1 ENOENT (No such file or directory)
stat64("/lib/libch02.so", 0xbef9ea58)   = -1 ENOENT (No such file or directory)
mmap2(NULL, 4096, PROT_READ|PROT_WRITE, MAP_PRIVATE|MAP_ANONYMOUS, -1, 0) = 0x40000000
mprotect(0x40000000, 4096, PROT_READ)   = 0
fstat64(1, {st_mode=S_IFCHR|0600, st_rdev=makedev(136, 1), ...}) = 0
brk(0)                                  = 0x11000
brk(0x11000)                            = 0x11000
brk(0x12000)                            = 0x12000
mprotect(0x40000000, 4096, PROT_READ|PROT_WRITE) = 0
mprotect(0x40000000, 4096, PROT_READ)   = 0
ioctl(1, SNDCTL_TMR_TIMEBASE or TCGETS, {B38400 opost isig icanon echo ...}) = 0
write(1, "bionic/linker/linker.c:1581| ERR"..., 70bionic/linker/linker.c:1581| ERROR:    835
could not load 'libch02.so'
) = 70
write(1, "bionic/linker/linker.c:1641| ERR"..., 61bionic/linker/linker.c:1641| ERROR: failed
to link ./testlib
) = 61
write(1, "bionic/linker/linker.c:1741| ERR"..., 71bionic/linker/linker.c:1741| ERROR: CANNOT
LINK EXECUTABLE './testlib'
) = 71
exit_group(-1)                          = ?
Process 835 detached
```

The following lines give a clue to the source of the problem:

```
stat64("/system/lib/libch02.so", 0xbef9ea58) = -1 ENOENT (No such file or directory)
stat64("/lib/libch02.so", 0xbef9ea58)   = -1 ENOENT (No such file or directory)
```

The linker first tries to open the library from the device /system/lib folder. This is a read-only file system, and user-defined libraries cannot be saved there. Next, the linker searches the /lib folder, which doesn't exist, thus the link fails. The linker is not searching in the current directory—that is the problem!

The good news is that this will not prevent the library from loading within the Java application, as long as there are no missing symbols.

If you run the same sequence in a version 1.0 R2 of the SDK, you will see that the second line becomes the following:

```
stat64("./libch02.so", 0xbef9ea58)   = 0 OK
```

Thus, the program runs successfully.

■ **Note** It is hard to say what has changed from version 1.0 to 1.5 in the file bionic/linker/linker.c, as Google provides no support in this matter. I can only speculate, but my guess is that either the developers forgot to search in the current folder or some new compilation option can be used to tell the linker where to search.

Compiling Statically

Finally, if you wish to write a command-line tool to run in the device, you must do so statically. Consider the simple program in Listing 2-10 to print the command-line arguments to stdout.

Listing 2-10. Simple Command-Line Program

```
#include <stdio.h>

int main(int argc, char **argv)
{
    int i;

    for ( i = 0 ; i < argc ; i++ ) {
        printf("Main argv[%d]=%s\n", i, argv[i]);
    }

    printf("Hello World\n");
    exit( 0);
}
```

If you compile the program with -static using the helper scripts, you get the following error:

```
agcc -c    main.c
ald -static -o a.out main.o
arm-none-linux-gnueabi-ld: cannot find -lc
```

The linker cannot find the C runtime libc.so, even though the path to the library is correct. Remember that ald uses -nostdlib to bypass linking against standard libraries.

When compiling statically (using -static), you must remove -nostdlib from the loader. Thus, the correct linking command should be as follows:

```
user@ubuntu:~/ch02.Project/native$ arm-none-linux-gnueabi-ld
 --dynamic-linker=/system/bin/linker
 -rpath /system/lib
 -rpath /home/user/tmp/android/system/lib
 -L/home/user/tmp/android/system/lib
 -static -o a.out main.o -lc -lm
```

```
/home/user/mydroid/prebuilt/darwin-x86/toolchain/
 arm-eabi-4.2.1/lib/gcc/arm-eabi/4.2.1/libgcc.a
 arm-none-linux-gnueabi-ld: warning: cannot find entry symbol _start;
 defaulting to 000080e0
```

Now you can test a.out in the device:

```
$ make pushbin
$ adb shell
# ./a.out test
Main[0]=test
Hello World
```

Testing the Native Application

With the compiled library, you can test the phone application and see if the library is loaded by JNI. From the command line, run the make command:

```
$ make lib
```

It will compile the library and also copy it to the assets folder in the Java project, so it can be installed when the application runs. Don't forget to refresh the project folder (press F5 on the main folder), so the IDE will pack it before running it.

Now let's create a run configuration and start the application. Here is how:

1. Select Run ▸ Run Configurations from the main menu.

2. In the Run Configurations dialog box, right-click Android Application in the left tree and choose New.

3. Enter a configuration name (ch02) and select a project (ch02.Project), as shown in Figure 2-6. Then click Run.

Figure 2-6. *Run Configurations dialog box for the project*

The application will run in the emulator and display the text "Hello Chapter2!". There is nothing out of the ordinary here. We must look at the logcat view to see the messages from the native layer. Figure 2-7 shows the output of the device log.

Figure 2-7. *logcat output for the project*

In the output, notice the following lines:

```
Trying to load lib /data/data/ch02.project/files/libch02.so ...
Added shared lib /data/data/c69+h02.project/files/libch02.so ...
```

These are JNI messages that tell us the library loaded successfully and the native methods can now be invoked within Java. The lines in **green** represent the callbacks performed by the native library calling the jni.Natives.OnMessage() method. Success! You have taken the first and most difficult step in building hybrid games for Android.

What's Next?

In this chapter, you have taken the first steps for building a hybrid game using JNI by learning how to create the main Java activity and loading a native library within it. Next, you learned about Java native methods using the native keyword plus the C header file required to implement them. You also learned some useful C tricks, such as converting Java arrays to C arrays, getting the size of a Java array, and invoking Java methods within C.

You then learned how to troubleshoot common mistakes and test the native library in the emulator. Things are getting more exciting by the minute.

This and the previous chapter provide the basic foundation if you are planning to port a game that has significant Linux C code to the Android platform. In the next chapter, you will learn how easy to use and powerful Android can be if you plan to build a Java-only game.

CHAPTER 3

■ ■ ■

Building a Java Game from Scratch

If you don't like C and want to stay as far away from it as possible, the next two chapters will show you how simple and fun writing a Java-only game can be. We start by taking a look at the differences between Android and the Java Micro Edition (Java ME), which is the standard for mobile development. Next, we take a look at some basic gaming techniques such as sprite rendering and sound manipulation, as an appetizer to the main course—building a real game called Space Blaster. In this fun game, you must shoot or duck incoming asteroids that threaten to destroy your space ship. A shield will also help you in your quest for a high score. Let's get started.

Android Gaming vs. Java ME Gaming

If you have written many Android applications, perhaps you have noticed how different the Android Java API is from the Java SE and Java ME APIs, the standards for Java and mobile development respectively. As a matter of fact, according to Wikipedia, this is a major source of criticism about Android (http://en.wikipedia.org/wiki/Android_(operating_system)).

- Android does not use a conventional Linux kernel. It does not have a native X Window system, nor does it support the standard GNU libraries, making reusing existing Linux applications or libraries difficult.

- Android does not use established Java standards (Java SE and Java ME). This prevents compatibility among Java applications. It does not provide the full set of Java SE or ME classes, libraries, and APIs.

- Android does not officially allow applications to be installed on or run from an SD card. This is a serious mistake as many advanced 3D games use big files to store graphics and sound. Storing these files in the main file system will quickly drain precious disk space.

These shortcomings are evident just by looking at the Android library within your IDE. Consider Figure 3-1, which displays the classes for the android.jar library. On the right side, you will notice that most of the packages of Java SE are included, which is good. However, some useful classes for games, such as java.awt.Polygon and java.awt.Dimension, are still missing. Although in version 1.5 of the SDK Google has added the important Java Bean property change support (see the java.beans package). The middle of the figure shows where Android and Java SE are two different animals—none of the classes in the Android package are part of the Java SE and ME standards. Finally, in the left view, you can see that

Google is reusing some neat libraries from the Apache Software Foundation (Commons HTTP and HTTP client) and the W3C XML APIs (under org.xml).

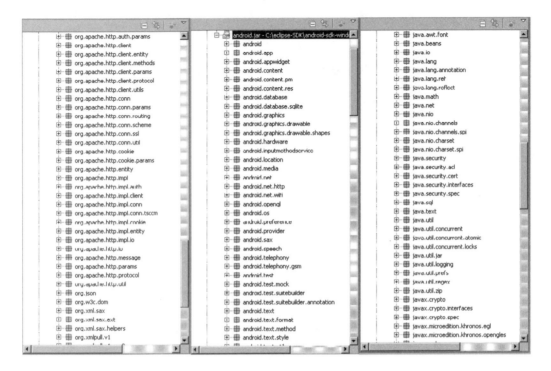

Figure 3-1. *The packages of the Android API (android.jar)*

The Android API breaks compatibility with Java SE/ME and makes it tough, but not impossible, to reuse Java code from standard Java games or applets. You'll find out how to reuse your Java code throughout this chapter.

Creating Space Blaster, Your First Java Game

It's time for the real thing. This section presents the pure Java game Space Blaster. Even though this is an Android game, some code has been reused from a Java applet.

Figure 3-2 shows the game in action. The objective of the game is to navigate a space ship through a field of meteors, shooting them up as you go. The ship has a laser weapon and a defensive shield. You can choose to shoot the meteor, dodge it by dragging the ship with your fingertips, or let the shield protect you, but whatever you choose, the power diminishes. As time passes, the power will replenish itself, and you will get points the longer you stay in the game. You can maneuver the ship with the keypad arrows or drag it across the field with your fingers. Tapping the background will fire the laser, pressing E will end the game, and pressing Q will terminate the application.

Figure 3-2. *Space Blaster running on the emulator*

Let's take a look at the class hierarchy for this application.

Understanding Game Architecture

Space Blaster is a relatively simple game. It has three main classes:

- SpaceBlaster.java: This is the main activity that bonds the game code with the Android platform. Its job is to load the game layout and process Activity events.

- SpaceBlasterGame.java: This is where all the meat resides. This class has all the game logic, and it processes key and touch events. SpaceBlasterGame extends ArcadeGame.

- ArcadeGame.java: This abstract class encapsulates common functionality. It also uses a standard Java TimerTask to define a game loop, which will repeat itself infinitely until the user quits the application.

These classes interact with each other and local resources as shown in Figure 3-3.

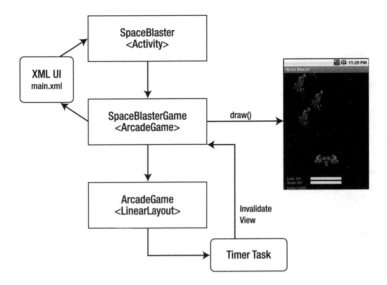

Figure 3-3. *The Space Blaster architecture*

The main activity class loads the XML UI from the file main.xml. The XML UI defines a basic Android LinearLayout that draws all the sprites on the game. The position of a sprite is controlled using X and Y coordinates within the LinearLayout::onDraw() method. Note that SpaceBlasterGame extends ArcadeGame, which in turn extends LinearLayout. This inheritance hierarchy allows you to define your own class to use as a LinearLayout, where you can draw by simply overloading the onDraw() method (see Listing 3-1).

Listing 3-1. *User-Defined LinearLayout (main.xml)*

```xml
<?xml version="1.0" encoding="utf-8"?>

<!-- User Defined Linear Layout -->
<ch03.game.sb.SpaceBlasterGame
  xmlns:android="http://schemas.android.com/apk/res/android"
  android:id="@+id/ll_absolute"
  android:orientation="vertical"
  android:layout_width="fill_parent"
  android:layout_height="fill_parent"
  android:background="#FF000000">

</ch03.game.sb.SpaceBlasterGame>
```

The XML in Listing 3-1 creates a LinearLayout with the ID ll_absolute whose width and height will fill the screen (fill_parent). It has a vertical orientation, so child controls will be aligned vertically. Other utility classes in the project follow:

- AudioClip.java: This sound handler class deals with the device's media player.

- Tools.java: This simple class has utility methods to display messages to the user.

To get started, you will need the chapter source that comes along with this book, which contains all the resources for the next sections.

Creating the Project

Create a project to host the game. Here is how:

1. Click New Android Project from the toolbar, and enter the following information (see Figure 3-4):

   - Name: **ch03.SpaceBlaster**

   - Build Target: **Android 1.1** or **Android 1.5**

   - Application Name: **Space Blaster**

   - Package Name: ch03.game.sb

   - Activity: **SpaceBlaster**

   - Min SDK version: **3** for 1.5, **2** for 1.1

2. Click Finish.

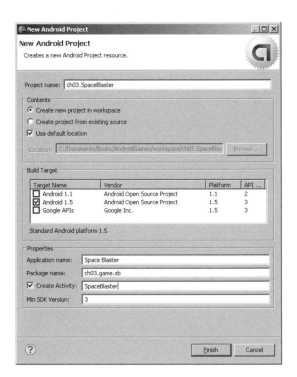

Figure 3-4. *The Space Blaster New Adroid Project dialog*

Now, let's work on the main activity and layout classes.

Creating the Game's Activity Class

Listing 3-2 shows the game activity class, ch03.game.sb.SpaceBlaster. This is the core class that will be executed when the game starts. When an instance of the game is created, the onCreate() method will be called once. This method loads the user-defined layout described in Listing 3-1.

Listing 3-2. *Space Blaster's Main Activity Class*

```
package ch03.game.sb;

import android.app.Activity;
import android.os.Bundle;
import android.view.LayoutInflater;
import android.view.View;

public class SpaceBlaster extends Activity {
    private View view;

    @Override
    protected void onCreate(Bundle savedInstanceState) {
        super.onCreate(savedInstanceState);

        LayoutInflater factory = LayoutInflater.from(this);

        // Set game layout
        view = factory.inflate(R.layout.main, null);
        setContentView(view);

        // Enable view key events
        view.setFocusable(true);
        view.setFocusableInTouchMode(true);

    }

    @Override
    protected void onStop() {
        super.onStop();
        ((ArcadeGame) view).halt();
    }

    @Override
    protected void onPause() {
        super.onPause();
        onStop();
    }

    @Override
    protected void onRestart() {
```

```
        super.onRestart();
        ((ArcadeGame) view).resume();
    }
}
```

The class keeps a reference to the layout (using the view class variable). This variable is used to halt the game when the user exists or restart it, as shown in the onStop and onRestart methods. To manually load the user-defined layout, we use the LayoutInfalter class:

```
LayoutInflater factory = LayoutInflater.from(this);
```

```
// Set game layout
view = factory.inflate(R.layout.main, null);
setContentView(view);
```

Two important lines are used to cascade key and touch events to the inner layout:

```
view.setFocusable(true);
view.setFocusableInTouchMode(true);
```

setFocusable tells the view (the user-defined layout) that it can receive focus and thus events in key or touch modes. These two lines are critical; if they are commented out, the game will not receive events.

Creating the Game Layout

As mentioned before, the class SpaceBlasterGame extends ArcadeGame, which in turn extends the Android layout LinearLayout. In this way, we can define a game thread to update the state of the game and simply draw sprites in the onDraw method of LinearLayout, thus gaining a finer control over the drawing process. SpaceBlasterGame performs the drawing, and it has all the game logic. This class is relatively complex compared to the others, but before we take a look at it, let's see how the game thread is handled by ArcadeGame.

ArcadeGame is the abstract base class for SpaceBlasterGame, and it deals with the game loop. This loop is infinite and invalidates the view to force a redraw of the display (see Listing 3-3).

Listing 3-3. *Abstract Class ArcadeGame*

```
package ch03.game.sb;

import java.util.Timer;
import java.util.TimerTask;

import ch03.common.AudioClip;

import android.content.Context;
import android.graphics.Bitmap;
import android.graphics.BitmapFactory;
import android.util.AttributeSet;
import android.widget.LinearLayout;

/**
```

```
 * Base class for all games. Extends {@link LinearLayout} and uses a
 * {@link TimerTask} to invalidate the view
 *
 * @author V. Silva
 *
 */
public abstract class ArcadeGame extends LinearLayout {
    // App context
    private Context mContex;

    // Update timer used to invalidate the view
    private Timer mUpdateTimer;

    // Timer period
    private long mPeriod = 1000;

    /**
     * C
     *
     * @param context
     */
    public ArcadeGame(Context context) {
        super(context);
        mContex = context;
    }

    public ArcadeGame(Context context, AttributeSet attrs) {
        super(context, attrs);
        mContex = context;
    }

    /**
     * Fires on layout
     */
    protected void onLayout(boolean changed, int l, int t, int r, int b) {
        super.onLayout(changed, l, t, r, b);
        try {
            // Init game
            initialize();

            /**
             * start update task. Which will fire onDraw in the future
             */
            startUpdateTimer();
        } catch (Exception e) {
            // bug
            e.printStackTrace();
        }
    }

    /**
```

```java
 * Set the update period
 *
 * @param period
 */
public void setUpdatePeriod(long period) {
    mPeriod = period;
}

/**
 * A timer is used to move the sprite around
 */
protected void startUpdateTimer() {
    mUpdateTimer = new Timer();
    mUpdateTimer.schedule(new UpdateTask(), 0, mPeriod);
}

protected void stopUpdateTimer() {
    if (mUpdateTimer != null) {
        mUpdateTimer.cancel();
    }
}

public Context getContex() {
    return mContex;
}

/**
 * Load an image
 *
 * @param id
 * @return
 */
protected Bitmap getImage(int id) {
    return BitmapFactory.decodeResource(mContex.getResources(), id);
}

/**
 * Get AudioClip
 *
 * @param id
 * @return
 */
protected AudioClip getAudioClip(int id) {
    return new AudioClip(mContex, id);
}

/**
 * Overload this to update the sprites on the game
 */
abstract protected void updatePhysics();
```

```java
    /**
     * Overload to initialize the game
     */
    abstract protected void initialize();

    abstract protected boolean gameOver();

    abstract protected long getScore();

    /**
     * Canvas update task
     *
     * @author vsilva
     *
     */
    private class UpdateTask extends TimerTask {

        @Override
        public void run() {
            updatePhysics();

            /**
             * Cause an invalidate to happen on a subsequent cycle
             * through the event loop. Use this to invalidate the View
             * from a non-UI thread. onDraw will be called sometime
             * in the future.
             */
            postInvalidate();
        }

    }

    /**
     * Halt game. Stops the update task. Called by a parent activity to halt
     *
     */
    public void halt() {
        stopUpdateTimer();
    }

    /**
     * Resume Game
     */
    public void resume() {
        initialize();
        startUpdateTimer();
    }
}
```

Any user-defined layout must define constructors with an Android Context and set of attributes for being able to be processed properly by the system:

```java
public ArcadeGame(Context context) {
    super(context);
    mContex = context;
}

public ArcadeGame(Context context, AttributeSet attrs) {
    super(context, attrs);
    mContex = context;
}
```

Note that ArcadeGame extends LinearLayout and sends its arguments to the parent via super(context) and super(context, attrs). This class also overloads the parent's method onLayout(), which fires when the view should assign a size and position to each of its children:

```java
/**
 * Fires on layout
 */
protected void onLayout(boolean changed, int l, int t, int r, int b) {
    super.onLayout(changed, l, t, r, b);
    try {
        // Init game
        initialize();

        /**
         * start update task. Which will fire onDraw in the future
         */
        startUpdateTimer();
    } catch (Exception e) {
        // bug
        e.printStackTrace();
    }
}
```

onLayout is in charge of initializing the game and starting the update timer. Note that initialize() is an abstract method that must be overloaded by the child class (SpaceBlasterGame) to perform initialization. The update timer, on the other hand, will be defined within AbstractGame. To define a game loop, we can use a simple TimerTask that will update itself using a period, as shown in Listing 3-4.

Listing 3-4. *Defining a Game Loop Using a Timer Task*

```java
// Timer period
private long mPeriod = 1000;

/**
 * Canvas update task
 *
 * @author vsilva
 *
 */
private class UpdateTask extends TimerTask {
    @Override
```

```
        public void run() {
            updatePhysics();

            /**
             * Cause an invalidate to happen on a subsequent cycle
             * through the event loop. Use this to invalidate the View
             * from a non-UI thread. onDraw will be called sometime
             * in the future.
             */
            postInvalidate();
        }

    }

    /**
     * A timer is used to move the sprite around
     */
    protected void startUpdateTimer() {
        mUpdateTimer = new Timer();
        mUpdateTimer.schedule(new UpdateTask(), 0, mPeriod);
    }

    protected void stopUpdateTimer() {
        if (mUpdateTimer != null) {
            mUpdateTimer.cancel();
        }
    }

    /**
     * Set the update period
     *
     * @param period
     */
    public void setUpdatePeriod(long period) {
        mPeriod = period;
    }
```

When the layout initializes, the onLayout() method will fire and call initialize() and startUpdateTimer(). These methods will start the Timertask:run() method, which updates the physics of the child class and invalidates the view by calling postInvalidate(). Invalidating the view will, in turn, tell the system UI thread to refresh the display. This cycle will repeat itself until the value of the update period (mPeriod) is reached, and this value can be set by the main class (SpaceBlaster) using the setUpdatePeriod method. In this way, we have created a simple refresh loop for the game.

Implementing the Game

The previous sections showed you the foundation for the main class, SpaceBlasterGame. Here is where all the meat resides. Let's take a closer look at the most important sections of SpaceBlaster.java. Note that the class has been stripped for simplicity in Listing 3-5, but the chapter source contains the full implementation.

Listing 3-5. *The Main Game Class*

```
package ch03.game.sb;

import ch03.common.AudioClip;
import ch03.common.Tools;
import android.content.Context;
import android.graphics.Bitmap;
import android.graphics.Canvas;
import android.graphics.Paint;
import android.graphics.RectF;
import android.util.AttributeSet;
import android.view.KeyEvent;
import android.view.MotionEvent;

public class SpaceBlasterGame extends ArcadeGame
{
    // Game name
    public static final String NAME = "SpaceBlaster";

    // Refresh rate (ms)
    private static final long UPDATE_DELAY = 40;

    private Context mContext;

    // For text
    private Paint mTextPaint = new Paint();

    // For Bitmaps
    private Paint mBitmapPaint = new Paint();

    private Paint mLaserBarPaint = new Paint();
    private Paint mShieldBarPaint = new Paint();
    private Paint mShieldPaint = new Paint();

    /**
     * Constructor
     *
     * @param context
     */
    public SpaceBlasterGame(Context context) {
        super(context);
        mContext = context;
        super.setUpdatePeriod(UPDATE_DELAY);
    }

    public SpaceBlasterGame(Context context, AttributeSet attrs) {
        super(context, attrs);
        mContext = context;
        super.setUpdatePeriod(UPDATE_DELAY);
    }
```

```
    // Code removed for simplicity
    // See chapter source
    // ...
}
```

The class constructor `SpaceBlasterGame` starts by initializing the Android context by calling `super(context)` and setting the game update delay to 40 milliseconds. Note that the context is critical for all the UI thread operations. A series of `Paint` objects is also defined to hold the style and color information about how to draw geometries, text, and bitmaps:

- `mTextPaint` holds style and color information for the text. It will be initialized as white.

- `mBitmapPaint` holds style and color information for all bitmaps.

- `mLaserBarPaint` holds style and color information for the laser bar at the bottom of the screen.

- `mShieldBarPaint` holds style and color information for the shield bar at the bottom of the screen.

- `mShieldPaint` holds style and color information for the ship's shield. It will be used to draw an oval filled with a semitransparent light blue color around the ship.

Initializing Sprites and Sounds

Game initialization occurs in the `initialize` method overloaded from the parent abstract class `ArcadeGame` (see Listing 3-6). The call sequence goes as follows: `LinearLayout.onLayout` calls `ArcadeGame.initilize`, which calls `SpaceBlasterGame.initilize`. This last method performs the following tasks:

- Set the screen size.

- Set the style and color attributes for the Paint objects: text, laser bar, and shield bar.

- Load the game bitmap sprites: ship, meteor, laser bullet, and explosion sequence.

- Load the audio clips.

Listing 3-6. *Game Initialization*

```
    public void initialize() {
        int n;

        // Screen size
        int width = getWidth();
        int height = getHeight();

        // Text Paints
        mTextPaint.setARGB(255, 255, 255, 255);
        mShieldPaint.setARGB(125, 0, 255, 255);
```

```java
    // Laser Bar Energy
    mLaserBarPaint.setARGB(255, 0, 255, 96);
    mLaserBarPaint.setStyle(Paint.Style.FILL);

    // Shield Bar Energy
    mShieldBarPaint.setARGB(255, 0, 255, 255);
    mShieldBarPaint.setStyle(Paint.Style.FILL);

    ship = getImage(R.drawable.sb_ship);
    bullet = getImage(R.drawable.sb_bullet);
    fire = new Bitmap[fireframe];

    // Load fire image sprites
    int[] ids = new int[] { R.drawable.sb_fire0, R.drawable.sb_fire1 };

    for (n = 0; n < fireframe; n++) {
        fire[n] = getImage(ids[n]);
    }

    // Load meteor explosion sequence sprites
    ids = new int[] { R.drawable.sb_boom0, R.drawable.sb_boom1,
            R.drawable.sb_boom2, R.drawable.sb_boom3,
            R.drawable.sb_boom4 };

    boom = new Bitmap[bframes + 1];

    for (n = 0; n <= bframes; n++) {
        boom[n] = getImage(ids[n]);
    }
    // ...

    // Meteor initialize
    meteor = getImage(R.drawable.sb_meteor);

    // ...

    // Load Audio clips
    try {
        blast = getAudioClip(R.raw.sb_blast);
        crash = getAudioClip(R.raw.sb_collisn);
        kill = getAudioClip(R.raw.sb_mdestr);
    } catch (Exception e) {
        Tools.MessageBox(mContext, "Audio Error: " + e.toString());
    }

    initStars();
    // ...

}
```

Loading Bitmap Sprites

Bitmap sprites are loaded by SpaceBlasterGame.initialize from the drawables section of the project using the getImage(RESOURCEID) method. getImage is defined in the base class ArcadeGame, so it'll be easy for child classes to reuse. For example, the game's explosion is simply an array of bitmaps loaded from the drawables folder (shown in Figure 3-5). To create an explosion, the game manipulates the explosion frame number when the display is drawn. The tricky part is keeping track of many explosions and their X and Y coordinates. Consider the next fragment, which loads bitmaps for the ship, laser bullet and explosion frames:

```
// Ship
ship = getImage(R.drawable.sb_ship);

// Laser Bullet
bullet = getImage(R.drawable.sb_bullet);

// Load meteor explosion sequence sprites
ids = new int[] { R.drawable.sb_boom0, R.drawable.sb_boom1,
        R.drawable.sb_boom2, R.drawable.sb_boom3,
        R.drawable.sb_boom4 };

boom = new Bitmap[bframes + 1];

for (n = 0; n <= bframes; n++) {
    boom[n] = getImage(ids[n]);
}
```

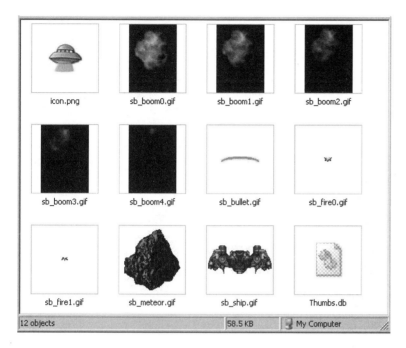

Figure 3-5. *Game sprites in the drawables folder*

Creating the Star Field

Another neat trick is to create a random star field in the background (see Figure 3-6). We can do this by using arrays of X and Y coordinates for each star. But we must also set style and colors using Paint objects. Listing 3-7 demonstrates how to create the random star field and styles for SpaceBlaster.

Listing 3-7. *A Random Star Field*

```
/**
 * create the star field in the background
 */
public void initStars() {
    starsX = new int[numStars];
    starsY = new int[numStars];
    starsC = new Paint[numStars];
    for (int i = 0; i < numStars; i++) {
        starsX[i] = (int) ((Math.random() * xSize - 1) + 1);
        starsY[i] = (int) ((Math.random() * ySize - 1) + 1);
        starsC[i] = newColor();
    }
}

public Paint newColor() {
```

```
    int r = Math.random() * 255;
    int g = Math.random() * 255;
    int b = Math.random() * 255;
    Paint p = new Paint();
    p.setARGB(255, r, g, b);
    return p;
}
```

Figure 3-6. *The star field with game sprites*

Playing Audio Clips

A good sound implementation is critical for any successful game. Android gives you two choices when dealing with game sound:

- Implement the sound logic in Java using Android's MediaPlayer API.

- Implement the sound natively (in C or C++). This could be an option if you have native code and wish to reuse it. This can be though as, by the time of this writing, Google provides no support for native development.

Java sound must be implemented using the MediaPlayer API. This is a powerful media tool, but it has some drawbacks when dealing with game sound:

- The MediaPlayer can only open raw resources (sound files within your project) or files located in the file system. This is a serious caveat if the game packs sprites and sounds in a single file. 3D games like Doom and Wolf 3D use a single file for sprites and sounds, and they use a mixer device to combine streams of bytes simultaneously. This solution is not possible with the MediaPlayer.

- The MediaPlayer API has some annoying idiosyncrasies when developing. For example, playing a resource sound is easy:

```
MediaPlayer mPlayer = MediaPlayer.create(Context, RESOURCEID);
mPlayer.start();
```

- However if you attempt to pause a sound before it plays or issue two simultaneous play commands, the MediaPlayer throws an IllegalState exception. The same thing happens if you try to replay a sound before preparing or making sure the player has been paused. These limitations make dealing with the player annoying and difficult for a game where multiple sounds must be replayed continuously.

- The MediaPlayer consumes significant resources and can slow things down quite a bit, especially if you have lots of sounds.

Listing 3-8 shows the AudioClip sound class. It is designed to mirror the Java SE class of the same name by wrapping an instance of the MediaPlayer and dealing with the media events behind the scenes.

Listing 3-8. *An Audio Helper Class*

```
package ch03.common;

import android.content.Context;
import android.media.MediaPlayer;

public class AudioClip {
    private MediaPlayer mPlayer;
    private String name;

    private boolean mPlaying = false;
    private boolean mLoop = false;

    public AudioClip(Context ctx, int resID)
    {
        // clip name
        name = ctx.getResources().getResourceName(resID);

        // Create a media player
        mPlayer = MediaPlayer.create(ctx, resID);

        // Listen for  completion events
        mPlayer.setOnCompletionListener(
            new MediaPlayer.OnCompletionListener() {
```

```java
            @Override
            public void onCompletion(MediaPlayer mp) {
                mPlaying = false;

                if (mLoop) {
                    mp.start();
                }
            }

        });
    }


    public synchronized void play() {
        if (mPlaying)
            return;

        if (mPlayer != null) {
            mPlaying = true;
            mPlayer.start();
        }
    }

    public synchronized void stop() {
        try {
            mLoop = false;
            if (mPlaying) {
                mPlaying = false;
                mPlayer.pause();
            }

        } catch (Exception e) {
            System.err.println("AduioClip::stop " + name + " "
                    + e.toString());
        }
    }

    public synchronized void loop() {
        mLoop = true;
        mPlaying = true;
        mPlayer.start();

    }

    public void release() {
        if (mPlayer != null) {
            mPlayer.release();
            mPlayer = null;
        }
    }
}
```

AudioClip wraps and instance of MediaPlayer and is aware of the state of the sound: paying, paused, or looping. This awareness is necessary for dealing with IllegalState exceptions explained previously. AudioClip also listens for completion events via setOnCompletionListener(OnCompletionListener), and if the loop flag is set, it will replay the sound. Space Blaster has three sounds that can be loaded with the code:

```
blast = getAudioClip(R.raw.sb_blast);      // Laser shot
crash = getAudioClip(R.raw.sb_collisn);  // Ship collision
kill = getAudioClip(R.raw.sb_mdestr);    // meteor destruction
```

getAudioClip takes a sound resource ID as argument, and it is defined in the abstract class ArcadeGame as follows:

```
protected AudioClip getAudioClip(int id) {
return new AudioClip(mContex, id);
}
```

■ **Tip** Audio resources must be saved in the res/raw folder within the project.

About Native Sound

Native games like Doom and Wolf 3D, shown in later chapters, pack sound resources in their own formats and manipulate the sound device at the operating system level. Even though Android runs a Linux kernel behind the scenes, it is not a standard Linux distribution, especially with dealing with low-level devices, for example:

- The standard Linux sound device (/dev/dsp) and mixer (/dev/mixer) are not supported, making reusing sound logic very difficult for native games. For some reason, Google decided to use the Sonivox Enhanced Audio System (EAS) via the /dev/eac device. This caveat is compounded by the fact that Google provides no support for native development. Nevertheless, a solution is to cascade the sound name back to Java via JNI and play it using AudioClip. This technique is explained in detail in Chapters 6 and 7.

- If you have native code that uses OpenAL/OpenGL for accelerated sound and graphics, you are in trouble. Google wants all development done in its Java-based version of OpenGL and doesn't support OpenAL. This leaves you with the painful task of translating OpenGL logic line by line from C to Java. Nevertheless, all is not lost. I found a neat trick to leave your C-based OpenGL code intact and still be able to run it from Java, and I explain my trick in 21.330Chapter 5.

Handling Key and Touch Events

Key and touch events can be handled by overloading the following methods (as shown in Listing 3-9):

- onKeyDown: This event fires when a key is pressed. The event receives two arguments: an integer representing the key code and a KeyEvent. Note that the key code is an integer value defined by Android not related to the standard ASCII keys. To test for a specific key, simply compare the value with the static key constants in KeyEvent.

- onKeyUp: This event fires when a key is released, and it receives the same arguments as onKeUp. Furthermore, you can also check the status of the Shift or Alt keys using event.isShiftPressed() or event.isAltPressed() respectively.

- onTouchEvent: This event fires when you tap the screen, and it receives a MotionEvent. Tap events have two states: DOWN and UP just like key events. You can check the tap state by comparing event.getAction() with MotionEvent.ACTION_DOWN or MotionEvent.ACTION_UP. You can also get the X and Y coordinates relative to the upper-left corner of the screen.

Listing 3-9. *Handling Touch and Key Events*

```java
/**
 * Android Key events
 */
@Override
public boolean onKeyUp(int keyCode, KeyEvent event) {
    keyUp(keyCode);
    return true;
}

@Override
public boolean onKeyDown(int keyCode, KeyEvent event) {
    keyDown(keyCode);
    return true;
}

public boolean onTouchEvent(MotionEvent event) {
    int tx = (int)event.getX();
    int ty = (int)event.getY();

    // Has the ship been touched. if so move it
    if ( tx >= x && tx <= x + ship.getWidth()
        && ty >= y && ty <= y + ship.getHeight()){
        x = tx - (ship.getWidth()/2);
        y = ty - (ship.getHeight()/2);

    }
    // else handle tap
    else if ( event.getAction() == MotionEvent.ACTION_UP)
    {
```

```java
            // if not in game, start
            if ( !ingame ) {
                ingame = true;
                GameStart();
            }
            else {
                // fire gun
                keyDown(KeyEvent.KEYCODE_SPACE);
            }
        }
    }
    return true;
}

/**
 * Process key down event
 * @param key Android Key code
 * @return
 */
public boolean keyDown( int key) {
    if (ingame) {
        mousex = -1;
        if (key == KeyEvent.KEYCODE_DPAD_LEFT
                || key == KeyEvent.KEYCODE_Q)
            dx = -1;
        if (key == KeyEvent.KEYCODE_DPAD_RIGHT
                || key == KeyEvent.KEYCODE_W)
            dx = 1;
        if (key == KeyEvent.KEYCODE_DPAD_UP
                || key == KeyEvent.KEYCODE_O)
            dy = -1;
        if (key == KeyEvent.KEYCODE_DPAD_DOWN
                || key == KeyEvent.KEYCODE_L)
            dy = 1;
        if ( (key ==  KeyEvent.KEYCODE_SPACE) ) {
            if (bcur > 0) {
                fireGun();
            }
        }
    } else {
        if (key == KeyEvent.KEYCODE_S) {
            ingame = true;
            GameStart();
        }
    }
    if (key == KeyEvent.KEYCODE_E){
        ingame = false;
    }

    if (key == KeyEvent.KEYCODE_Q){
        // Arggg!! There should be a better wayt to quit!
        System.exit(0);
```

```
        }
        return true;
    }

    /**
     * Process key up event
     * @param e Key event
     * @param key key code
     * @return
     */
    public boolean keyUp(int key) {
        if (key == KeyEvent.KEYCODE_DPAD_LEFT
                || key == KeyEvent.KEYCODE_DPAD_RIGHT
                || key == KeyEvent.KEYCODE_Q
                || key == KeyEvent.KEYCODE_W)
            dx = 0;
        if (key == KeyEvent.KEYCODE_DPAD_UP
                || key == KeyEvent.KEYCODE_DPAD_DOWN
                || key == KeyEvent.KEYCODE_O
                || key == KeyEvent.KEYCODE_L)
            dy = 0;
        return true;
    }
```

In SpaceBlaster, when the pad arrows are pressed, the position of the ship is shifted by 1 unit in the corresponding direction. S stars the game; E ends it, and Q terminates the application. The onTouchEvent allows the ship to be dragged around the device screen using your fingertips. When the game is running, tapping anywhere on the device screen (other than the ship) will start the game if it's not already started or fire the laser gun if the game is already running.

At this point, the project, including all files and resources, should look as shown 24.251in Figure 3-7.

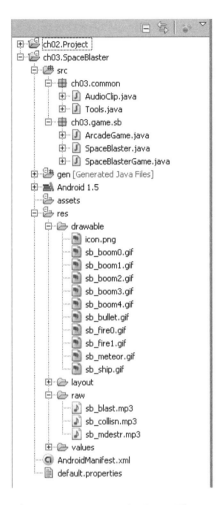

Figure 3-7. *Resources for Space Blaster*

Testing on the Emulator

We can finally start gaming! Start your emulator, and run the game like so:

1. From the Eclipse main menu, click Run   Run Configurations.

2. On the left side, right-click Android Application   New.

3. Enter a name (**SpaceBlaster**), and select the project ch03.SpaceBlaster (see Figure 3-8).

4. Click Run.

Figure 3-6 shows how the game should look on the emulator. To play, tap the screen and use the arrows to move the ship around. Press the space bar to fire the gun.

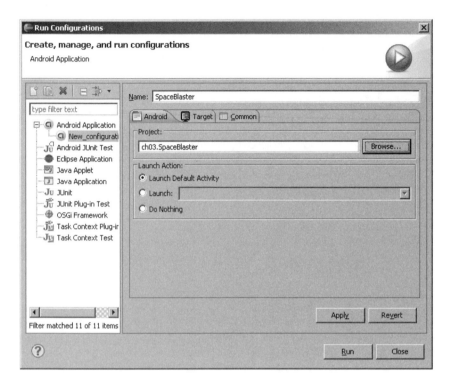

Figure 3-8. *The Run Configurations dialog for SpaceBlaster*

What's Next?

In this chapter, you have taken the first steps in writing a simple Java game and looked at the different issues that affect Java game development for Android, such as the significant differences between the Android API and the Java ME standard and how that influences code reuse and multiplatform support. You also learned gaming tricks, including creating an XML user-defined linear layout, using a timer task to simulate a game loop, invalidating a view layout within a user-defined (non-UI) thread, loading sprites and sounds, and dealing with the idiosyncrasies of the media player. You also saw some drawing techniques for creating sprite animations and simple objects and setting text styles and colors using the Paint object. Finally, I showed you how to deal with key and touch events.

In the next chapter, we take things further to create an arcade classic—Asteroids, a game that presents a new set of challenges when dealing with drawing techniques.

CHAPTER 4

■ ■ ■

Java Games Continued: Fun with Polygons

In this chapter, we take things to the next level with an arcade classic: Asteroids. The goal of this chapter is to illustrate a polygon-based game (Asteroids), as opposed to the previous chapter's sprite-based game (Space Blaster). Using polygons presents a new set of challenges due to the limited polygon capabilities of Android, as you'll see in the next section. Nevertheless, Asteroids is a relatively simple game that takes advantage of the high portability of the Java language by reusing code from the standard Java SE Abstract Windowing Toolkit (AWT). Let's get started.

About the Chapter Layout

This chapter has a different layout than previous chapters, as it doesn't start with a description of the game implementation but a series of caveats I found when trying to create Asteroids:

- *Caveats of drawing polygons and rectangles*: It turns out that, at the time of this writing, there is no polygon support in Android. This made creating this game tougher than the previous chapter's, as I found the need to create three brand new classes: Rectangle, Polygon, and PolygonSripte. Lucky for me, I was able to take advantage of the high portability of the Java language and reuse most of the code of the Rectangle and Polygon classes of Java SE (this is one of the reasons I like the Java language). PolygonSprite is a class I created from the ground up.

- *Game architecture and implementation*: In this section, the actual game implementation starts. I chose to do this because the game cannot be described without the previous foundation classes. Here you will learn about resource description, game life cycle, processing key press and touch events plus Testing in the emulator. Let's get started.

Understanding the Caveats of Drawing Polygons in Android

Before starting work on Asteroids, let's take a look at the caveats of drawing polygons in Android. This section represents the foundation over which the game itself will be built. There is a little problem when thinking of building a polygon-based game in Android—the API has no polygons. This would be like designing a house just to find out there is no land to build on. In the previous chapter, we used the onDraw method of the LinearLayout class to render bitmaps. Asteroids will use the same technique to draw polygons instead of bitmaps. To illustrate this concept, consider the following code snippet to draw the Android canvas:

```
class MyLayout extends Linearlayout {
    // ...
  protected void onDraw(Canvas canvas)
  {
      // draw a point
      canvas.drawPoint(x, y, aPaint);

      // Draw lines
      canvas.drawLines(float[] points, aPaint);
  }
}
```

The Canvas class holds many draw calls. To draw something, you need four basic components: a bitmap to hold the pixels, a Canvas to host the draw calls, a drawing primitive (e.g., Rect, Path, Text, or Bitmap), and a Paint to describe the colors and styles for the drawing. The basic primitives that could help when drawing polygons follow:

- drawPoint(float x, float y, Paint paint) draws a single point given X and Y coordinates and a paint style.

- drawArc (RectF oval, float startAngle, float sweepAngle, boolean useCenter, Paint paint) draws the specified arc, which will be scaled to fit inside the specified rectangle. oval defines the bounds of the rectangle used to define the shape and size of the arc. startAngle is the starting angle (in degrees) where the arc begins. sweepAngle is the sweep angle (in degrees) measured clockwise. useCenter, if true, includes the center of the oval in the arc and closes it if it is being stroked drawing a wedge.

- drawCircle (float cx, float cy, float radius, Paint paint) draws a circle using the specified paint. cx and cy define the X and Y coordinates of the center. The circle will be filled or framed based on the Style in the paint.

- drawLine (float startX, float startY, float stopX, float stopY, Paint paint) draws a line segment with the specified start and stop coordinates, using the specified paint. The style paint is ignored because a line is always framed.

- drawLines (float[] pts, int offset, int count, Paint paint) draws a series of lines. Each line is taken from four consecutive values in the pts array. Thus to draw one line, the array must contain at least four values. These are the X and Y coordinates of each point: X0, Y0, X1, Y1,...,Xn,Yn.

- drawRect (Rect r, Paint paint) draws the specified Rect using the specified Paint. The rectangle will be filled or framed based on the style in the paint.

- drawRoundRect (RectF rect, float rx, float ry, Paint paint) draws the specified rounded rectangle using the specified paint. The rounded rectangle will be filled or framed based on the style in the paint. rx and ry define the xy radius of the oval used to round the corners.

These are the most important methods for drawing shapes in the Canvas class, but we need more. For example, for a polygon-based game, a basic technique is to inscribe shapes within rectangles. In this way, operations such as collision detection and rendering can be applied. Thus, we need three basic shapes for our Asteroids game that are missing from the Android API: a rectangle, a polygon, and a polygon sprite.

■ **Tip** The Android API defines the classes Rect and RectF for rectangles, but it does not define polygons or polygon sprites.

Understanding the Caveats of Drawing Rectangles

From the drawing methods in the previous section, we could use Canvas.drawLines to draw our polygons directly. However, we also need extra functionally:

- A way to detect if a polygon is inside another in the (X, Y) coordinate system, which is necessary to detect collisions within the game

- A way to assign style and color to the polygon

Thus, using Canvas.drawLines is insufficient to manipulate polygons directly. We need a more elegant solution; we need to create Rectangle, Polygon, and PolygonSprite classes.

Android already has the classes Rect and RectF that could be reused. Nevertheless these classes lack the functionality to check if the rectangle is inscribed within another (a critical requirement for Asteroids).

Listing 4-1 shows the class Rectangle capable of remembering its (X, Y) coordinates plus width and height. It can also check if its bounds contain or are inside another rectangle. As a matter of fact this code is taken from the Java SE java.awt.Rectangle class (taking advantage of the high portability of Java).

The Rectangle class in Listing 4-1 is the basis for the polygon sprite we need for Asteroids.

Listing 4-1. *The Rectangle Class Used by Polygon*

```
package ch04.common;

public class Rectangle {

    public int x;
    public int y;
    public int width;
    public int height;

    public Rectangle() {
        this(0, 0, 0, 0);
    }
```

```java
/**
 * Constructs a new <code>Rectangle</code> whose top-left corner is
 * specified as (<code>x</code>, <code>y</code>) and whose width
 * and height are specified by the arguments of the same name.
 *
 * @param x
 *              the specified x coordinate
 * @param y
 *              the specified y coordinate
 * @param width
 *              the width of the <code>Rectangle</code>
 * @param height
 *              the height of the <code>Rectangle</code>
 */
public Rectangle(int x, int y, int width, int height) {
    this.x = x;
    this.y = y;
    this.width = width;
    this.height = height;
}

public boolean contains(int X, int Y, int W, int H) {
    int w = this.width;
    int h = this.height;

    if ((w | h | W | H) < 0) {
        // At least one of the dimensions is negative...
        return false;
    }
    // Note: if any dimension is zero, tests below must return false...
    int x = this.x;
    int y = this.y;
    if (X < x || Y < y) {
        return false;
    }
    w += x;
    W += X;
    if (W <= X) {
        // X+W overflowed or W was zero, return false if...
        // either original w or W was zero or
        // x+w did not overflow or
        // the overflowed x+w is smaller than the overflowed X+W
        if (w >= x || W > w) {
            return false;
        }
    } else {
        // X+W did not overflow and W was not zero, return false if...
        // original w was zero or
```

```
            // x+w did not overflow and x+w is smaller than X+W
            if (w >= x && W > w) {
                return false;
            }
        }
        h += y;
        H += Y;
        if (H <= Y) {
            if (h >= y || H > h) {
                return false;
            }
        } else {
            if (h >= y && H > h) {
                return false;
            }
        }
        return true;
    }

    public boolean contains(int x, int y) {
        return inside(x, y);
    }

    public boolean inside(int X, int Y) {
        int w = this.width;
        int h = this.height;
        if ((w | h) < 0) {
            // At least one of the dimensions is negative...
            return false;
        }
        // Note: if either dimension is zero, tests below must return false...
        int x = this.x;
        int y = this.y;
        if (X < x || Y < y) {
            return false;
        }
        w += x;
        h += y;
        // overflow || intersect
        return ((w < x || w > X) && (h < y || h > Y));
    }
}
```

Creating a Polygon Class for Asteroids

The standard J2SE API has the neat class Polygon that we can reuse for Asteroids. It is hard to understand why Google has not included such useful classes from java.awt into the Android API. Listing 4-2 shows the modified Polygon class (it is the same as the Java SE Polygon stripped for running in Android and Asteroids). Some of the most interesting methods of this class follow:

- *Constructors*: The default constructor will create a four-sided polygon. You can also define an N-sided polygon by giving two arrays representing the X0,X1,. . .Xn and Y0,Y1,. . .Yn coordinates of the vertices where (X0,Y0) represents the coordinates of the first vertex and so forth, The constructor also takes the number of sides.

- calculateBounds(int xpoints[], int ypoints[], int npoints): This method calculates the bounds of the polygon given a set of X and Y coordinates and number of points with respect to maximum integer values.

- addPoint(int x, int y): This one adds a point to the polygon given its X and Y coordinates.

- updateBounds(int x, int y): This method updates the bounds of the polygon to include a new point (X,Y).

- getBoundingBox(): This returns the rectangular bounds of the polygon.

- contains(int x, int y): This one checks if the polygon contains a given point (X,Y).

- float[] getPoints(): This method returns the X and Y coordinates of the vertices of the polygon.

Both the Polygon and Rectangle classes are used by the next class, PolygonSprite, to define all game objects.

Listing 4-2. The Polygon Class for Asteroids

```
package ch04.common;

public class Polygon {

    public int npoints;
    public int[] ypoints;
    public int[] xpoints;

    protected Rectangle bounds;

    public Polygon() {
        xpoints = new int[4];
        ypoints = new int[4];
    }

    public Polygon(int xpoints[], int ypoints[], int npoints) {
        // Fix 4489009: should throw IndexOutofBoundsException instead
        // of OutofMemoryException if npoints is huge
        // and > {x,y}points.length
        if (npoints > xpoints.length || npoints > ypoints.length) {
            throw new IndexOutOfBoundsException(
                    "npoints > xpoints.length || npoints > ypoints.length");
        }
```

```java
        this.npoints = npoints;
        this.xpoints = new int[npoints];
        this.ypoints = new int[npoints];
        System.arraycopy(xpoints, 0, this.xpoints, 0, npoints);
        System.arraycopy(ypoints, 0, this.ypoints, 0, npoints);
    }

    void calculateBounds(int xpoints[], int ypoints[], int npoints) {
        int boundsMinX = Integer.MAX_VALUE;
        int boundsMinY = Integer.MAX_VALUE;
        int boundsMaxX = Integer.MIN_VALUE;
        int boundsMaxY = Integer.MIN_VALUE;

        for (int i = 0; i < npoints; i++) {
            int x = xpoints[i];
            boundsMinX = Math.min(boundsMinX, x);
            boundsMaxX = Math.max(boundsMaxX, x);
            int y = ypoints[i];
            boundsMinY = Math.min(boundsMinY, y);
            boundsMaxY = Math.max(boundsMaxY, y);
        }

        bounds = new Rectangle(boundsMinX, boundsMinY, boundsMaxX
                - boundsMinX, boundsMaxY - boundsMinY);
    }

    public void reset() {
        npoints = 0;
        bounds = null;
    }

    /**
     * Appends the specified coordinates to this <code>Polygon</code>.
     *
     * @param x
     * @param y
     */
    public void addPoint(int x, int y) {
        if (npoints == xpoints.length) {
            int tmp[];

            tmp = new int[npoints * 2];
            System.arraycopy(xpoints, 0, tmp, 0, npoints);
            xpoints = tmp;

            tmp = new int[npoints * 2];
            System.arraycopy(ypoints, 0, tmp, 0, npoints);
            ypoints = tmp;
        }
        xpoints[npoints] = x;
        ypoints[npoints] = y;
```

```java
            npoints++;
            if (bounds != null) {
                updateBounds(x, y);
            }
        }

    void updateBounds(int x, int y) {
        if (x < bounds.x) {
            bounds.width = bounds.width + (bounds.x - x);
            bounds.x = x;
        } else {
            bounds.width = Math.max(bounds.width, x - bounds.x);
        }

        if (y < bounds.y) {
            bounds.height = bounds.height + (bounds.y - y);
            bounds.y = y;
        } else {
            bounds.height = Math.max(bounds.height, y - bounds.y);
        }
    }

    public Rectangle getBoundingBox() {
        if (npoints == 0) {
            return new Rectangle();
        }
        if (bounds == null) {
            calculateBounds(xpoints, ypoints, npoints);
        }
        return bounds;
    }

    /**
     * Determines if the specified coordinates are inside this
     * <code>Polygon</code>.
     *
     * @param x
     * @param y
     * @return
     */
    public boolean contains(int x, int y) {
        if (npoints <= 2 || !getBoundingBox().contains(x, y)) {
            return false;
        }
        int hits = 0;

        int lastx = xpoints[npoints - 1];
        int lasty = ypoints[npoints - 1];
        int curx, cury;
```

```java
// Walk the edges of the polygon
for (int i = 0; i < npoints; lastx = curx, lasty = cury, i++) {
    curx = xpoints[i];
    cury = ypoints[i];

    if (cury == lasty) {
        continue;
    }

    int leftx;
    if (curx < lastx) {
        if (x >= lastx) {
            continue;
        }
        leftx = curx;
    } else {
        if (x >= curx) {
            continue;
        }
        leftx = lastx;
    }

    double test1, test2;
    if (cury < lasty) {
        if (y < cury || y >= lasty) {
            continue;
        }
        if (x < leftx) {
            hits++;
            continue;
        }
        test1 = x - curx;
        test2 = y - cury;
    } else {
        if (y < lasty || y >= cury) {
            continue;
        }
        if (x < leftx) {
            hits++;
            continue;
        }
        test1 = x - lastx;
        test2 = y - lasty;
    }

    if (test1 < (test2 / (lasty - cury) * (lastx - curx))) {
        hits++;
    }
}
```

```java
        return ((hits & 1) != 0);
    }

    @Override
    public String toString() {
        if (npoints == 0)
            return null;
        String s = ""; //

        for (int i = 0; i < xpoints.length; i++) {
            s += "(" + xpoints[i] + "," + ypoints[i] + ") ";
        }
        return s;
    }

    /**
     * Get polygon points (x0y0, x1y1,.....) for rendering Each point pair will
     * render 1 line so the total # of points must be num sides * 4
     *
     * @return
     */
    public float[] getPoints() {
        int size = npoints * 4;
        float[] points = new float[size];
        int j = 1;

        if (size == 0 || xpoints == null || ypoints == null)
            return null;

        points[0] = xpoints[0];
        points[1] = ypoints[0];

        for (int i = 2; i < points.length - 2; i += 4) {

            points[i] = xpoints[j];
            points[i + 1] = ypoints[j];
            points[i + 2] = xpoints[j];
            points[i + 3] = ypoints[j];
            j++;
        }
        points[size - 2] = xpoints[0];
        points[size - 1] = ypoints[0];

        return points;
    }
}
```

Creating a PolygonSprite Class for Asteroids

PolygonSprite is the final foundation class of the game (see Listing 4-3). It is used to describe all game objects including the ship, asteroids, and flying saucer. Furthermore, it tracks information such as the following for all of these game objects:

- X and Y coordinates

- Angle of rotation

- Position in the screen

In this class, two polygons are used: one to keep the basic shape, and the other to apply the final translation and rotation and to paint on screen.

Listing 4-3. *The PolygonSprite Class Used by Asteroids*

```
package ch04.game;

import ch04.common.Polygon;
import android.graphics.Canvas;
import android.graphics.Paint;

/**********************************************************
 * The PolygonSprite class defines a game object, including it's shape,
 * position, movement and rotation. It also can determine if two objects
 * collide.
 **********************************************************/

public class PolygonSprite
{

    // Base sprite shape, centered at the origin (0,0).
    public Polygon shape;

    // Final location and shape of sprite after
    // applying rotation and translation to get screen
    // position. Used for drawing on the screen and in
    // detecting collisions.
    public Polygon sprite;

    boolean active; // Active flag.
    double angle; // Current angle of rotation.
    double deltaAngle; // Amount to change the rotation angle.
    double deltaX, deltaY; // Amount to change the screen position.

    // coords
    int x;
    int y;

    // Constructors:
```

```java
    public PolygonSprite() {

        this.shape = new Polygon();
        this.active = false;
        this.angle = 0.0;
        this.deltaAngle = 0.0;
        this.x = 0;
        this.y = 0;
        this.deltaX = 0.0;
        this.deltaY = 0.0;
        this.sprite = new Polygon();
    }

    public void render(int width, int height) {

        int i;

        // Render the sprite's shape and location by rotating it's
        // base shape and moving it to its proper screen position.

        this.sprite = new Polygon();
        for (i = 0; i < this.shape.npoints; i++) {
            this.sprite.addPoint((int) Math.round(this.shape.xpoints[i]
                    * Math.cos(this.angle) + this.shape.ypoints[i]
                    * Math.sin(this.angle))
                    + (int) Math.round(this.x) + width / 2,
                    (int) Math.round(this.shape.ypoints[i]
                            * Math.cos(this.angle) - this.shape.xpoints[i]
                            * Math.sin(this.angle))
                            + (int) Math.round(this.y) + height / 2);
        }
    }

    public boolean isColliding(PolygonSprite s) {

        int i;

        // Determine if one sprite overlaps with another, i.e., if any vertice
        // of one sprite lands inside the other.

        for (i = 0; i < s.sprite.npoints; i++) {
            if (this.sprite.contains(s.sprite.xpoints[i],
                    s.sprite.ypoints[i])) {
                return true;
            }
        }
        for (i = 0; i < this.sprite.npoints; i++) {
            if (s.sprite.contains(this.sprite.xpoints[i],
                    this.sprite.ypoints[i])) {
                return true;
            }
```

```java
    }

    return false;
}

/**
 * Advance Sprite
 *
 * @param width screen width
 * @param height screen height
 * @return
 */
public boolean advance(int width, int height) {

    boolean wrapped;

    // Update the rotation and position of the sprite based on the delta
    // values. If the sprite moves off the edge of the screen, it is wrapped
    // around to the other side and TRUE is returned.

    this.angle += this.deltaAngle;
    if (this.angle < 0)
        this.angle += 2 * Math.PI;
    if (this.angle > 2 * Math.PI)
        this.angle -= 2 * Math.PI;
    wrapped = false;
    this.x += this.deltaX;
    if (this.x < -width / 2) {
        this.x += width;
        wrapped = true;
    }
    if (this.x > width / 2) {
        this.x -= width;
        wrapped = true;
    }
    this.y -= this.deltaY;
    if (this.y < -height / 2) {
        this.y += height;
        wrapped = true;
    }
    if (this.y > height / 2) {
        this.y -= height;
        wrapped = true;
    }
    return wrapped;
}

@Override
public String toString() {
    return "Sprite: " + sprite + " Shape:" + shape;
}
```

```
/**
 * Draw Sprite using polygon points
 *
 * @param canvas
 * @param paint
 */
void draw(Canvas canvas, Paint paint) {
    float[] points = sprite.getPoints();

    if (points != null) {
        canvas.drawLines(points, paint);
    }
}
}
```

PolygonSprite defines the following methods:

- render(int width, int height) computes the shape of the sprite given the width and height of the screen. It also translates the polygon to the proper screen position and applies rotation. Note that this method has nothing to do with the actual screen painting (so perhaps "render" was not the best name choice).

- isColliding(PolygonSprite s) checks if the sprite is colliding with another by checking if the vertices of the sprite are inside the other (see Figure 4-1).

- advance(int width, int height) moves the sprite around based on the delta X and Y values. It also updates the sprites rotation values. The width and height arguments represent the size of the screen. Note that the sprite will be wrapped around if it moves off the screen.

- draw(Canvas canvas, Paint paint) does the actual drawing of the sprite in the Android layout. Its arguments are a Canvas object where the points will be drawn and a Paint object for style and color information.

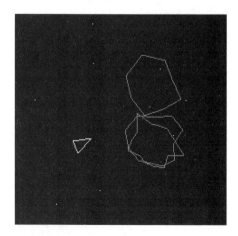

Figure 4-1. Polygon sprites about to collide

We have discussed the caveats of using polygons in Android. The goal of this section has been to illustrate the missing pieces we need to start building the game itself. We now have the foundation classes for Asteroids, so let's look at the actual game architecture.

Understanding the Game's Architecture

The architecture of Asteroids is almost identical to Space Blaster from the last chapter. When the program starts, the main class AsteroidsActivity will be loaded by Android. This activity will load the user-defined layout in the Asteroids class. This class, in turn, inherits from the abstract class ArcadeGame, which extends LinearLayout. Note that the user-defined layout is bound with the system by the XML file asteroids.xml (see Figure 4-2).

Here, you realize why ArcadeGame has been defined as Abstract. By incorporating common functionality in this class, we can implement multiple arcade games in the same project. As a matter of fact, you can merge SpaceBlaster and Asteroids into the same project and build your own arcade system.

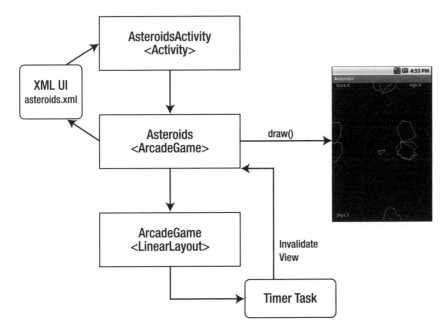

Figure 4-2. *The Asteroids game architecture*

Let's take a closer look at the actual project.

Creating the Project

We'll start by creating an Android project called Asteroids. Here is how:

1. Click the New Android Project button from the Eclipse toolbar.

2. Enter the project information:

   - *Name*: ch04.Asteroids

   - *Build Target*: **Android 1.5**

   - *Application Name*: **Asteroids**

   - *Package name*: ch04.game

   - *Create Activity*: **AsteroidsActivity**

   - *Min SDK Version:* **3**

3. Click Finish (see Figure 4-3).

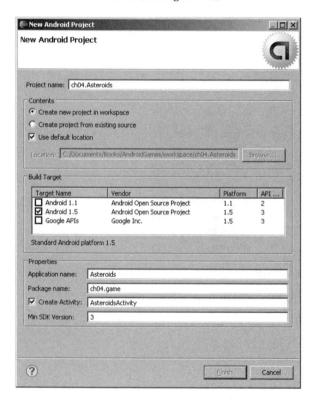

Figure 4-3. *The Asteroids project information*

Creating the Game Layout

We must create the user-defined layout using XML and the Asteroids class. Rename the main.xml file created by the wizard as asteroids.xml and insert the code in Listing 4-4.

Listing 4-4. *The XML Layout of Asteroids*

```
<?xml version="1.0" encoding="utf-8"?>

<ch04.game.Asteroids
 xmlns:android="http://schemas.android.com/apk/res/android"
    android:id="@+id/ll_asteroids"
    android:orientation="vertical"
    android:layout_width="fill_parent"
    android:layout_height="fill_parent"
    android:background="#FF000000">
</ch04.game.Asteroids>
```

Note that ch04.game.Asteroids is a required Java class that extends ArcadeGame, which in turn extends LinearLayout. A detailed list of files and resources is shown in the next section.

Looking at the Resources

Besides code, we need resources such as sounds, XML string messages, and a game icon (see Figure 4-4). Here is a list of resources used by Asteroids and what they do:

- Java classes

    - AsteroidsActivity: This is the master class called by Android when the user starts the game. It contains life cycle events such as onCreate, onResume, and onStop.

    - Asteroids: This class contains all game code. It extends ArcadeGame.

    - ArcadeGame: This is an abstract class with the game loop and game life cycle events initialize, updatePhysics, getScore, halt, and resume.

    - Constants: This class contains many game constants such as game delay, frames per second, number of ships, and sprite speeds.

- Polygon classes

    - PolygonSprite: This class represents any game sprite. It has methods to detect collisions using the classes Polygon and Rectangle.

    - Polygon: This class represents an N-sided polygon. It code is taken from the Java SE java.awt.Polygon class with most of the code stripped for simplicity.

    - Rectangle: This is also a stripped version of the Java SE java.awt.Rectangle class. It describes a rectangle by X and Y coordinates, as well as width and height. It can also check if the rectangle contains or is inside another.

- Other classes
  - AudioClip: This class deals with the Android MediaPlayer and is capable of playing, stopping, or looping a sound clip.
  - Tools: This class contains miscellaneous help methods such as message boxes, dialogs, and a browser launcher.
- Other resources
  - Asteroids.xml: This is the user-defined layout of the game. It points to the ch04.game.Asteroids class.
  - Asteroids.png: This is the game icon that you will see in your phone window. Clicking this icon will start the game.
  - Strings.xml: This file contains game strings, such as the game name and other messages.
- Raw sounds
  - a_crash.mp3: Played when an asteroid explodes
  - a_explosion.mp3: Played when the ship explodes
  - a_fire.mp3: Played when the ship fires the gun
  - a_missile.mp3: Played when the ship fires the missile
  - a_saucer.mp3: Played when the UFO shows up on screen
  - a_thrusters.mp3: Played when the ship moves around
  - a_warp.mp3: Played when the ship jumps into hyperspace (To avoid a collision, a ship vanishes from one point and reappears in another.)

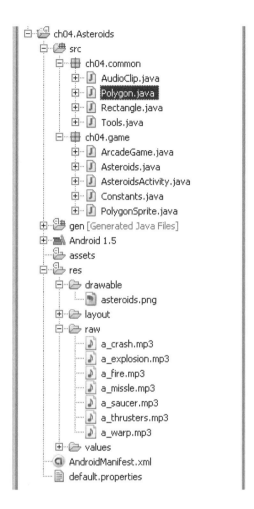

Figure 4-4. *The Asteroids resources*

Understanding the Game Life Cycle

As mentioned earlier, we use a LinerLayout to paint sprites on screen using a continuous game loop. The layout and loop—both controlled using Timers—are described by the abstract class ArcadeGame (see Listing 4-5). This class also defines the life cycle of the game using abstract methods that must be overridden by the child class Asteroids. This life cycle contains the following methods:

- void initialize() fires on game initialization. This is where sounds are loaded and sprites are created.

- void onDraw() must be overridden to paint sprites on screen. All painting is done using a Canvas and one or more Paint objects for font, color, and style information.

- void updatePhysics() fires once on every step of the loop. Use this method to update the sprites on the game.

- boolean gameOver() can be used to check if the user has terminated the game and perhaps get a final score. Its implementation is mostly optional.

- long getScore() can be used to get the user's final score.

Listing 4-5. *The Game Loop Using Timer Tasks*

```java
public abstract class ArcadeGame extends LinearLayout
{
    // Update timer used to invalidate the view
    private Timer mUpdateTimer;

    // Timer period
    private long mPeriod = 1000;

    // ....

    protected void onLayout(boolean changed, int l, int t, int r, int b) {
        super.onLayout(changed, l, t, r, b);
        try {
            // Init game
            initialize();

            /**
             * start update task. Which will fire onDraw in the future
             */
            startUpdateTimer();
        } catch (Exception e) {
            e.printStackTrace();
        }
    }

    // ...

    /**
     * A timer is used to move the sprite around
     */
    protected void startUpdateTimer() {
        mUpdateTimer = new Timer();
        mUpdateTimer.schedule(new UpdateTask(), 0, mPeriod);
    }

    private class UpdateTask extends TimerTask {
        @Override
        public void run() {
            updatePhysics();

            /**
             * Cause an invalidate to happen on a subsequent cycle through
```

```
                * the event loop. Use this to invalidate the View from
                * a non-UI thread. onDraw will be called sometime
                * in the future.
                */
               postInvalidate();
           }
       }

       /**
        * Overridden these to process game events (life-cycle)
        */

       // Update sprites here
       abstract protected void updatePhysics();

       // Init game
       abstract protected void initialize();

       // Game over
       abstract protected boolean gameOver();

       // Get score
       abstract protected long getScore();

}
```

Let's take a closer look at the game life cycle of Asteroids.

Initializing the Game

Game initialization occurs by overriding the initialize method in the Asteroids class (see Listing 4-6). It starts by loading sounds from the res/raw folder as follows:

```
Context ctx = getContext();
crashSound = new AudioClip(ctx, R.raw.a_crash);
clipTotal++;
explosionSound = new AudioClip(ctx, R.raw.a_explosion);
clipTotal++;
```

Here is where we use the AudioClip class to quickly load the raw resource using its ID. Note that we also need the application Context. The game also keeps track of the total number of clips in the game.

Next, we create the star background using an array of Points and the size of the screen:

```
void createStarts() {
    int width = getWidth();
    int height = getHeight();

    // Generate the starry background.
    numStars = width * height / 5000;
    stars = new Point[numStars];
```

```
    for (i = 0; i < numStars; i++) {
        // random XY Point
        stars[i] = new Point((int) (Math.random() * width)
                , (int) (Math.random() * height) );
    }
}
```

The stars are created using random Points with X and Y coordinates defined using the getWidth and getHeight methods. Note that getWidth and getHeight are built-in methods provided by the LinerLayout class.

Next, we create all polygon sprites in the game:

- The ship

- The ship's thrusters

- Photons (the ship's bullets)

- The flying saucer

- Asteroids and asteroid explosions

Note that all elements in the game are polygons, even the tiny photons and asteroid explosions. Finally, miscellaneous data is initialized and the game is put in Game Over mode.

Listing 4-6. *Game Initialization*

```
protected void initialize() {

    // Load sounds
    try {
        loadSounds();
        loaded = true;
    } catch (Exception e) {
        Tools.MessageBox(mContex, "Sound Error: " + e.toString());
    }

    // create star background
    createStarts();

    // Create shape for the ship sprite.
    ship = new PolygonSprite();
    ship.shape.addPoint(0, -10);
    ship.shape.addPoint(7, 10);
    ship.shape.addPoint(-7, 10);

    // Create thruster shapes
    createThrusters();

    // Create shape for each photon sprites.
    for (i = 0; i < Constants.MAX_SHOTS; i++) {
```

```java
        photons[i] = new PolygonSprite();
        photons[i].shape.addPoint(1, 1);
        photons[i].shape.addPoint(1, -1);
        photons[i].shape.addPoint(-1, 1);
        photons[i].shape.addPoint(-1, -1);
    }

    // Create shape for the flying saucer.
    ufo = new PolygonSprite();
    ufo.shape.addPoint(-15, 0);
    ufo.shape.addPoint(-10, -5);
    ufo.shape.addPoint(-5, -5);
    ufo.shape.addPoint(-5, -8);
    ufo.shape.addPoint(5, -8);
    ufo.shape.addPoint(5, -5);
    ufo.shape.addPoint(10, -5);
    ufo.shape.addPoint(15, 0);
    ufo.shape.addPoint(10, 5);
    ufo.shape.addPoint(-10, 5);

    // Create shape for the guided missile.
    missile = new PolygonSprite();
    missile.shape.addPoint(0, -4);
    missile.shape.addPoint(1, -3);
    missile.shape.addPoint(1, 3);
    missile.shape.addPoint(2, 4);
    missile.shape.addPoint(-2, 4);
    missile.shape.addPoint(-1, 3);
    missile.shape.addPoint(-1, -3);

    // Create asteroid sprites.
    for (i = 0; i < Constants.MAX_ROCKS; i++)
        asteroids[i] = new PolygonSprite();

    // Create explosion sprites.
    for (i = 0; i < Constants.MAX_SCRAP; i++)
        explosions[i] = new PolygonSprite();
    // Initialize game data and put it in 'game over' mode.
    highScore = 0;
    sound = true;
    detail = true;
    initGame();
    endGame();
}
```

Drawing Sprites

Drawing 23.70the sprites is the next step in the game life cycle and the most important too. Here is where all polygon sprites are drawn (see Listing 4-7). The most important steps are as follows:

1. The size of the screen is queried using the layout's getWidth and getHeight methods. The size is required to render elements on screen

2. The stars are drawn using an array of star sprites and calling canvas.drawPoint. Each sprite is drawn using its X and Y coordinates and a Paint object for style information.

3. Photons are drawn only if they are active. A photon becomes active when the user presses the space bar to fire the gun. Each photon is aware of its position on the canvas.

4. Missiles, a UFO, and the user's ship are drawn if they are active. When the user reaches a score threshold, the UFO will show up. Users must watch out for the missiles fired against them by the UFO. Note that the ship's thrusters must be drawn when the user presses the arrow keys to move the ship around.

5. Asteroids and explosion debris are drawn. Note that each bit of debris is an independent sprite.

6. Status messages are drawn. Messages include the score in the upper-left corner, the number of ships left in the lower-left, and the high score in the upper-right.

7. Other messages are displayed depending on the state of the game, including Game Over, Game Paused, or Sound Muted.

■ **Tip** Remember that each sprite is aware of its X and Y coordinates on screen and angle of rotation? The key method that performs all the magic is PolygonSprite.draw(Canvas canvas, Paint paint). Within this method, the polygon lines are drawn using canvas.drawLines(float[] points, Paint paint).

Listing 4-7. The Drawing Subroutine for Asteroids

```
protected void onDraw(Canvas canvas)
{
    // get screen size
    int width = getWidth();
    int height = getHeight();

    // draw stars
    for (i = 0; i < numStars; i++) {
        canvas.drawPoint(stars[i].x, stars[i].y, mPaint);
    }

    // Draw photon bullets.
    for (i = 0; i < Constants.MAX_SHOTS; i++) {
        if (photons[i].active) {
            photons[i].draw(canvas, mPaint);
```

```java
        }
    }

    // Draw the guided missile,
    if (missile.active) {
        missile.draw(canvas, mPaint);
    }

    // Draw the flying saucer.
    if (ufo.active) {
        ufo.draw(canvas, mRedPaint);
    }

    // Draw the ship
    if (ship.active) {
        // draw ship
        ship.draw(canvas, mPaint);

        // Draw thruster exhaust if thrusters are on. Do it randomly to get
        // a flicker effect.

        if (!paused && Math.random() < 0.5) {
            if (up) {
                fwdThruster.draw(canvas, mPaint);
            }
            if (down) {
                revThruster.draw(canvas, mPaint);
            }
        }
    }

    // Draw the asteroids.
    for (i = 0; i < Constants.MAX_ROCKS; i++) {
        if (asteroids[i].active) {
            asteroids[i].draw(canvas, mGreenPaint);
        }
    }
    // Draw any explosion debris.
    for (i = 0; i < Constants.MAX_SCRAP; i++) {
        if (explosions[i].active) {
            explosions[i].draw(canvas, mGreenPaint);
        }
    }

    // Display status messages.
    float fontSize = mPaint.getTextSize();

    // upper left
    canvas.drawText("Score: " + score, fontSize, mPaint.getTextSize(),
            mPaint);
```

```java
    // Lower Left
    canvas.drawText("Ships: " + shipsLeft, fontSize, height - fontSize,
            mPaint);

    // Upper right
    String str = "High: " + highScore;

    canvas.drawText("High: " + highScore, width
                - (fontSize / 1.2f * str.length()), fontSize, mPaint);

    if (!sound) {
        str = "Mute";
        canvas.drawText(str, width - (fontSize * str.length()), height
                - fontSize, mPaint);
    }

    if ( ! playing) {
        if (loaded) {
            str = "Game Over";
            final float x = (width - (str.length() * fontSize / 2)) / 2;

            canvas.drawText(str, x, height / 4, mPaint);

        }
    }
    else if ( paused ) {
        str = "Game Paused";

        final float x = (width - (str.length() * fontSize / 2)) / 2;
        canvas.drawText(str, x, height / 4, mPaint);
    }
}
```

Updating Game Physics

The third step in the game life cycle is to update the game physics. This simply means updating the positions of all sprites in the game. Listing 4-8 shows the implementation for Asteroids. Let's take a closer look at this method:

1. First, update the game sprites including the ship, photons, UFO, missile, asteroids, and explosions.

2. Update the scores.

3. Start the UFO if the score reaches the UFO score threshold.

4. Create a new batch of asteroids if all have been destroyed.

Listing 4-8 also shows the method used to update the ship: updateShip() (note that sections have been stripped from Listing 4-8 for simplicity). This method performs the following tasks:

1. Rotate or move the ship on screen depending on the value of the class variables: left, right, up, or down. These variables are updated depending on the key pressed by the user. The actual movement or rotation is performed by updating the delta values of the ship's X and Y coordinates and its angle of rotation.

2. Update other sprites, like the thrusters (which are independent sprites), as the ship moves around.

3. Perform other physics checks:

    • Do not let the ship exceed a speed limit.

    • If the ship has exploded, update the ship counter, and create a new ship or end the game depending on the number of ships left.

Listing 4-8. *Updating the Game Physics*

```java
protected void updatePhysics() {
    // Update Sprites
    updateShip();
    updatePhotons();
    updateUfo();
    updateMissile();
    updateAsteroids();
    updateExplosions();

    // Check the score and advance high score,
    if (score > highScore)
        highScore = score;

    // add a new ship if score reaches Constants.NEW_SHIP_POINTS
    if (score > newShipScore) {
        newShipScore += Constants.NEW_SHIP_POINTS;
        shipsLeft++;
    }

    // start the flying saucer as necessary.
    if (playing && score > newUfoScore && ! ufo.active) {
        newUfoScore += Constants.NEW_UFO_POINTS;
        ufoPassesLeft = Constants.UFO_PASSES;
        initUfo();
    }

    // If all asteroids have been destroyed create a new batch.
    if (asteroidsLeft <= 0)
        if (--asteroidsCounter <= 0)
            initAsteroids();

}

// Update Ship
```

```java
public void updateShip() {
    int width = getWidth();
    int height = getHeight();

    double dx, dy, speed;

    if (!playing)
        return;

    /**
     * Rotate the ship if left or right cursor key is down.
     */
    if (left) {
        ship.angle += Constants.SHIP_ANGLE_STEP;
        if (ship.angle > 2 * Math.PI)
            ship.angle -= 2 * Math.PI;
    }
    if (right) {
        ship.angle -= Constants.SHIP_ANGLE_STEP;
        if (ship.angle < 0)
            ship.angle += 2 * Math.PI;
    }

    /**
     * Fire thrusters if up or down cursor key is down.
     */
    dx = Constants.SHIP_SPEED_STEP * -Math.sin(ship.angle);
    dy = Constants.SHIP_SPEED_STEP * Math.cos(ship.angle);
    if (up) {
        ship.deltaX += dx;
        ship.deltaY += dy;
    }
    if (down) {
        ship.deltaX -= dx;
        ship.deltaY -= dy;
    }

    /**
     * Don't let ship go past the speed limit.
     */
    if (up || down) {
        speed = Math.sqrt(ship.deltaX * ship.deltaX + ship.deltaY
                * ship.deltaY);
        if (speed > Constants.MAX_SHIP_SPEED) {
            dx = Constants.MAX_SHIP_SPEED * -Math.sin(ship.angle);
            dy = Constants.MAX_SHIP_SPEED * Math.cos(ship.angle);
            if (up)
                ship.deltaX = dx;
            else
                ship.deltaX = -dx;
            if (up)
```

```
                ship.deltaY = dy;
            else
                ship.deltaY = -dy;
        }
    }

    /**
     * Move the ship. If it is currently in hyper space, advance the
     * count down.
     */
    if (ship.active) {
        ship.advance(width, height);
        ship.render(width, height);
        if (hyperCounter > 0)
            hyperCounter--;

        // Update the thruster sprites to match the ship sprite.

        fwdThruster.x = ship.x;
        fwdThruster.y = ship.y;
        fwdThruster.angle = ship.angle;
        fwdThruster.render(width, height);
        revThruster.x = ship.x;
        revThruster.y = ship.y;
        revThruster.angle = ship.angle;
        revThruster.render(width, height);
    }

    /**
     * Ship is exploding, advance the countdown or create a new ship if it
     * is done exploding. The new ship is added as though it were in
     * hyper space. This gives the player time to move the ship if it is
     * in imminent danger. If that was the last ship, end the game.
     */
    else {
        if (--shipCounter <= 0) {
            if (shipsLeft > 0) {
                initShip();
                hyperCounter = Constants.HYPER_COUNT;
            } else {
                endGame();
            }
        }
    }
}
```

Getting Scores

Scoring is the final step in the life cycle of Asteroids and is usually an optional step. In this step, a check
is performed too see if the game is over and, if so, get a final score and do something with it (such as

create a high score listing). Listing 4-9 shows two boolean variables used to check if the game is over and a long variable used to return the score.

Listing 4-9. *Getting the Game Score*

```java
protected boolean gameOver() {
    return loaded && !playing;
}

@Override
protected long getScore() {
    return score;
}
```

Responding to Key Press and Touch Events

The final piece of the puzzle is listening for user events such as key press and touch events and taking the appropriate action. We do this by overriding the onKeyUp, onKeyDown, and onTouchEvent methods. The following tasks are performed:

- Update the class variables: up, down, left, or right depending on which arrow key is pressed.

- Fire photons when the space bar is pressed.

- Jump into hyperspace when H is pressed. The ship will disappear from one point and appear in a random location on the screen.

- Toggle the pause mode when P is pressed.

- Toggle sound (mute the game) when M is pressed.

- Start the game when S is pressed.

- Quit the game when E is pressed.

When the screen is tapped, the game will start if and only if the game resources are loaded and the game is not playing already.

Listing 4-10. *Responding to Key Press and Touch Events*

```java
@Override
public boolean onKeyUp(int keyCode, KeyEvent event) {
    keyReleased(event);
    return true;
}

@Override
public boolean onKeyDown(int keyCode, KeyEvent event) {
    keyPressed(event);
    return true;
```

```java
    }

    /**
     * OnTap Start Game
     */
    @Override
    public boolean onTouchEvent(MotionEvent event) {
        if (loaded && !playing) {
            initGame();
        }
        return true;
    }

    public void keyPressed(KeyEvent e) {
        final int keyCode = e.getKeyCode();

        /**
         * Check if any cursor keys have been pressed and set flags.
         */
        if (keyCode == KeyEvent.KEYCODE_DPAD_LEFT
                || keyCode == KeyEvent.KEYCODE_Q)
            left = true;
        if (keyCode == KeyEvent.KEYCODE_DPAD_RIGHT
                || keyCode == KeyEvent.KEYCODE_W)
            right = true;
        if (keyCode == KeyEvent.KEYCODE_DPAD_UP
                || keyCode == KeyEvent.KEYCODE_O)
            up = true;
        if (keyCode == KeyEvent.KEYCODE_DPAD_DOWN
                || keyCode == KeyEvent.KEYCODE_L)
            down = true;

        if ((up || down) && ship.active  && !thrustersPlaying) {
            if (sound && !paused) {
                thrustersSound.loop();
            }
            thrustersPlaying = true;
        }

        /**
         * Spacebar: fire a photon and start its counter.
         */
        if ( (keyCode == KeyEvent.KEYCODE_SPACE) && ship.active)
        {
            if (sound & !paused) {
                fireSound.play();
            }

            photonTime = System.currentTimeMillis();
            photonIndex++;
```

111

```java
    if (photonIndex >= Constants.MAX_SHOTS)
        photonIndex = 0;

    photons[photonIndex].active = true;
    photons[photonIndex].x = ship.x;
    photons[photonIndex].y = ship.y;
    photons[photonIndex].deltaX = 2 * Constants.MAX_ROCK_SPEED
            * -Math.sin(ship.angle);
    photons[photonIndex].deltaY = 2 * Constants.MAX_ROCK_SPEED
            * Math.cos(ship.angle);
}

/**
 * 'H' key: warp ship into hyperspace by moving to a random location and
 * starting counter. Note: keys are case independent
 */
if (keyCode == KeyEvent.KEYCODE_H && ship.active && hyperCounter <= 0) {
    ship.x = (int) (Math.random() * getWidth());
    ship.y = (int) (Math.random() * getHeight());
    hyperCounter = Constants.HYPER_COUNT;

    if (sound & !paused)
        warpSound.play();
}

/**
 * 'P' key: toggle pause mode and start or stop any active looping sound
 * clips.
 */
if (keyCode == KeyEvent.KEYCODE_P) {
    if (paused) {
        if (sound && misslePlaying)
            missileSound.loop();
        if (sound && saucerPlaying)
            saucerSound.loop();
        if (sound && thrustersPlaying)
            thrustersSound.loop();
    } else {
        if (misslePlaying)
            missileSound.stop();
        if (saucerPlaying)
            saucerSound.stop();
        if (thrustersPlaying)
            thrustersSound.stop();
    }
    paused = !paused;
}

/**
 * 'M' key: toggle sound on or off and stop any looping sound clips.
 */
```

```java
        if (keyCode == KeyEvent.KEYCODE_M && loaded) {
            if (sound) {
                crashSound.stop();
                explosionSound.stop();
                fireSound.stop();
                missileSound.stop();
                saucerSound.stop();
                thrustersSound.stop();
                warpSound.stop();
            } else {
                if (misslePlaying && !paused)
                    missileSound.loop();
                if (saucerPlaying && !paused)
                    saucerSound.loop();
                if (thrustersPlaying && !paused)
                    thrustersSound.loop();
            }
            sound = !sound;
        }

        /**
         * 'S' key: start the game, if not already in progress.
         */
        if (keyCode == KeyEvent.KEYCODE_S && loaded && !playing) {
            initGame();
        }

        /**
         * 'E' Exit game
         */
        if (keyCode == KeyEvent.KEYCODE_E ) {
            stopUpdateTimer();
            releaseSounds();

            System.exit(0); // Ouch!
        }
    }
}
```

Our arcade game is now complete, and we can run it in the emulator.

Testing Asteroids on the Emulator

Let's fire the emulator and play some Asteroids! Here is how:

1. Create a new launch configuration. From the Eclipse main menu, click Run ➤ Run Configurations.

2. Enter a configuration name, Asteroids.

3. Select the project, ch04.Asteroids.

4. Set the Launch Action as Launch Default Activity, and click Run.

Stand by for the emulator window. You should see the game starting with the message Game Over and some asteroids floating around the screen. Press S to start the game and try some of the game's features (see Figure 4-5):

- Move the ship around using the arrow keys. You should see the thrusters fire and hear the thrusters' sound. The ship should wrap around when it goes off the screen.

- Press the space bar to fire the gun. Make sure the photons display (and that the sound plays) and the asteroids are destroyed when hit.

- Press the H to jump into hyperspace. The ship should disappear and reappear in a random location. Make sure the sound effect is played.

- Try to get a high score, and make sure the UFO shows up on screen and fires the missile against you.

- Press E to terminate the game when you get bored.

Figure 4-5. *The Asteroids game in action*

What's Next?

In this chapter, we looked at the polygon-based game Asteroids. This game presented new challenges due to the lack of polygon support in the Android API. To overcome this limitation, we created two helper classes: Rectangle and Polygon. This code has been ported from the Java SE API and slightly modified for this game. You also learned how to build a PolygonSprite capable of remembering X and Y coordinates and an angle of rotation. PolygonSprite is also capable of detecting collisions with other PolygonSprites and drawing itself in the Android canvas.

With these classes, we have built the arcade classic Asteroids. Furthermore, we have looked at the game's inner workings such as a user-defined XML layout and manipulation of game resources such as audio files and icons.

You have also taken a look at the critical steps in the game life cycle: initialization, drawing, and updating physics, as well as the caveats of drawing the polygons in the Android canvas. Finally, you learned at how to process key and touch events, and you tested Asteroids in the emulator.

I hope that you have learned new interesting techniques in building pure Java games. In the following chapters, I switch gears to concentrate in hybrid games, which mix Java and C thru JNI for maximum performance. We'll begin with the always-interesting subject of OpenGL.

CHAPTER 5

■ ■ ■

Hybrid 3D Graphics with OpenGL and JNI

The classic Asteroids arcade game presented in the previous chapter provided a great introduction to drawing techniques in Android, using polygons and user-defined layouts. Now it's time to ramp things up a notch.

In this chapter, you will learn a neat trick to mix OpenGL code in Java and C. This is a key step in reusing large portions of OpenGL C code along with Java code, thus using the best features of each language for maximum savings in time and costs.

Any game developer knows that OpenGL is the holy grail of advanced game development. You won't find any powerful games that are not written with this API, because it takes advantage of hardware acceleration, which is infinitely superior to any kind of software renderer.

OpenGL can be a scary subject to the newcomer due to its complexity. But you don't have to be an OpenGL guru to understand what it does and how to draw elements with this API. All you need is the desire to learn a powerful and exciting tool for gaming.

The goal of this chapter is not to teach you OpenGL (a whole book wouldn't be enough for that), but to show you how you can take the Android OpenGL sample provided by Google and modify it in a completely different way by mixing OpenGL API calls in both Java and native C for maximum reusability.

Some may say this is simply another OpenGL chapter for a mobile device (dime a dozen, right?). Well, it is not. This chapter presents a technique for OpenGL in Android that is unique, and at the time of this writing, not available anywhere in the Android sphere (on the Web). This is a technique I stumbled on by accident when thinking about porting the game Quake to Android. In a nutshell, the technique consists of creating the OpenGL context, display, and surface objects in Java, and performing all drawing operations natively in C. At the end of the rendering cycle, a JNI callback is used by the C engine to tell the Java side to swap the buffers (render the image). The cycle then repeats itself. This technique is extremely useful when you have a 200,000-line code game like Quake, and rewriting this code in Java is simply not feasible.

The chapter starts by examining the OpenGL tumbling cubes sample to expose how OpenGL works in Java. Next, we will look at how sections of the rendering process can be implemented in the native layer, and how everything is bound by JNI. The final section discusses some of the limitations of the OpenGL OpenGL Embedded System when it comes to advanced 3D games.

Let's get started.

Need An OpenGL Refresher?

For this chapter, you'll need a basic understanding of OpenGL. If your OpenGL is a bit rusty, I suggest referring to the best tutorials I have found on the Web:

- Greg Sidelnikov's tutorial about the OpenGL coordinate system. It covers the basics such as perspectives, orthographic projections, 3D camera, graphics pipeline, variable and function naming conventions, and more. It is a good place to start:

http://www.falloutsoftware.com/tutorials/gl/glo.htm

- If you are confused about OpenGL projections, MathWorld has some good information about all kinds of 3D projections used in OpenGL:

http://mathworld.wolfram.com/OrthographicProjection.html

- NeHe Productions has compiled a comprehensive set of tutorials that cover pretty much everything you need to write an OpenGL application. These are very popular:

http://nehe.gamedev.net/

The Power of Mobile Devices

Mobile Android devices have become pretty powerful for graphics development. Check out the following hardware stats for the T-Mobile G1:

- ARM processor running at 500MHz

- Graphics processing unit (GPU) with 256KB of RAM

- 320-by-480 pixel display

To make good use of the GPU, Google has included the OpenGL Embedded System (ES) within Android. OpenGL ES provides the software API to make high-performance, hardware-accelerated games possible. This is a Java API, which is good news for Java developers who wish to create 3D games from scratch, but bad news for C developers who wish to reuse 3D engines written in C. 3D game engines are very complex and large, and are mostly written in C. Rewriting these engines in Java would be a very difficult task, consuming significant development and time resources.

Consider how easy it is to reuse OpenGL code in C. Let's look at another powerful smart phone: Apple's iPhone. If you search the iPhone App Store (or the Web), you will find that dozens of OpenGL-based 3D games have already been ported to the platform, including some of the greatest 3D shooters for the PC: Wolfenstein 3D, Doom, and Quake I. Even Quake III Arena—a game that has extremely advanced 3D graphics for a mobile device—has been ported! What do all these games have in common? They are written in C. Furthermore, Apple provides a C toolchain that makes it easy to have the games running in the platform. Clearly, Android is at a big disadvantage in this field. Nevertheless, porting these games to Android is still possible.

Even though Android supports only Java development, the Android OS is built in a stripped version of GNU Linux featuring a C runtime. Using an ARM C toolchain, you can write and compile C code and bind it to Java using JNI.

■ **Note** As noted in previous chapters, Google doesn't support this type of native development, but it seems Google is being pushed by the overwhelming number of 3D games being ported to the iPhone and other mobile devices. So much so, that Google has recently released the Android NDK, a set of tools and header files for native development, introduced in Chapter 1.

A Head Start: The Source Code for this Chapter

In this chapter, we'll use the Android 3D cubes sample in its original Java language, but we will also move code to the native side. This sample is available from the Android site; however, the sample is composed of many resources, which are bundled as part of the overall Android samples pack. To make things simpler, I have packed the required files, plus the changes described throughout this chapter, in the chapter source code.

If you wish, you can import the project into your workspace. To do so, select File → Import. In the dialog box, select Existing Projects into Workspace. Next, navigate to the chapter source ch06.OpenGL. Optionally, check Copy project into workspace. When you click Finish, the automated build will load.

Try to familiarize yourself with the project layout, especially with the following folders:

- src contains the Java classes used by the project.

- native contains the cube renderer and the cube-drawing subroutines.

OpenGL the Java Way

Let's look at how OpenGL graphics are done within Java. For this exploration, you need to create a project to hold the GL tumbling cubes application from the Android samples. Here is how:

1. Click the New Android Project button.

2. In the New Android Project dialog box, enter a project name, such as ch05.OpenGL.

3. Specify the build target as Android 1.5.

4. Enter an application name, such as OpenGL Java.

5. Enter a package name, such as opengl.test.

6. Select Create Activity and enter JavaGLActivity.

7. Specify the minimum SDK version as 3. Figure 5-1 shows the completed dialog box for this example.

8. Click Finish.

■ **Note** The original sample code will be modified to fit the changes described throughout this chapter.

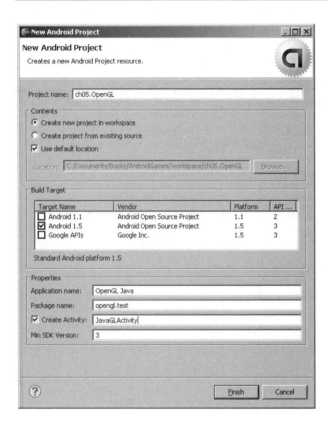

Figure 5-1. *New Android project for the OpenGL sample*

The Android cubes sample consists of the following Java classes (see Figure 5-2):

- GLSurfaceView: This is an implementation of SurfaceView that uses a dedicated surface for displaying an OpenGL animation. The animation will run in a separate thread (GLThread).

- GLThread: This is a generic thread with a loop for GL operations. Its job is to perform resource initialization. It also delegates rendering to an instance of the Renderer interface.

- Renderer: This is a generic interface for rendering objects. In this case, we will be rendering two tumbling cubes.

- EglHelper: This is a GL helper class used to do the following:

- Initialize the EGL context.

- Create the GL surface.

- Swap buffers (perform the actual drawing).

- CubeRenderer: This is an implementation of the Renderer interface to draw the cubes.

- Cube: This class encapsulates a GL cube, including vertices, colors, and indices for each face.

Because the sample needs to be slightly modified to illustrate the concepts of the chapter, the following classes have been added for this purpose:

- JavaGLActivity: This is the Android activity that will start the Java-only version of the application.

- NativeGLActivity: This activity will start the hybrid version of the sample (with Java/C/JNI code).

- Natives: This class defines the native methods used by this sample.

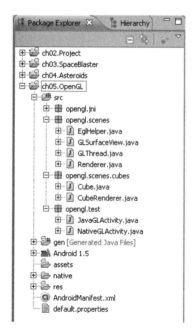

Figure 5-2. *Resource list for the OpenGL sample*

The Android manifest needs to be updated to include the new activities defined in the previous paragraph, as shown in bold in Listing 5-1.

Listing 5-1. *Manifest File for This Chapter's Example*

```
<?xml version="1.0" encoding="utf-8"?>
<manifest xmlns:android="http://schemas.android.com/apk/res/android"
      package="opengl.test"
      android:versionCode="1"
      android:versionName="1.0">
    <application android:icon="@drawable/icon"
        android:label="@string/app_name">
        <activity android:name=".JavaGLActivity"
                  android:label="OpenGL Java">
            <intent-filter>
                <action android:name="android.intent.action.MAIN" />
                <category android:name="android.intent.category.LAUNCHER" />
            </intent-filter>
        </activity>
        <activity android:name=".NativeGLActivity"
                  android:label="OpenGL Native">
            <intent-filter>
                <action android:name="android.intent.action.MAIN" />
                <category android:name="android.intent.category.LAUNCHER" />
            </intent-filter>
        </activity>
    </application>
    <uses-sdk android:minSdkVersion="3" />
</manifest>
```

The following lines tell Android to create two application launchers in the device launchpad, one for each of the activities OpenGL Java and OpenGL Native:

```
<action android:name="android.intent.action.MAIN" />
<category android:name="android.intent.category.LAUNCHER" />
```

Let's start with the Java-only implementation. Figure 5-3 defines the basic workflow of the OpenGL application. The figure shows the main activity (JavaGLActivity), which creates the rendering surface (GLSurfaceView). The surface creates a thread (GLThread) and renderer (CubeRenderer). GLThread contains the loop that invokes the renderer draw() method that draws the tumbling cubes seen on the device display.

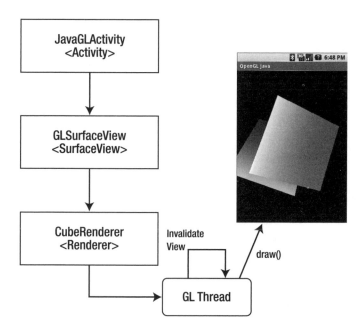

Figure 5-3. *Workflow of the Java-only cubes sample*

Java Main Activity

When the user starts the application, the JavaGLActivity.onCreate() method will be called (see Listing 5-2). Here is where the surface view (mGLSurfaceView) is initialized and set as the application content:

```
mGLSurfaceView = new GLSurfaceView(this);
mGLSurfaceView.setRenderer(new CubeRenderer(true));
setContentView(mGLSurfaceView);
```

Note that the GL surface view must use a renderer (CubeRenderer in this case), which implements the Renderer interface and takes a Boolean argument indicating if a translucent background should be used.

Listing 5-2. *Main Activity for the Java-Only Version of the GL Cubes Sample*

```
package opengl.test;

import opengl.scenes.GLSurfaceView;
import opengl.scenes.cubes.CubeRenderer;
import android.app.Activity;
import android.os.Bundle;

public class JavaGLActivity extends Activity
{
```

```java
private GLSurfaceView mGLSurfaceView;

/** Called when the activity is first created. */
@Override
public void onCreate(Bundle savedInstanceState) {
    super.onCreate(savedInstanceState);

    mGLSurfaceView = new GLSurfaceView(this);

    try {
        mGLSurfaceView.setRenderer(new CubeRenderer(true));
        setContentView(mGLSurfaceView);

    } catch (Exception e) {
        e.printStackTrace();
    }
}

@Override
protected void onPause() {
    // Ideally a game should implement onResume() and onPause()
    // to take appropriate action when the activity loses focus
    super.onPause();
    mGLSurfaceView.onPause();
}

@Override
protected void onResume() {
    super.onResume();
    mGLSurfaceView.onResume();
}
}
```

When the application loses focus or resumes, the onPause() or onResume() method will be called, respectively. These methods delegate to the surface view (GLSurfaceView) to take the appropriate action, such as saving application state or suspending/resuming the rendering process.

Surface View

The class GLSurfaceView (see Listing 5-3) defines the surface where the tumbling cubes animation will take place. The class constructor starts by initializing a callback to receive notifications when the surface is changed, created, or destroyed:

```java
mHolder = getHolder();
mHolder.addCallback(this);
mHolder.setType(SurfaceHolder.SURFACE_TYPE_GPU);
```

By implementing SurfaceHolder.Callback and calling SurfaceHolder.addCallback(), the class will receive the events:

- `surfaceCreated(SurfaceHolder holder)`: This is called immediately after the surface is first created. In this case, the surface delegates to the inner thread `GLThread.surfaceCreated()`.

- `surfaceDestroyed(SurfaceHolder holder)`: This method is called immediately before a surface is being destroyed. After returning from this call, the surface should not be accessed. In this case, the method delegates to the rendering thread `GLThread.surfaceDestroyed()`.

- `surfaceChanged(SurfaceHolder holder, int format, int w, int h)`: This method is called immediately after any structural changes (format or size) have been made to the surface. Here is where you tell the inner thread that the size has changed. This method is always called at least once, after `surfaceCreated()`. The second argument of this method (format) is the pixel format of the graphics defined in the `PixelFormat` class.

Listing 5-3. *Surface View for the GL Cubes Sample*

```
package opengl.scenes;

import opengl.jni.Natives;
import android.content.Context;
import android.util.AttributeSet;
import android.view.SurfaceHolder;
import android.view.SurfaceView;

/**
 * An implementation of SurfaceView that uses the dedicated surface for
 * displaying an OpenGL animation. This allows the animation to run in a
 * separate thread, without requiring that it be driven by the update
 * mechanism of the view hierarchy.
 *
 * The application-specific rendering code is delegated to a GLView.Renderer
 * instance.
 */
public class GLSurfaceView extends SurfaceView
  implements  SurfaceHolder.Callback
{
    public GLSurfaceView(Context context) {
        super(context);
        init();
    }

    public GLSurfaceView(Context context, AttributeSet attrs) {
        super(context, attrs);
        init();
    }

    private void init() {
        // Install a SurfaceHolder.Callback so we get notified when the
        // underlying surface is created and destroyed
```

```java
        mHolder = getHolder();
        mHolder.addCallback(this);
        mHolder.setType(SurfaceHolder.SURFACE_TYPE_GPU);
    }

    public SurfaceHolder getSurfaceHolder() {
        return mHolder;
    }

    public void setRenderer(Renderer renderer) {
        mGLThread = new GLThread(renderer, mHolder);
        mGLThread.start();
    }

    public void surfaceCreated(SurfaceHolder holder) {
        mGLThread.surfaceCreated();
    }

    public void surfaceDestroyed(SurfaceHolder holder) {
        // Surface will be destroyed when we return
        mGLThread.surfaceDestroyed();
    }

    public void surfaceChanged(SurfaceHolder holder, int format, int w,
            int h) {
        // Surface size or format has changed. This should not happen in
        // this example.
        mGLThread.onWindowResize(w, h);
    }

    /**
     * Inform the view that the activity is paused.
     */
    public void onPause() {
        mGLThread.onPause();
    }

    /**
     * Inform the view that the activity is resumed.
     */
    public void onResume() {
        mGLThread.onResume();
    }

    /**
     * Inform the view that the window focus has changed.
     */
    @Override
    public void onWindowFocusChanged(boolean hasFocus) {
        super.onWindowFocusChanged(hasFocus);
        mGLThread.onWindowFocusChanged(hasFocus);
    }
```

```
/**
 * Queue an "event" to be run on the GL rendering thread.
 *
 * @param r
 *            the runnable to be run on the GL rendering thread.
 */
public void queueEvent(Runnable r) {
    mGLThread.queueEvent(r);
}

@Override
protected void onDetachedFromWindow() {
    super.onDetachedFromWindow();
    mGLThread.requestExitAndWait();
}

private SurfaceHolder mHolder;
private GLThread mGLThread;
```
}

Other important methods in the surface view include the following:

- setRenderer(): This method creates the inner thread that does all the work and
  starts it. The thread keeps a reference to the surface holder available by calling
  getHolder().

```
public void setRenderer(Renderer renderer) {
    mGLThread = new GLThread(renderer, mHolder);
    mGLThread.start();
}
```

- queueEvent(Runnable r): This method sends an event to be run by the inner
  thread.

- onDetachedFromWindow(): This method is called when the view is detached from a
  window. At this point, it no longer has a surface for drawing.

GL Thread

The main loop of the animation is performed by GLThread. When started, this thread performs the
following steps:

1. It creates a semaphore:

```
sEglSemaphore.acquire();
guardedRun();    // Only 1 thread can access this code
sEglSemaphore.release();
```

2. It runs the critical animation loop. Within the loop, the actual drawing is
   delegated to the CubeRenderer.

3.   When asked to quit, the loops terminates, and the OpenGL resources are released.

■ **Note** A *semaphore* is an object often used to restrict the number of threads than can access the OpenGL context. When the Android framework launches a second instance of an activity, the new instance's onCreate() method may be called before the first instance returns from onDestroy(). A semaphore ensures that only one instance at a time accesses the GL API. We must do this because OpenGL is a single-threaded API (which means that only one thread can access the GLContext at a time).

Listing 5-4 shows a fragment of the GLThread class taken from the GL cubes sample. When the thread starts, the run() method will be invoked, and a semaphore used to ensure that guardedRun() can be accessed by one thread only. guardedRun() performs other important steps, such as the following:

- Initialize the Embedded OpenGL (EGL) for a given configuration specification. The configuration specification defines information, such as pixel format and image depth.

- Create the OpenGL surface and tell the renderer about it.

- Check if the size of the surface has changed and tell the renderer about it.

- Queue and get events to be run on the GL rendering thread.

Listing 5-4. *Rendering Thread for the GL Cubes Sample*

```java
package opengl.scenes;

// ...

/**
 * A generic GL Thread. Takes care of initializing EGL and GL.
 * Delegates to a Renderer instance to do the actual drawing.
 */
public class GLThread extends Thread
{
    public GLThread(Renderer renderer, SurfaceHolder holder) {
        super();
        mDone = false;
        mWidth = 0;
        mHeight = 0;
        mRenderer = renderer;
        mHolder = holder;
        setName("GLThread");
    }
```

```java
@Override
public void run() {
    try {
        try {
            sEglSemaphore.acquire();
        } catch (InterruptedException e) {
            return;
        }
        guardedRun();
    } catch (Exception ex) {
        ex.printStackTrace();
    } finally {
        sEglSemaphore.release();
    }
}

private void guardedRun() throws InterruptedException {
    mEglHelper = new EglHelper();

    // Specify a configuration for our OpenGL session
    int[] configSpec = mRenderer.getConfigSpec();
    mEglHelper.start(configSpec);

    GL10 gl = null;
    boolean tellRendererSurfaceCreated = true;
    boolean tellRendererSurfaceChanged = true;

    // This is our main activity thread's loop,
    while (!mDone) {

        // Update the asynchronous state (window size)
        int w, h;
        boolean changed;
        boolean needStart = false;
        synchronized (this) {
            Runnable r;
            while ((r = getEvent()) != null) {
                r.run();
            }
            if (mPaused) {
                mEglHelper.finish();
                needStart = true;
            }
            if (needToWait()) {
                while (needToWait()) {
                    wait();
                }
            }
            if (mDone) {
                break;
            }
            changed = mSizeChanged;
```

```
                w = mWidth;
                h = mHeight;
                mSizeChanged = false;
            }
            if (needStart) {
                mEglHelper.start(configSpec);
                tellRendererSurfaceCreated = true;
                changed = true;
            }
            if (changed) {
                // Create the surface
                gl = (GL10) mEglHelper.createSurface(mHolder);
                tellRendererSurfaceChanged = true;
            }
            if (tellRendererSurfaceCreated) {
                mRenderer.surfaceCreated(gl);
                tellRendererSurfaceCreated = false;
            }
            if (tellRendererSurfaceChanged) {
                mRenderer.sizeChanged(gl, w, h);
                tellRendererSurfaceChanged = false;
            }
            if ((w > 0) && (h > 0)) {
                /* draw a frame here */
                mRenderer.drawFrame(gl);

                // Call swapBuffers() to instruct the system to display
                mEglHelper.swap();
            }
        }

        // Clean up...
        mEglHelper.finish();
    }

    // …
    private static final Semaphore sEglSemaphore = new Semaphore(1);
    private EglHelper mEglHelper;
}
```

Cube Renderer

CubeRenderer is the class that renders the pair of tumbling cubes (see Listing 5-5). It implements the Renderer interface and does some very interesting things.

The void drawFrame(GL10 gl) method does the actual drawing and gets called many times per second. The method starts by setting the matrix mode to GL_MODELVIEW. This essentially says to render things in a 3D perspective (model view). Next, it clears all screen buffers by calling glLoadIdentity().

```
        gl.glMatrixMode(GL10.GL_MODELVIEW);
        gl.glLoadIdentity();
```

Next, the perspective is translated in the z axis by three units toward the eye viewpoint (also known as the camera):

```
gl.glTranslatef(0, 0, -3.0f);
```

The next two instructions tell the pipeline to rotate the perspective in the y and x axes by an angle given in radians (0-6.28, 0 meaning zero degrees, and 6.28, meaning 360 degrees).

```
gl.glRotatef(mAngle, 0, 1, 0);
gl.glRotatef(mAngle * 0.25f, 1, 0, 0);
```

Next, it requests that vertices and colors be rendered. These are defined within the Cube class:

```
gl.glEnableClientState(GL10.GL_VERTEX_ARRAY);
gl.glEnableClientState(GL10.GL_COLOR_ARRAY);
```

Then the cube is drawn:

```
mCube.draw(gl);
```

The perspective is rotated again in the y and z axes, and translated half a unit away from the eye:

```
gl.glRotatef(mAngle * 2.0f, 0, 1, 1);
gl.glTranslatef(0.5f, 0.5f, 0.5f);
```

The second cube is drawn, and the angle of rotation is increased for the next iteration.

```
mCube.draw(gl);
mAngle += 1.2f;
```

The int[] getConfigSpec() method initializes the pixel format and the depth of the display. The pixel format describes the size of the ARGB values used to describe a pixel. The depth indicates the maximum number of colors used. For example, the following integer array requests 32 bits per pixel (ARGB 32bpp) with a depth of 16 (2^{16} colors).

```
int[] configSpec = {
EGL10.EGL_RED_SIZE,      8,
EGL10.EGL_GREEN_SIZE,    8,
EGL10.EGL_BLUE_SIZE,     8,
EGL10.EGL_ALPHA_SIZE,    8,
EGL10.EGL_DEPTH_SIZE,    16,
EGL10.EGL_NONE
};
```

The following are two other interesting methods in the cube renderer:

- void sizeChanged(GL10 gl, int width, int height): This method fires when the size of the viewport changes. It scales the cubes by setting the ratio of the projection matrix and resizing the viewport.

- void surfaceCreated(GL10 gl): This method fires when the surface is created. Here, some initialization is performed, such as setting a translucent background (if requested) and miscellaneous OpenGL renderer tweaking.

When the code in drawFrame() is executed many times per second, the result is two tumbling cubes (see Figure 5-4).

Listing 5-5. *Cube Renderer for the Pair of Tumbling Cubes*

```
package opengl.scenes.cubes;

import javax.microedition.khronos.egl.EGL10;
import javax.microedition.khronos.opengles.GL10;

import opengl.jni.Natives;
import opengl.scenes.Renderer;

/**
 * Render a pair of tumbling cubes.
 */
public class CubeRenderer implements Renderer {

    public CubeRenderer(boolean useTranslucentBackground) {
        mTranslucentBackground = useTranslucentBackground;
        mNativeDraw = nativeDraw;
        mCube = new Cube();
    }

    public void drawFrame(GL10 gl) {
        /*
         * Usually, the first thing one might want to do is to clear
         * the screen. The most efficient way of doing this is
         * to use glClear().
         */
        gl.glClear(GL10.GL_COLOR_BUFFER_BIT | GL10.GL_DEPTH_BUFFER_BIT);

        /*
         * Now we're ready to draw some 3D objects
         */
        gl.glMatrixMode(GL10.GL_MODELVIEW);
        gl.glLoadIdentity();
        gl.glTranslatef(0, 0, -3.0f);
        gl.glRotatef(mAngle, 0, 1, 0);
        gl.glRotatef(mAngle * 0.25f, 1, 0, 0);

        gl.glEnableClientState(GL10.GL_VERTEX_ARRAY);
        gl.glEnableClientState(GL10.GL_COLOR_ARRAY);

        mCube.draw(gl);

        gl.glRotatef(mAngle * 2.0f, 0, 1, 1);
```

```java
        gl.glTranslatef(0.5f, 0.5f, 0.5f);

        mCube.draw(gl);

        mAngle += 1.2f;
    }

    public int[] getConfigSpec() {
        if (mTranslucentBackground) {
            // We want a depth buffer and an alpha buffer
            int[] configSpec = { EGL10.EGL_RED_SIZE, 8,
                    EGL10.EGL_GREEN_SIZE, 8, EGL10.EGL_BLUE_SIZE, 8,
                    EGL10.EGL_ALPHA_SIZE, 8, EGL10.EGL_DEPTH_SIZE, 16,
                    EGL10.EGL_NONE };
            return configSpec;
        } else {
            // We want a depth buffer, don't care about the
            // details of the color buffer.
            int[] configSpec = { EGL10.EGL_DEPTH_SIZE, 16,
                    EGL10.EGL_NONE };
            return configSpec;
        }
    }

    public void sizeChanged(GL10 gl, int width, int height) {
        gl.glViewport(0, 0, width, height);

        /*
         * Set our projection matrix. This doesn't have to be done each time we
         * draw, but usually a new projection needs to be set when the viewport
         * is resized.
         */
        float ratio = (float) width / height;
        gl.glMatrixMode(GL10.GL_PROJECTION);
        gl.glLoadIdentity();
        gl.glFrustumf(-ratio, ratio, -1, 1, 1, 10);
    }

    public void surfaceCreated(GL10 gl) {
        /*
         * By default, OpenGL enables features that improve quality but reduce
         * performance. One might want to tweak that especially on software
         * renderer.
         */
        gl.glDisable(GL10.GL_DITHER);

        /*
         * Some one-time OpenGL initialization can be made here probably based
         * on features of this particular context
         */
        gl.glHint(GL10.GL_PERSPECTIVE_CORRECTION_HINT
            , GL10.GL_FASTEST);
```

133

```
        if (mTranslucentBackground) {
            gl.glClearColor(0, 0, 0, 0.5f);
        } else {
            gl.glClearColor(1, 1, 1, 0.5f);
        }

        gl.glEnable(GL10.GL_CULL_FACE);
        gl.glShadeModel(GL10.GL_SMOOTH);
        gl.glEnable(GL10.GL_DEPTH_TEST);
    }

    private boolean mTranslucentBackground;
    private Cube mCube;
    private float mAngle;
}
```

Cube Class

CubeRenderer delegates drawing to the Cube class (see Listing 5-6). This class defines a 12-sided cube with 8 vertices (8 * x,y,z coordinates), 32 colors (8 vertices * 4 ARGB values), and 36 indices for the x,y,z coordinates of each side. The class consists of two methods:

- Cube(): This is the class constructor. It initializes arrays for the vertices, colors, and indices required to draw. It then uses direct Java buffers to place the data on the native heap, where the garbage collector cannot move them. This is required by the gl*Pointer() API functions that do the actual drawing.

- draw(): To draw the cube, we simply set the vertices and colors, and issue a call to glDrawElements using triangles (GL_TRIANGLES). Note that a cube has 6 faces, 8, vertices, and 12 sides:

```
gl.glVertexPointer(3, GL10.GL_FIXED, 0, mVertexBuffer);
gl.glColorPointer(4, GL10.GL_FIXED, 0, mColorBuffer);
gl.glDrawElements(GL10.GL_TRIANGLES, 36
    , GL10.GL_UNSIGNED_BYTE,  mIndexBuffer);
```

Listing 5-6. *Cube Class for the GL Cubes Sample*

```
package opengl.scenes.cubes;

import java.nio.ByteBuffer;
import java.nio.ByteOrder;
import java.nio.IntBuffer;
import javax.microedition.khronos.opengles.GL10;

/**
 * A vertex shaded cube.
 */
public class Cube {
    public Cube() {
        int one = 0x10000;
```

```
    // 8 vertices each with 3 xyz coordinates
    int vertices[] = { -one, -one, -one
            , one, -one, -one
            , one, one,  -one
            , -one, one, -one
            , -one, -one, one
            , one, -one, one
            , one, one, one
            , -one, one, one };

    // 8 colors each with  4 RGBA values
    int colors[] = { 0, 0, 0, one
            , one, 0, 0, one
            , one, one, 0, one
            , 0, one, 0, one
            , 0, 0, one, one
            , one, 0, one, one
            , one, one, one, one
            , 0, one, one, one};
    // 12 indices each with 3 xyz coordinates
    byte indices[] = { 0, 4, 5, 0, 5, 1, 1, 5, 6, 1, 6, 2, 2, 6, 7,
            2, 7, 3, 3, 7, 4, 3, 4, 0, 4, 7, 6, 4, 6, 5, 3, 0, 1,
            3, 1, 2 };


    ByteBuffer vbb = ByteBuffer.allocateDirect(vertices.length * 4);
    vbb.order(ByteOrder.nativeOrder());
    mVertexBuffer = vbb.asIntBuffer();
    mVertexBuffer.put(vertices);
    mVertexBuffer.position(0);

    ByteBuffer cbb = ByteBuffer.allocateDirect(colors.length * 4);
    cbb.order(ByteOrder.nativeOrder());
    mColorBuffer = cbb.asIntBuffer();
    mColorBuffer.put(colors);
    mColorBuffer.position(0);

    mIndexBuffer = ByteBuffer.allocateDirect(indices.length);
    mIndexBuffer.put(indices);
    mIndexBuffer.position(0);
}

public void draw(GL10 gl) {
    gl.glFrontFace(GL10.GL_CW);
    gl.glVertexPointer(3, GL10.GL_FIXED, 0, mVertexBuffer);
    gl.glColorPointer(4, GL10.GL_FIXED, 0, mColorBuffer);
    gl.glDrawElements(GL10.GL_TRIANGLES, 36, GL10.GL_UNSIGNED_BYTE,
            mIndexBuffer);
}

private IntBuffer mVertexBuffer;
private IntBuffer mColorBuffer;
```

```
    private ByteBuffer mIndexBuffer;
}
```

Figure 5-4 shows the sample in action. In the next section, you'll see how portions of this code can be implemented natively.

Figure 5-4. *Tumbling cubes from the Java sample*

OpenGL the Native Way

In the previous section, you saw how a pure Java OpenGL application works from the ground up. This applies if you write an application from scratch in Java. However, if you already have a C OpenGL renderer and wish to interface with Android, you probably don't want to rewrite your application (especially if it has thousands of lines of code). This would consume significant time and resources, and more than likely, give you terrible headache. To understand how you can maximize the return on your investment, let's look at the general steps used to create an OpenGL application.

Any OpenGL application can be divided into the following major steps:

1. *Initialization*: OpenGL is a single-threaded system that requires a GLContext to be initialized. Only one thread can access this context at a time. In EGL, this step is subdivided as follows:

   a. Get an EGL instance. In Android, this can be done using the EGLContext class:

```
mEgl = EGLContext.getEGL();
```

   b. Get a default display. The display is required for the rendering process. In Android, use this call:

```
mEglDisplay = mEgl.eglGetDisplay(EGL10.EGL_DEFAULT_DISPLAY);
```

   c. Initialize the display, as follows:

```
int[] version = new int[2];
mEgl.eglInitialize(mEglDisplay, version);
```

   d. You must also specify the pixel format and image depth you wish to use. The following requests a 32bpp pixel format with an image depth of 16:

```
EGLConfig[] configs = new EGLConfig[1];
int[] num_config = new int[1];

int[] configSpec = {
  EGL10.EGL_RED_SIZE,      8,
  EGL10.EGL_GREEN_SIZE,    8,
  EGL10.EGL_BLUE_SIZE,     8,
  EGL10.EGL_ALPHA_SIZE,    8,
  EGL10.EGL_DEPTH_SIZE,    16,
  EGL10.EGL_NONE
};
mEgl.eglChooseConfig(mEglDisplay, configSpec, configs, 1, num_config);
```

2. *Main loop*: This is usually a user-defined thread that performs or delegates drawing operations.

3. *Drawing*: In the drawing process, a set of GL operations is performed for each iteration of the *loop*. At the end of each iteration, buffers must be swapped to display the rendered surface on the screen.

4. *Cleanup*: In this step, the GLContext is destroyed and resources released back to the system.

All these steps can be performed in Java. So it happened that one day I wanted to port an OpenGL-based game to Android written in C, and wondered if some steps could be done in Java and some in C. I was very happy to discover that this is indeed possible. For example, the following steps can be performed in Java within an Android activity:

• *Initialization*: Get the EGL instance, initialize the default display, and set the pixel format and image depth.

- *Main loop*: The main loop can be a combination of a Java thread that calls a native game loop. Here is where things get interesting.

■ **Note** OpenGL operations can be performed natively after the GLContext is initialized by an Android activity if, and only if, the native code is loaded by the activity as a shared library through JNI.

- *Swap buffers*: This step can be performed in Java, provided that the native library issues a callback after all GL operations have been completed. This is simply using JNI callbacks and will result in a rendered surface on the screen.

This is great news. You don't need to rewrite large portions of an OpenGL game. You simply need to initialize the GLContext within your Java activity, load the shared library, do all the rendering operations natively, and issue a swap buffers callback to Java on each iteration of the game loop.

Let's apply this concept by rewriting portions of the GL cubes Java sample in C. The portion that will be rewritten is the rendering of the cubes. The rest—initialization, main loop, and swap buffers—will remain in Java. To accomplish this, you must make some simple changes to the sample classes and add a new native activity.

Main Activity

You must create a new activity (with its own launcher) to load the native code (see Listing 5-7). This activity is almost identical to its Java counterpart, except for the following:

- A native library is loaded using System.load("/data/libgltest_jni.so").

- The Renderer constructor has been modified to accept a second Boolean argument (use native rendering): mGLSurfaceView.setRenderer(new CubeRenderer(true, true)). This tells the cube renderer to use a translucent background and native rendering.

Listing 5-7. *Native Cubes Activity*

```
package opengl.test;

import opengl.scenes.GLSurfaceView;
import opengl.scenes.cubes.CubeRenderer;
import android.app.Activity;
import android.os.Bundle;

public class NativeGLActivity extends Activity {
    private GLSurfaceView mGLSurfaceView;

    {
        final String LIB_PATH = "/data/libgltest_jni.so";

        System.out
```

```
            .println("Loading JNI lib using abs path:" + LIB_PATH);
        System.load(LIB_PATH);
    }

    /** Called when the activity is first created. */
    @Override
    public void onCreate(Bundle savedInstanceState) {
        super.onCreate(savedInstanceState);

        mGLSurfaceView = new GLSurfaceView(this);

        try {
            mGLSurfaceView.setRenderer(new CubeRenderer(true, true));
            setContentView(mGLSurfaceView);

        } catch (Exception e) {
            e.printStackTrace();
        }
    }

    @Override
    protected void onResume() {
        // Ideally a game should implement onResume() and onPause()
        // to take appropriate action when the activity loses focus
        super.onResume();
        mGLSurfaceView.onResume();
    }

    @Override
    protected void onPause() {
        // Ideally a game should implement onResume() and onPause()
        // to take appropriate action when the activity loses focus
        super.onPause();
        mGLSurfaceView.onPause();
    }
}
```

The following new files will be added to the project (see Figure 5-5):

- *Native activity*: This is the main entry point to the application. It can be run from its own launcher on the device.

- *Native interface class*: This is a new Java class that contains the native methods to be invoked within the renderer thread.

- *Native cube renderer* (cuberenderer.c): This is the C equivalent of CubeRenderer.java. It initializes the scene and draws a frame. It also contains all the JNI callbacks.

- *Native cube* (cube.c): This file is equivalent to Cube.java; it draws the cube.

Three files will be updated to accommodate the native calls: CubeRenderer, GLSurfaceView, and GLThread.

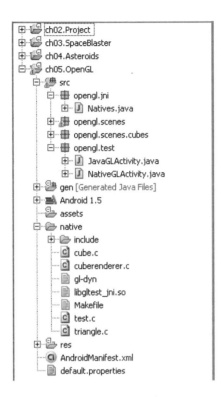

Figure 5-5. *GL native cubes sample file layout*

Native Interface Class

The native interface class defines native methods to be invoked within the application thread (see Listing 5-8). It includes one native method and two callbacks:

- `static native int NativeRender()`: This is the actual native method that will render the cube. It is implemented natively in C and executed through JNI.

- `static void OnMessage(String text)`: This is a callback invoked within the native layer to display a message back to the application.

- `static void GLSwapBuffers()`: This is a callback invoked within the native layer to request a buffer swap (render it). For this sample, this method will not be actually invoked (as the loop is defined in Java), but it could be useful in other situations (when the main loop is implemented natively).

■ **Tip** As you may know, using JNI, you can invoke C functions from Java. You may not know that you can also load classes and invoke Java methods within C.

Listing 5-8. *Native Interface for the GL Cubes Sample*

```
package opengl.jni;

public class Natives {

    private static EventListener listener;

    public static interface EventListener {
        void OnMessage(String text);
        void GLSwapBuffers();
    }

    public static void setListener(EventListener l) {
        listener = l;
    }

    /**
     * Native Render test
     *
     * @return
     */
    public static native int NativeRender();

    @SuppressWarnings("unused")
    private static void OnMessage(String text) {
        if (listener != null)
            listener.OnMessage(text);
    }

    @SuppressWarnings("unused")
    private static void GLSwapBuffers() {
        if (listener != null)
            listener.GLSwapBuffers();
    }
}
```

This class needs a way to notify components (the activity, for example) that some message has been received from the native layer. You do this by creating the interface EventListener. In this way, a class that wants to receive messages must implement EventListener and issue a call to Natives.setListener(this).

Before we jump to the C code, let's take a look at the Java changes required to the classes CubeRenderer, GLSurfaceView, and GLThread for the sample.

Changes to the Original Sample

The class CubeRenderer has been modified to accept a Boolean argument in its constructor to request a native draw (see Listing 5-9).

Listing 5-9. *Changes for CubeRenderer Class*

```
public class CubeRenderer implements Renderer
{
    private boolean mNativeDraw = false;

    public CubeRenderer(boolean useTranslucentBackground,
            boolean nativeDraw)
    {
        mTranslucentBackground = useTranslucentBackground;
        mNativeDraw = nativeDraw;
        mCube = new Cube();
    }

    public void drawFrame(GL10 gl) {
        if (mNativeDraw)
            doNativeDraw();
        else
            doJavaDraw(gl);
    }

    private void doJavaDraw(GL10 gl) {
        // Same as before
        // ...
    }

    public void doNativeDraw() {
        Natives.NativeRender();
    }

    // ...
}
```

When drawFrame() is invoked and mNativeDraw is true, the cube will be rendered from C (by calling Natives.NativeRender()). Otherwise, the Java implementation will be used.

When the surface is created, and a renderer is set for that surface using GLSurfaceView.setRenderer(Renderer renderer), you must tell the native interface class (Natives.java) that you wish to listen for messages by sending a reference to the loop thread:

```
public void setRenderer(Renderer renderer) {
    mGLThread = new GLThread(renderer, mHolder);
    mGLThread.start();
    Natives.setListener(mGLThread);
}
```

Note that GLThread must implement Natives.EventListener for this to work.

Finally, the last class to be updated is GLThread (see Listing 5-10), which contains the main loop.

Listing 5-10. *Changes for GLThread.java*

```
public class GLThread extends Thread implements EventListener
{
    // ...
    @Override
    public void GLSwapBuffers() {
        if ( mEglHelper != null ) {
            mEglHelper.swap();
        }
    }

    @Override
    public void OnMessage(String text) {
        System.out.println("GLThread::OnMessage " + text);
    }
}
```

GLThread implements EventListener. This allows the C code to send text messages if something is wrong. The method GLSwapBuffers() will be invoked when the C code requests a buffer swap.

This takes care of the Java portion of the sample. Now let's look at the C files: cuberenderer.c and cube.c.

Native Cube Renderer

The native cube renderer (cuberenderer.c) is similar to the Java class CubeRenderer. This file performs the following tasks (see Listings 5-11 through 5-14):

- It initializes the scene. This function is almost identical to CubeRenderer.surfaceCreated().

- It draws a frame using the drawFrame() function. This function is similar in nature to CubeRenderer.drawFrame().

- It contains the native implementation of the native interface class opengl.jni.Natives.NativeRender (mapped in C as Java_opengl_jni_Natives_NativeRender). This function will be invoked every time a frame is rendered from the GLThread Java class.

- It contains the Java callbacks (functions that will invoke Java methods):

  - jni_printf(char *format, ...) sends a text message back.

  - jni_gl_swap_buffers () requests a buffer swap within Java.

■ **Caution** Before the `cuberenderer.c` file can be compiled, the header file `opengl_jni_Natives.h` must be created. This header contains the prototypes for the native methods in `opengl.jni.Natives.java`. To do this, use the `javah` command: `javah -cp [CLASS_PATH] -d include opengl.jni.Natives`, where `CLASS_PATH` points to the project `bin` folder.

Scene Initialization

Scene initialization is performed by the `init_scene()` function (see Listing 5-11). Its job is to perform trivial GL initialization calls, such as setting a perspective correction hint, background color, and shade model, and in this case, enabling face culling and depth tests.

init_scene()is meant to mirror the Java method CubeRenderer.surfaceCreated, which initializes the scene after the surface is created. Note that Java lines such as gl.glDisable(GL10.GL_DITHER) become glDisable(GL_DITHER). Because the context is already initialized in Java, you can simply make the GL commands you need in the equivalent C function.

Listing 5-11. Scene Initialization from cuberenderer.c

```
#include <stdlib.h>
#include <stdio.h>
#include <stdarg.h>
#include <string.h>
#include <math.h>

#include <EGL/egl.h>
#include <GLES/gl.h>
#include <GLES/glext.h>

#include "include/opengl_jni_Natives.h"

#define ONE   1.0f
#define FIXED_ONE 0x10000

// Prototypes
void jni_printf(char *format, ...);
void jni_gl_swap_buffers ();

// Rotation Angle
static float mAngle = 0.0;

extern void Cube_draw();

static void init_scene(void)
{
        glDisable(GL_DITHER);

        /*
         * Some one-time OpenGL initialization can be made here
```

```
   * probably based on features of this particular context
   */
  glHint(GL_PERSPECTIVE_CORRECTION_HINT,GL_FASTEST);

  glClearColor(.5f, .5f, .5f, 1);

  glEnable(GL_CULL_FACE);
  glShadeModel(GL_SMOOTH);
  glEnable(GL_DEPTH_TEST);
}
```

Drawing Frames

Drawing the actual frames is performed by the drawFrame() function. This function performs the following steps:

- It clears the screen via glClear().

- It sets the framework to draw 3D objects via the glMatrixMode(GL_MODELVIEW) system call.

- It performs an initial translation—a rotation to be applied to the first cube.

- It draws the first cube by calling Cube_draw(). Note that vertices and colors must be enabled via glEnableClientState().

- It performs a second rotation/translation and draws a second cube by calling Cube_draw() again.

- It increases the angle for the next interaction.

drawFrame() is meant to mirror the Java method CubeRenderer.drawFrame(), which includes the code in the next fragment:

```
gl.glClear(GL10.GL_COLOR_BUFFER_BIT | GL10.GL_DEPTH_BUFFER_BIT);
gl.glMatrixMode(GL10.GL_MODELVIEW);
gl.glLoadIdentity();
gl.glTranslatef(0, 0, -3.0f);
gl.glRotatef(mAngle,        0, 1, 0);
gl.glRotatef(mAngle*0.25f,  1, 0, 0);

gl.glEnableClientState(GL10.GL_VERTEX_ARRAY);
gl.glEnableClientState(GL10.GL_COLOR_ARRAY);

mCube.draw(gl);

gl.glRotatef(mAngle*2.0f, 0, 1, 1);
gl.glTranslatef(0.5f, 0.5f, 0.5f);

mCube.draw(gl);

mAngle += 1.2f;
```

In C, the preceding code simply becomes the following:

```
glDisable(GL_DITHER);

glTexEnvx(GL_TEXTURE_ENV,
        GL_TEXTURE_ENV_MODE,GL_MODULATE);
glClear(GL_COLOR_BUFFER_BIT | GL_DEPTH_BUFFER_BIT);

glMatrixMode(GL_MODELVIEW);
glLoadIdentity();

glTranslatef(0, 0, -3.0f);
glRotatef(mAngle,        0, 0, 1.0f);
glRotatef(mAngle*0.25f,  1, 0, 0);

glEnableClientState(GL_VERTEX_ARRAY);
glEnableClientState(GL_COLOR_ARRAY);

Cube_draw();

glRotatef(mAngle*2.0f, 0, 1, 1);
glTranslatef(0.5f, 0.5f, 0.5f);

Cube_draw();

mAngle += 1.2f;
```

Note that drawFrame() is defined as static, which tells the compiler that this function will be visible only by functions within cuberenderer.c (a bit similar to the private keyword in Java). Furthermore, the function Cube_draw() is implemented in cube.c.

Listing 5-12. *Drawing Frames from cuberenderer.c*

```
static void drawFrame()
{
        /*
         * By default, OpenGL enables features that improve quality
         * but reduce performance. One might want to tweak that
         * especially on software renderer.
         */
        glDisable(GL_DITHER);
        glTexEnvx(GL_TEXTURE_ENV,
            GL_TEXTURE_ENV_MODE,GL_MODULATE);

        /*
         * Usually, the first thing one might want to do is to clear
         * the screen. The most efficient way of doing this is to use
         * glClear().
         */
        glClear(GL_COLOR_BUFFER_BIT | GL_DEPTH_BUFFER_BIT);
```

```
    /*
     * Now we're ready to draw some 3D objects
     */
    glMatrixMode(GL_MODELVIEW);
    glLoadIdentity();

    glTranslatef(0, 0, -3.0f);
    glRotatef(mAngle,        0, 0, 1.0f);
    glRotatef(mAngle*0.25f,  1, 0, 0);

    glEnableClientState(GL_VERTEX_ARRAY);
    glEnableClientState(GL_COLOR_ARRAY);

    Cube_draw();

    glRotatef(mAngle*2.0f, 0, 1, 1);
    glTranslatef(0.5f, 0.5f, 0.5f);

    Cube_draw();

    mAngle += 1.2f;
}
```

Java Callbacks

The Java callbacks are used to send messages from the native layer to the Java layer (see Listing 5-13). The cube renderer implements two callbacks:

- jni_send_str(const char * text): This callback sends a string message to Java (mostly for debugging purposes). It does so by attaching to the current thread. This step must be done if you call JNI in a C function outside a JNI native implementation. The callback then loads the Java class opengl.jni.Natives.java. Finally, it calls the Java method opengl.jni.Natives.OnMessage(String).

- jni_gl_swap_buffers (): This is the most important callback. It tells Java that it is time to swap the OpenGL buffers. In OpenGL lingo, that means render the graphics. This step must be performed at the end of each frame of the rendering loop. The callback implementation is similar to the previous one. The main difference is that it invokes the Java method opengl.jni.Natives.GLSwapBuffers ().

Listing 5-13. *Java Callbacks from cuberenderer.c*

```
/**
 * Send a string back to Java
 */
static jmethodID mSendStr;
static jclass jNativesCls;
static JavaVM *g_VM;
```

```
static void jni_send_str( const char * text)
{
    JNIEnv *env;

    if ( !g_VM) {
        return;
    }

    (*g_VM)->AttachCurrentThread (g_VM, (void **) &env, NULL);


    if ( !jNativesCls ) {
        jNativesCls = (*env)->FindClass(env, "opengl/jni/Natives");

    }
    if ( jNativesCls == 0 ) {
            return;
    }

    // Call opengl.jni.Natives.OnMessage(String)
    if (! mSendStr ) {
        mSendStr = (*env)->GetStaticMethodID(env, jNativesCls
            , "OnMessage"
            , "(Ljava/lang/String;)V");
    }
    if (mSendStr) {
        (*env)->CallStaticVoidMethod(env, jNativesCls
                , mSendStr
                , (*env)->NewStringUTF(env, text) );
    }
}

void jni_gl_swap_buffers () {
    JNIEnv *env;

    if ( !g_VM) {
        return;
    }

    (*g_VM)->AttachCurrentThread (g_VM, (void **) &env, NULL);


    if ( !jNativesCls ) {
        jNativesCls = (*env)->FindClass(env, "opengl/jni/Natives");

    }
    if ( jNativesCls == 0 ) {
            return;
    }

    // Call opengl.jni.Natives.GLSwapBuffers ()
    jmethodID mid = (*env)->GetStaticMethodID(env, jNativesCls
```

```
                , "GLSwapBuffers"
                , "()V");

    if (mid) {
        (*env)->CallStaticVoidMethod(env, jNativesCls
                , mid
                );
    }
}


/**
 * Printf into the java layer
 * does a varargs printf into a temp buffer
 * and calls jni_sebd_str
 */

void jni_printf(char *format, ...)
{
    va_list             argptr;
    static char               string[1024];

    va_start (argptr, format);
    vsprintf (string, format,argptr);
    va_end (argptr);

    jni_send_str (string);
}
```

Let's take a closer look at the anatomy of a JNI Java callback. To start using JNI, a C program must include the system header:

```
#include <jni.h>
```

Now, if your function is called from a different place than the one that started Java_opengl_jni_Natives_NativeRender, you must attach to the current thread with the following:

```
(*g_VM)->AttachCurrentThread (g_VM, (void **) &env, NULL);
```

This is required if, for example, your program implements its own game loop, and then sends messages back to Java through JNI. This isn't the case in our example, but I've included it so the function can be invoked either way. g_VM is a global reference to the JVM, which must be saved within the very first call to Java_opengl_jni_Natives_NativeRender. Next, to load a Java class opengl.jni.Natives within C, you use the following:

```
jclass jNativesCls = (*env)->FindClass(env, "opengl/jni/Natives");
```

Here, env is a reference to the JNI environment obtained from then previous call. Note that the class name must be separated using /, not ..

Now, with a reference to the natives class, you can call the static void method OnMessage:

```
jmethod mSendStr = (*env)->GetStaticMethodID(env, jNativesCls, "OnMessage"
, "(Ljava/lang/String;)V");
(*env)->CallStaticVoidMethod(env, jNativesCls, mSendStr
            , (*env)->NewStringUTF(env, text) );
```

Note that to call this method, you need to obtain its JNI method ID using its name (OnMessage) and its signature (Ljava/lang/String;)V. The signature describes the method's arguments (a string in this case) and the return type (void). With this information, you call the static void method sending the corresponding arguments.

■ **Note** C strings must be converted into Java strings before invoking Java methods, using (*env)-> NewStringUTF(env, MyCString).

Native Interface Call

The native interface function (see Listing 5-14) is the C implementation of the Java native method opengl.jni.Natives.NativeRender(). This function performs the following tasks:

- It saves a reference to the Java VM, required by the Java callbacks of the previous section.

- It initializes the scene.

- It renders one frame. This function is meant to be called multiple times within the rendering thread (implemented by GLThread.java).

Listing 5-14. *Native Interface Function from cuberenderer.c*

```
/*
 * Class:     opengl_jni_Natives
 * Method:    RenderTest
 * Signature: ()V
 */
JNIEXPORT jint JNICALL Java_opengl_jni_Natives_NativeRender
  (JNIEnv * env, jclass cls)
{

    (*env)->GetJavaVM(env, &g_VM);
    static int initialized = 0;

    if ( ! initialized ) {
        jni_printf("Native:RenderTest initscene");
        init_scene();

        initialized = 1;

    }
```

```
    drawFrame();
    return 1;
}
```

Native Cube

Native cube (cube.c) is the last file in the lot (see Listing 5-15). This file is a carbon copy of Cube.java. It defines the vertices, colors, and indices of the cube, and draws it in the same way as its Java counterpart.

Listing 5-15. Native Implementation of Cube.java

```c
#include <stdio.h>
#include <unistd.h>
#include <stdlib.h>
#include <GLES/gl.h>

#define FIXED_ONE 0x10000
#define one 1.0f

typedef unsigned char byte;

extern void jni_printf(char *format, ...);

// Cube vertices
static GLfloat vertices[24] = {
        -one, -one, -one,
        one, -one, -one,
        one,  one, -one,
        -one,  one, -one,
        -one, -one,  one,
        one, -one,  one,
        one,  one,  one,
        -one,  one,  one,
};

// Colors
static GLfloat colors[] = {
        0,    0,    0,   one,
        one,    0,    0,   one,
        one,  one,    0,   one,
        0,  one,    0,   one,
        0,    0,  one,   one,
        one,    0,  one,   one,
        one,  one,  one,   one,
        0,  one,  one,   one,
};

static byte indices[] = {
        0, 4, 5,    0, 5, 1,
        1, 5, 6,    1, 6, 2,
```

```
        2, 6, 7,    2, 7, 3,
        3, 7, 4,    3, 4, 0,
        4, 7, 6,    4, 6, 5,
        3, 0, 1,    3, 1, 2
};


void Cube_draw()
{
    glFrontFace(GL_CW);

    glVertexPointer(3, GL_FLOAT, 0, vertices);
    glColorPointer(4, GL_FLOAT, 0 , colors);

    glDrawElements(GL_TRIANGLES, 36, GL_UNSIGNED_BYTE, indices);
}
```

Compiling and Running the Sample

You have the code in place, and now you must compile it. To do so, use the helper scripts agcc and ald described in Chapter 1, and the Makefile shown in Listing 5-16.

Listing 5-16. *Makefile for This Chapter's Example*

```
#############################################
# Android Makefile for CH05
#############################################

# Android source: Contains GL C headers
SYS_DEV             = /home/user/mydroid

# Compiler script
CC          = agcc

# Linker script
LINKER           = ald

# C files
MAIN_OBJS        = cuberenderer.o cube.o

# Library name, dynamic executable
LIB             = libgltest_jni.so
DYN             = gl-dyn

# Compilation flags & libs
INCLUDES          = -I$(SYS_DEV)/frameworks/base/opengl/include
CFLAGS        = -DNORMALUNIX -DLINUX -DANDROID
LIBS               = -lGLES_CM -lui

# Compile the main library (ibgltest_jni.so)
```

```
lib: $(MAIN_OBJS) # jni
        @echo
        $(LINKER) -shared -o $(LIB) $(MAIN_OBJS) $(LIBS)
        @echo Done. Out file is $(LIB)

# Create JNI headers
jni:
        @echo "Creating JNI C headers..."
        javah -jni -classpath ../bin -d include opengl.jni.Natives

# Test dynamic exe
dyn:
        $(CC) -c test.c $(INCLUDES)
        $(LINKER) -o $(DYN) test.o  -lgltest_jni -L.
        @echo
        @echo Done. Out file is $(DYN)
        @echo

.c.o:
        @echo
        $(CC) -Wall -O2 -fpic -c $(CFLAGS) $(INCLUDES) $<

# Deploy lib to device /data folder
deploy-test:
        @echo "Deploying $(LIB) to /data"
        adb push $(LIB) /data

clean:
        rm -f *.o
```

First, generate the JNI headers for opengl.jni.Natives.java with the following:

```
$ make jni
```

Next, compile the library with the following:

```
user@ubuntu:~/workspace/ch05.OpenGL/native$ make
agcc -Wall -O2 -fpic -c -DNORMALUNIX -DLINUX -DANDROID -
I/home/user/mydroid/frameworks/base/opengl/include cuberenderer.c

agcc -Wall -O2 -fpic -c -DNORMALUNIX -DLINUX -DANDROID -
I/home/user/mydroid/frameworks/base/opengl/include cube.c

ald -shared -o libgltest_jni.so cuberenderer.o cube.o   -lGLES_CM -lui
arm-none-linux-gnueabi-ld: warning: library search path "/usr/lib/jvm/java-6-
sun/jre/lib/i386" is unsafe for cross-compilation
```

```
Done. Out file is libgltest_jni.so
```

Check for missing symbols with this code:

```
user@ubuntu:~/workspace/ch05.OpenGL/native$ make dyn
agcc -c test.c -I/home/user/mydroid/frameworks/base/opengl/include
ald -o gl-dyn test.o -lgltest_jni -L.
arm-none-linux-gnueabi-ld: warning: library search path "/usr/lib/jvm/java-6-
sun/jre/lib/i386" is unsafe for cross-compilation
arm-none-linux-gnueabi-ld: warning: cannot find entry symbol _start; defaulting to 000082e8

Done. Out file is gl-dyn
```

■ **Note** The compiler will complain about the local system JNI headers: "library search path "/usr/lib/jvm/
java-6-sun/jre/lib/i386" is unsafe for cross-compilation." This message can be ignored.

Finally, the library must be deployed to the device /data folder so the activity can load it:

```
user@ubuntu:~ ch05.OpenGL/native$ make deploy-test
Deploying libgltest_jni.so to /data
adb push libgltest_jni.so /data
87 KB/s (7389 bytes in 0.082s)
```

As shown in Figure 5-6, when the project is started in the device, two launchers will be placed in the device desktop: OpenGL Java and OpenGL Native.

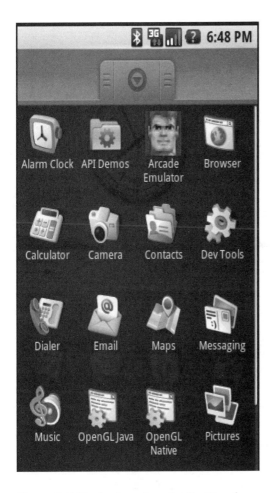

Figure 5-6. *Device launchers for the GL cubes sample*

Run both launchers and look at the device log (see Listing 5-17). On the native side, you should see the following messages:

```
DEBUG/dalvikvm(512): Trying to load lib /data/libgltest_jni.so 0x433a7258
DEBUG/dalvikvm(512): Added shared lib /data/libgltest_jni.so
```

This indicates that the native library has been successfully loaded by JNI. Now stop the activity using the Devices view (see Figure 5-7), and then try the other activity.

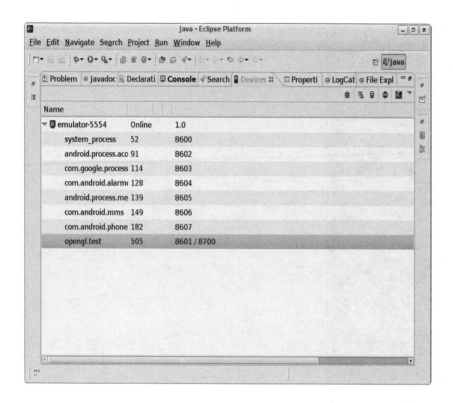

Figure 5-7. *Stopping an Android activity using the Devices view*

Listing 5-17. *Device Logs for the Java and Native Implementations of GL Cubes*

```
// Java Device Log
07-28 19:46:04.568: INFO/ActivityManager(52): Start proc opengl.test for activity
opengl.test/.JavaGLActivity: pid=505 uid=10021 gids={}
07-28 19:46:04.857: INFO/jdwp(505): received file descriptor 10 from ADB
07-28 19:46:05.677: INFO/System.out(505): GLSurfaceView::setRenderer setting
07-28 19:46:06.347: INFO/System.out(505): Vendor:Google Inc.
07-28 19:46:06.376: INFO/System.out(505): Renderer:Android PixelFlinger 1.0
07-28 19:46:06.376: INFO/System.out(505): Version:OpenGL ES-CM 1.0
07-28 19:46:06.416: INFO/System.out(505): Vendor:Google Inc.
07-28 19:46:06.436: INFO/System.out(505): Renderer:Android PixelFlinger 1.0
07-28 19:46:06.476: INFO/System.out(505): Version:OpenGL ES-CM 1.0
07-28 19:46:06.546: INFO/ARMAssembler(505): generated 07-28 19:46:06.638:
INFO/ActivityManager(52): Displayed activity opengl.test/.JavaGLActivity: 2202 ms

// Native Log
07-28 19:56:57.167: INFO/ActivityManager(52): Start proc opengl.test for activity
opengl.test/.NativeGLActivity: pid=512 uid=10021 gids={}
07-28 19:56:57.357: INFO/jdwp(512): received file descriptor 10 from ADB
```

```
07-28 19:56:58.247: INFO/System.out(512): Loading JNI lib using abs
path:/data/libgltest_jni.so
07-28 19:56:58.267: DEBUG/dalvikvm(512): Trying to load lib /data/libgltest_jni.so
0x433a7258
07-28 19:56:58.376: DEBUG/dalvikvm(512): Added shared lib /data/libgltest_jni.so 0x433a7258
07-28 19:56:58.387: DEBUG/dalvikvm(512): No JNI_OnLoad found in /data/libgltest_jni.so
0x433a7258
07-28 19:56:58.548: INFO/System.out(512): GLSurfaceView::setRenderer setting natives
listener
07-28 19:56:59.777: INFO/System.out(512): Vendor:Google Inc.
07-28 19:56:59.816: INFO/System.out(512): Renderer:Android PixelFlinger 1.0
07-28 19:56:59.916: INFO/System.out(512): Version:OpenGL ES-CM 1.0
07-28 19:57:00.056: INFO/System.out(512): Vendor:Google Inc.
07-28 19:57:00.158: INFO/System.out(512): Renderer:Android PixelFlinger 1.0
07-28 19:57:00.187: INFO/System.out(512): Version:OpenGL ES-CM 1.0
07-28 19:57:00.187: INFO/System.out(512): GLThread::OnMessage Native:RenderTest initscene
07-28 19:57:00.796: INFO/ActivityManager(52): Displayed activity
opengl.test/.NativeGLActivity: 3971 ms
```

Figure 5-7 shows the native renderer running in the emulator.

Figure 5-7. *GL cubes native renderer*

When it comes to advanced OpenGL games written for embedded devices, there are some caveats that you should be aware of before starting you porting work, which we'll look at in the next section.

Caveats of Porting OpenGL Games to Android

Today's smart phones have become pretty powerful. They feature a GPU capable of advanced graphics. Nevertheless, when it comes to writing advanced 3D games for embedded devices using OpenGL, several issues should be considered.

Consider a game like Quake, which has been ported to multiple smart phones. This game uses *immediate mode drawing* for specifying geometry. For example, consider the following snippet to render an arbitrary polygon and corresponding texture:

```
// Bind some texture
glBegin (GL_POLYGON);
glTexCoord2f (...);
glVertex3fv (...);
...
glEnd ();
```

This code is typical of a desktop application; however, it is not valid in Android (which implements OpenGL ES). This is because OpenGL ES does not support immediate mode (glBegin/glEnd) for simple geometry. Porting this code can consume significant resources (especially for a game like Quake, which has approximately 100,000 lines of source).

In OpenGL ES, geometry must be specified using vertex arrays, so the preceding code becomes something like this:

```
const GLbyte Vertices []= { ...};
const GLbyte TexCoords []= { ...};
...
glEnableClientState (GL_VERTEX_ARRAY);
glEnableClientState (GL_TEXTCOORD_ARRAY);

glVertexPointer (..., GL_BYTE , 0, Vertices);
glTexCoordPointer (..., GL_BYTE , 0, TexCoords);
glDrawArrays (GL_TRIANGLES, 0, ...);
```

You also must consider floating-point issues. OpenGL ES defines functions that use fixed-point values, as many devices do not have a floating-point unit (FPU). Fixed-point math is a technique to encode floating-point numbers using only integers. OpenGL ES uses 16 bits to represent the integer part, and another 16 bits to represent the fractional part. Here is an example of using a fixed-point translation function:

```
glTranslatex (10 << 16, 0, 0, 2 << 16); // glTranslatef (10.0f, 0.0f, 0.0f, 2.0f);
```

The following are other differences worth mentioning:

- OpenGL ES does not render polygons as wireframe or points (only solid).

- There is no GLU (OpenGL Utility Library). However, it is possible to find implementations of GLU functions on the Internet.

- The GL_QUADS, GL_QUAD_STRIP, and GL_POLYGON primitives are not supported.

These are some of the things to watch for when you decide to port your OpenGL game to an embedded device.

The Veil Has Been Lifted

The veil has been lifted to reveal a new frontier of 3D development for Android. The techniques demonstrated in this chapter can help you to bring a large number of 3D PC games to the platform, at an enormous savings in development costs.

In this chapter, you have learned a trick to mix OpenGL code in Java and C to enable the reuse of large portions of C code along with Java code. We started by looking at the OpenGL tumbling cubes sample provided by Google, and how sections of the rendering process can be implemented in C. You saw that the sample's rendering process included EGL initialization, the main loop, drawing, buffer swap, and cleanup. Then you saw how to reimplement the cube rendering invoked within the main loop. You created the new components:

- The native activity used to launch the application from the device

- The native interface class used to define the native methods and C callbacks

- The cube renderer and cube class used to render the cubes

Finally, we looked at the limitations of OpenGL ES when it comes to advanced 3D games. I hope this chapter will help you get your own 3D games for Android with minimal effort and maximum code reuse. This is a prelude to the next chapters, where we will look at two of the greatest 3D shooters for the PC, Wolfenstein 3D and Doom, and the minimal changes required to get them running on your phone.

■ ■ ■

## CHAPTER 6

3D Shooters Episode I: Wolfenstein 3D for Android

The next two chapters are my personal favorites and the most exciting of this book. We start by looking at the real thing: Wolfenstein 3D (also referred to as Wolf 3D), the godfather of all 3D shooters. The main goal of this chapter is to show you how easy is to bring Wolf 3D from the PC to the Android device, but also in this chapter, you will learn how to do the following:

- Maximize code reuse by compiling high-performance native code in a dynamic shared library.

- Write JNI code to connect Java and C subroutines.

- Cascade graphics back and forth the native and Java layers.

- Handle sound requests sent by the native layer with the Android media player.

- Build the Android project and test in the emulator.

Let's get started.

Gathering Your Tools

Some Java developers simply dismiss other languages, especially procedural languages like C. I believe that you should embrace the elegant object oriented features of Java and the raw power of C and there is nothing you cannot do in the gaming world.

Before we start, you will need to acquire the things explained in this section to make the most of this chapter.

Downloading the Chapter Source Code

My 1.210goal in here is to create a balance between the object-oriented features of the Java language and the power of C. Thus I have provided not only the Java source but the C code, neatly organized in this chapter source code. You should import the project to workspace as you move along this chapter. Some of the listings have been stripped for simplicity. To import the chapter source to your Eclipse workspace, follow these steps:

1. From the main menu click File ➤ Import.

2. In the Import dialog, select Existing Projects into Workspace. Click Next.

3. Navigate to the Chapter source ch06.Wolf3D.SW; optionally check "Copy project into workspace". Click Finish.

The automated build will kick in immediately; make sure there are no errors in the project. Next, try to familiarize yourself with the folder layout, which is divided in the following subfolders:

- src: This folder contains the Java layer of the game.

- assests: This folder contains the game files for the shareware version of Wolf 3D compressed in the zip file: wolfsw.zip.

- libs/armeabi: This folder contains the Wolf 3D native library libwolf_jni.so.

- native: This folder contains the source of the Wolf 3D C engine. The version I choose is Wolf 3D for the Game Park gaming device (a popular Korean handheld also known as GP32).

- res: This folder contains Android resources: graphics, sounds, layouts, and strings.

Introducing Wolf 3D

When Wolf 3D came to the game scene of the 1990s, it revolutionized PC gaming forever. It was the first game of its kind: a game with immersive 3D graphics where the player navigates the Nazi underground picking up weapons, opening secret doors, and shooting up rabid dogs and evil Nazis (see Figure 6-1).

Figure 6-1. Wolf 3D running on the emulator

Even though the game's environment appears to be 3D, it really is not. In reality, the game uses a technique called ray casting pioneered by John Carmack from id Software (one of the original creators of the game) to simulate a 3D environment. Ray casting is also called 2.5D and provides the geometry to render perspectives and other pseudo-3D elements.

■ **Tip** A nice ray casting tutorial by F. Permad discusses the basics such as drawing textures, floors, ceilings, walls, shading, and more. Plus, it has some neat Java examples. It can be found at

`http://www.permadi.com/tutorial/raycast/index.html`.

According to an article on Wikipedia at `http://en.wikipedia.org/wiki/Wolfenstein_3D`, Wolf 3D was released by id Software in 1992 to a huge success. It popularized the first-person shooter game for the PC. The source code was later released under a shareware strategy that helped the game to be ported to almost any platform imaginable, including these:

- Windows and Pocket PC

- Linux

- Nintendo Entertainment System (NES) and Super Nintendo (SNES)

- Atari Jaguar

- Mac OS

- Game Boy Advance

- PlayStation and PSP

- Xbox 360

- iPhone and iPod Touch

When I started fiddling with the idea of bringing Wolf 3D to Android, I knew the key of the project would be to find a highly portable version for Linux, because first, Android is built on Linux, and second, high portability will minimize potential compilation and optimization errors that are very common when using different versions of the GNU C compiler. The best two candidates I could find on the web follow:

- Wolfenstein 3D for GP32: This is a port to the Gamepark32, a Korean handheld device similar to the PSP. It is written in C. Wolf 3D for GP32 is available online at `http://sourceforge.net/projects/gp32wolf3d/`.

- Wolf3D S60: This is port of Wolfenstein 3D and Spear of Destiny for Nokia S60 cell phones. Wolf3D S60 is available online at `http://sourceforge.net/projects/wolf3d-s60/`.

Digging through the source of both projects, I realized that both were almost identical and based on a defunct port for Linux found on the Web. Of these two, the Gamepark32 version seemed the cleanest and easiest to understand, so I decided to use it. If you wish to understand why nobody has taken the time to port this code to Java, take a look at Listing 6-1.

Listing 6-1. *Total Number of Lines of Source and Headers for Wolf 3D for Gamepark32*

```
gp2xwolf3d>wc -l *.c
   1026 fmopl.c
   1127 id_ca.c
    507 id_us.c
    471 id_vh.c
    416 jni_wolf.c
    355 misc.c
    145 objs.c
    198 sd_comm.c
    166 sd_null.c
    758 sd_oss.c
     16 test.c
    399 vi_comm.c
    273 vi_null.c
    450 vi_sdl.c
    999 wl_act1.c
   2622 wl_act2.c
    801 wl_act3.c
   1483 wl_agent.c
    248 wl_debug.c
   1411 wl_draw.c
   1603 wl_game.c
   1424 wl_inter.c
   2453 wl_main.c
   3626 wl_menu.c
   1373 wl_play.c
   1483 wl_state.c
    731 wl_text.c
  26564 total

gp2xwolf3d>wc -l *.h
    121 audiosod.h
    137 audiowl6.h
    108 fmopl.h
    144 foreign.h
    171 gfxv_sdm.h
    242 gfxv_sod.h
    185 gfxv_wl1.h
    189 gfxv_wl6.h
    203 gfxv_wl6_92.h
     24 gp2xcont.h
     80 id_ca.h
     71 id_heads.h
     39 id_us.h
     60 id_vh.h
     69 misc.h
     47 sd_comm.h
     20 version.h
    176 vi_comm.h
```

```
 795 wl_act3.h
1401 wl_def.h
 212 wl_menu.h
4494 total
```

Listing 6-1 shows the total number of lines of code (.c files plus .h header files) of Wolf 3D for the Gamepark32. It's close to 30,000 lines of code. It doesn't seem that much for today's standards, but consider this: when I was in school, one of my computer ethics professors said that, statistically, a software developer can deliver ten lines of production-quality code per day. If you do the math, 3,000 days is the time that a single person would take to deliver a high-quality product. Compound this with the fact that that the work must be done pro bono. Wolf 3D falls under the GNU Public License (GPL), which would allow you to sell your Java version; however, the GPL also requires for you to give up the source, which will prevent you from reaping the product of your hard work.

In my quest to bring this game to Android, I even played with the idea of rewriting this code in Java. I found people who attempted a Java and JavaScript port of the game, but I was quickly discouraged after looking at the complexity and size of the source. These are the reasons why a pure Java port of this game is not feasible:

- *Size*: The code base is too big and complex (even for such an old game).

- *Licensing*: All work must be done for free, which is not good for business.

- *Time*: Writing the game will take too long even for a small team of developers.

The only solution with potential time and cost savings is to create a dynamic shared library of the game and cascade messages back and forth between Java and C using JNI. This is what you will learn in this chapter. Let's get started by looking at the game architecture from a high level perspective.

Understanding the Game Architecture

Figure 6-2 5.250shows the workflow of the application. When you start the game the main activity (WolfLauncher) will start. After some preliminary sanity checks, WolfLauncher will start a thread which loads the main subroutine from the dynamic shared object (DSO)—the native library). All interactions with the native library go thru the native interface class (Natives). The DSO loads all game data and runs the main game loop. In each iteration of this loop, two basic pieces of information are sent back to Java thru JNI:

- *An array of integers representing the video buffer for each frame of the game*: This array is encoded in Android's format, as a 32 bit integers with ARGB values.

- *An integer representing the index of a sound to be played by the Java audio API*: This value gets sent every time there is a sound event, such as firing the gun or opening a door.

■ **Tip** Because there is no native sound implementation, sound events are cascaded back to Java, which will load and play them on the fly. This Java sound implementation slows things down a bit. Unfortunately, because Android doesn't use the standard Linux audio device and mixer, native sound is not possible at the time of this writing. Furthermore, Google doesn't support native development, which makes things tough.

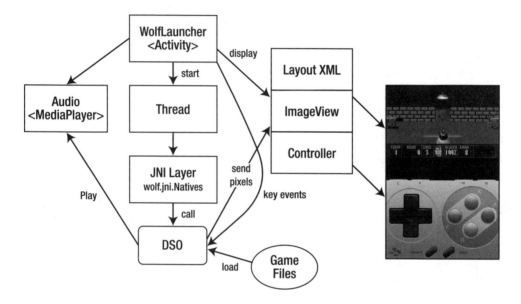

Figure 6-2. *The Wolf3D game architecture*

Other types of messages sent by the DSO layer include these:

- *Graphics initialization*: This message is sent when the video buffer is first created. Message contents include the width and height of the buffer.

- *Miscellaneous text messages*: These string messages are sent by the DSO to Java to display information to the user.

The game display is represented by an XML layout, which contains two visual components:

- *An image view*: This element displays the video buffer sent back by the DSO after an iteration of the game loop.

- *A controller layout*: This layout displays an SNES-style controller (see Figure 6-2), which listens for touch events such as navigation, gun firing, and others. These events are cascaded as scan codes back to the DSO, which process them and updates the game flow accordingly.

Game audio is handled by two Java classes that encapsulate multiple media players. These audio classes receive events from the DSO (thru JNI) when a sound event occurs and play it accordingly. Let's look at the Java classes in more detail.

Understanding the Java Classes for Wolf 3D

We have looked at the high-level game architecture of Wolf 3D for Android. Now, let's look at the classes that constitute the Java side. Before we get started, make sure you have imported the chapter source into your workspace. This will greatly help your understanding of this section. Figure 6-3 shows the layout of the Java files for the game. The most important ones follow:

- WolfLauncher: This is the game's main activity class, and it is created when the user starts the game. Its job is to display the UI, handle phone events, such as keyboard touch events, and send them to the Natives class. It also spawns the main thread that starts the native game loop.

- SNESController: This class encapsulates the SNES-style controller used to play the game without a keyboard.

- ControllerListener: This is an interface implemented by WolfLauncher and provides the means for listening for controller events.

- AudioClip: This class encapsulates the Android media player and has methods to play, stop, or loop a sound.

- AudioMananger: This class acts as an intermediary between the main activity and the audio clips. It has logic to load, start, and cache sounds for better performance.

- SoundNames: This class maps native sounds (represented by a number) to raw sounds resources within the project.

- Natives: This is a two-way interface with the DSO. It contains all the native functions that will be implemented in the DSO, plus callbacks that will be started when the DSO sends messages back to Java.

Figure 6-3. *Layout of Java Resources*

Other utility classes include the following:

- DialogTool: This class has utility methods to display messages back to the user, launch a browser, and create dialogs.

- LibraryLoader: This class is used to load the DSO from the main activity.

- ScanCodes: This class maps android key codes to PC scan codes and ASCII codes.

- WolfTools: This class has miscellaneous game information such as the name of the DSO, game, and subroutines to install game files.

Creating the Main WolfLauncher Class

The main activity class fires when the user starts the game (see Listing 6-2). This activity is defined by two resources: a layout XML file and the class itself (WolfLauncher.java)

Main Activity Layout

The activity layout defines the main user interface. Wolf 3D has a simple UI: an image view that displays the video buffer sent by the DSO and the controller layout explained in the "Movement Controller" section.

```
<?xml version="1.0" encoding="utf-8"?>
<RelativeLayout xmlns:android="http://schemas.android.com/apk/res/android"
    android:layout_width="fill_parent"
    android:layout_height="fill_parent"
    >
    <!-- GAME IMAGE -->
    <ImageView android:id="@+id/wolf_iv"
        android:layout_width="fill_parent"
        android:layout_height="wrap_content"
        android:focusableInTouchMode="true"
        android:focusable="true"
        android:layout_centerHorizontal="true"
        android:layout_centerVertical="false"/>
    <!-- Controller XML removed -->
</RelativeLayout>
```

Main Activity Class (WolfLauncher)

Here is where all the meat resides. When this class starts, the method onCreate executes performs several actions. First, it sets the window manager to full screen with:

```
getWindow().setFlags(
    WindowManager.LayoutParams.FLAG_FULLSCREEN,
    WindowManager.LayoutParams.FLAG_FULLSCREEN);
```

Next, it sets the content view XML for the application using R.layout.wolf. This represents the application layout XML containing the game image view and the controller components. It also keeps a reference to the image view representing the video buffer (R.id.wolf_iv):

```
setContentView(R.layout.wolf);
mView = (ImageView) findViewById(R.id.wolf_iv);
```

It then initializes the movement controller with initController.

Finally, it starts the game using the base folder (the folder that contains the game files), the game ID (Wolf 3D), and a Boolean value indicating if portrait or landscape mode should be used: startGame(mGameDir, WolfTools.GAME_ID, true).

Listing 6-2 shows the first part of WolfLauncher.java with the methods onCreate and intController.

Listing 6-2. *The First Section of the Wolf 3D Main Activity WolLauncher.java*

```
package game.wolfsw;

public class WolfLauncher extends Activity
```

```java
    implements Natives.EventListener, ControllerListener
{
    private static final String TAG = "Wolf3D";

    public static final Handler mHandler = new Handler();

    private static boolean mGameStarted = false;

    private static Bitmap mBitmap;
    private static ImageView mView;

    // Audio Manager
    private AudioManager mAudioMgr;

    // Sound? ( yes by default)
    private boolean mSound = true;

    private String mGameDir = WolfTools.WOLF_FOLDER;

    // Navigation
    public static enum eNavMethod {
        KBD, PANEL
    };

    public static eNavMethod mNavMethod = eNavMethod.KBD;

    private SNESController controller;

    /**
     * Called when the activity is first created.
     */
    @Override
    public void onCreate(Bundle savedInstanceState) {
        super.onCreate(savedInstanceState);

        // full screen
        getWindow().setFlags(
                WindowManager.LayoutParams.FLAG_FULLSCREEN,
                WindowManager.LayoutParams.FLAG_FULLSCREEN);

        // No title
        requestWindowFeature(Window.FEATURE_NO_TITLE);

        setContentView(R.layout.wolf);

        mView = (ImageView) findViewById(R.id.wolf_iv);

        initController();

        if (mGameStarted) {
            return;
        }
```

```
        mGameDir += getString(R.string.pkg_name) + File.separator
                + "files" + File.separator;

        if (!mGameStarted)
            DialogTool.Toast(this, "Menu for options");

        // Image size
        setImageSize(320, 200);

        // Start Game
        startGame(mGameDir, WolfTools.GAME_ID, true);
    }

    private void initController() {
        // No controller in landscape
        if (!isPortrait()) {
            return;
        }

        // init controller
        if (controller == null) {
            controller = new SNESController(this);
            controller.setListener(this);
        }

        findViewById(R.id.snes).setVisibility(View.VISIBLE);
        mNavMethod = eNavMethod.PANEL;
    }

    public boolean isPortrait() {
        return getWindowManager().getDefaultDisplay().getOrientation() == 0;
    }

    /**
     * This will set the size of the image view
     *
     * @param w
     * @param h
     */
    private void setImageSize(int w, int h) {
        LayoutParams lp = mView.getLayoutParams();
        lp.width = w;
        lp.height = h;
    }
```

Other tasks handled by Listing 6-2 include the following:

- It initializes the movement controller, setting WolfLauncher as the listener for controller events. It makes the controller visible, and sets the navigation method to PANEL. (see the section titled Movement Controller for more details on this class):

```
SNESController controller = new SNESController(this);
controller.setListener(this);

findViewById(R.id.snes).setVisibility(View.VISIBLE);
mNavMethod = eNavMethod.PANEL;
```

- It defines the method isPortrait() to query the orientation of the device:

```
public boolean isPortrait() {
  return getWindowManager().getDefaultDisplay().getOrientation() == 0;
}
```

- It defines a method to set the size of the video buffer (using the ImageView reference mView) and its layout parameters:

```
private void setImageSize(int w, int h) {
  LayoutParams lp = mView.getLayoutParams();
  lp.width = w;
  lp.height = h;
}
```

Creating the Wolf 3D Main Menu

The main menu in Wolf3D is implemented by overriding two methods: onCreateOptionsMenu and onOptionsItemSelected (see Listing 6-3). onCreateOptionsMenu is used to add menu options that will be displayed when the user presses the menu key on the device. Wolf3D has three options:

- *Toggle Screen*: This option toggles the screen size between 320 × 320 pixels and 480 × 320 (full screen). It works in landscape mode only.

- *Navigation*: This option displays the navigation method dialog. This dialog lets the user select between keyboard navigation and a game pad controller (useful for keyboardless phones).

- *Exit*: This option terminates the game.

The next method (onOptionsItemSelected) fires when the user selects an option from the menu. This method receives a MenuItem; using the item's menu ID (obtained by calling item.getItemId()), the method can proceed appropriately. Thus when the menu ID is 0, the screen size is toggled. When it is 1, the navigation method dialog is display. When it is 2, the game is terminated. Figure 6-3 shows the main menu of Wolf 3D plus the navigation method dialog in action.

Listing 6-3. *The Main Menu for Wolf 3D (from WolfLauncher.java).*

```
/**
 * Menu
 */
@Override
public boolean onCreateOptionsMenu(Menu menu) {
    super.onCreateOptionsMenu(menu);
    menu.add(0, 0, 0, "Toggle Screen").setIcon(R.drawable.view);
    menu.add(0, 1, 1, "Navigation").setIcon(R.drawable.nav);
```

```
        menu.add(0, 2, 2, "Exit").setIcon(R.drawable.exit);

        return true;
    }

    /**
     * Menu actions
     */
    @Override
    public boolean onOptionsItemSelected(MenuItem item) {
        super.onOptionsItemSelected(item);

        switch (item.getItemId()) {
        case 0:
            // Screen size
            LayoutParams lp = mView.getLayoutParams();

            // 0 == prt, 1 = land
            int orien = getWindowManager().getDefaultDisplay()
                    .getOrientation();

            if (orien == 1) {
                if (lp.width < 0 || lp.height < 0) {
                    lp.width = 480;
                    lp.height = 320;
                    return true;
                }

                lp.width = lp.width == 320 ? 480 : 320;
                lp.height = lp.height == 200 ? 320 : 200;
            } else {
                DialogTool.Toast(this, "Gotta be in landscape.");
            }
            return true;

        case 1:
            // navigation method
            DialogTool.showNavMethodDialog(this);
            return true;

        case 2:
            // Exit
            WolfTools.hardExit(0);
            return true;

        }
        return false;
    }
```

Figure 6-4. *Wolf 3D main menu and navigation options dialog*

Handling Key and Touch Events

Listing 6-4 shows the way the game handles key and touch events within the main activity.

- When the user presses a key, onKeyDown first checks if the menu key has been pressed. It ignores the event if so. Otherwise, it translates the Android key code to a PC scan code with ScanCodes.keySymToScancode(keyCode) and sends it to the DSO using the Natives class key press.

- When the key is released, onKeyUp will be called performing similar steps as before. Menu keys are ignored, and the key code gets translated to a scan code and sent to the DSO as a key release event.

- When the screen is touched, onTouchEvent will be called. This method will send a CONTROL scan code to the DSO, which indicates the gun should be fired.

Listing 6-4. *Event Handlers Within the Main Activity*

```
/**
 * Key down
 */
@Override
public boolean onKeyDown(int keyCode, KeyEvent event) {
    // Ignore MENU
    if (keyCode == KeyEvent.KEYCODE_MENU)
        return false;

    try {
        int sym = ScanCodes.keySymToScancode(keyCode);

        Natives.keyPress(sym);

    } catch (UnsatisfiedLinkError e) {
        System.err.println(e.toString());
```

```
        }
        return false;
    }

    /**
     * Key Released
     */
    @Override
    public boolean onKeyUp(int keyCode, KeyEvent event) {
        // Ignore MENU
        if (keyCode == KeyEvent.KEYCODE_MENU)
            return false;

        try {
            int sym = ScanCodes.keySymToScancode(keyCode);

            Natives.keyRelease(sym);

        } catch (UnsatisfiedLinkError e) {
            System.err.println(e.toString());
        }
        return false;
    }

    /**
     * Touch event
     */
    @Override
    public boolean onTouchEvent(MotionEvent event) {
        try {
            if (event.getAction() == MotionEvent.ACTION_DOWN) {
                // Fire on tap R-CTL
                Natives.keyPress(ScanCodes.sc_Control);
            } else if (event.getAction() == MotionEvent.ACTION_UP) {
                Natives.keyRelease(ScanCodes.sc_Control);
            } else if (event.getAction() == MotionEvent.ACTION_MOVE) {
                // Motion event
            }
            return true;
        } catch (UnsatisfiedLinkError e) {
            // Should not happen!
            Log.e(TAG, e.toString());
            return false;
        }
    }
}
```

Creating the Game Loop

In this section, we look at how the game starts within the main activity (see Listing 6-5). The startGame function performs the following steps:

- It checks for a valid base folder. This is the folder that contains the game files. By default it points to /data/data/PACKAGE_NAME/files.

- It installs the game files (if required). Game files for the shareware PC version of Wolf 3D follow:

  - *Audio*: audiohed.wl1 and audiot.wl1

  - *Graphics*: config.wl1, gamemaps.wl1, and maphead.wl1

  - *VGA*: vgadict.wl1, vgagraph.wl1, vgahead.wl1, and vswap.wl1

- It defines the game arguments: the game label, ID, and base folder. Game IDs are wolf (for the retail version) and wolfsw (for shareware).

- It loads the native library using the system call System.load(LIBRAY_NAME).

- It sets up a listener to the natives interface class. This allows the game to receive messages from the native layer.

- It creates an instance of the AudioManager. This class is in charge of playing background music or sound events received from the native layer.

- It starts a new thread with the main game loop. The thread is required because the native game loop will block execution.

At this point, the game will start, and native events will begin cascading into the Java layer.

Listing 6-5. *The Game Loop from the Main Activity*

```
/**
 * Start the main game loop
 * @param baseDir
 * @param game
 * @param portrait
 */
private void startGame(String baseDir, String game, boolean portrait) {
    File dir = new File(baseDir);

    if (!dir.exists()) {
        if (!dir.mkdir()) {
            MessageBox("Invalid game base folder: " + baseDir);
            return;
        }
    }

    // setup game files
    try {
        WolfTools.installGame(this, dir);
    } catch (Exception e) {
        MessageBox("Fatal Error", "Unable to set game files:"
                + e.toString());
```

```
        return;
    }

    Log.d(TAG, "Start game base dir: " + baseDir + " game=" + game
            + " port:" + portrait);

    // Args
    final String argv[] = { "wolf3d", game, "basedir", baseDir };

    // Load lib
    if (!loadLibrary()) {
        // this should not happen
        return;
    }

    Natives.setListener(this);

    // Audio?
    if (mSound)
        mAudioMgr = AudioManager.getInstance(this);

    new Thread(new Runnable() {
        public void run() {
            mGameStarted = true;
            Natives.WolfMain(argv);
        }
    }).start();
}
```

Making Native Callbacks

After the startGame function completes, the following events will cascade from the native layer (see Listing 6-6):

- OnSysError: This event will fire whenever an unrecoverable system error occurs. The receiver should display the incoming message to the user and quit the application.

- OnImageUpdate: This event will fire every time there is a native video update. Depending on the frame rate, it may occur around 10 to 20 times per second. The incoming arguments include:

  - *Android pixels*: This is an array of 32-bit integers representing a packed ARGB pixel.

  - *Frame X and Y coordinates*: These are the left and top coordinates of the video frame.

  - *Frame width and height*: These are the width and height of the video frame respectively.

- OnInitGraphics: This event fires once on graphics initialization and will always fire before the first call to OnImageUpdate. It receives the width and height of the video buffer that will be used to create the game bitmap in the Java layer.

- OnMessage: This event fires whenever there is a text message from the native layer. It is mostly used to check what is going on in the native side.

- OnStartSound and OnStartMusic: See the next section for details.

Listing 6-6. *Native Callbacks from Main Activity*

```
/****************************************************
 * Native Events
 ****************************************************/
@Override
public void OnSysError(final String text) {
    mHandler.post(new Runnable() {
        public void run() {
            MessageBox("System Message", text);
        }
    });

    // Wait for the user to read the box
    try {
        Thread.sleep(8000);
    } catch (InterruptedException e) {

    }
    // Ouch !
    WolfTools.hardExit(-1);
}

@Override
public void OnImageUpdate(int[] pixels, int x, int y, int w, int h) {
    mBitmap.setPixels(pixels, 0, w, x, y, w, h);

    mHandler.post(new Runnable() {
        public void run() {
            try {
                mView.setImageBitmap(mBitmap);

            } catch (Throwable e) {
                e.printStackTrace();
            }
        }
    });
}

@Override
public void OnInitGraphics(int w, int h) {
    Log.d(TAG, "OnInitGraphics creating Bitmap of " + w + " by "
```

```
                 + h);
    mBitmap = Bitmap.createBitmap(w, h, Config.ARGB_8888);
}

@Override
public void OnMessage(String text) {
    System.out.println("** Wolf Message: " + text);
}

/**
 * Load JNI library. Native lib lives in ProjectFolder/libs/armeabi/libwolf_jni.so
 */
private boolean loadLibrary() {
    Log.d(TAG, "Loading JNI librray from " + WolfTools.WOLF_LIB);
    LibraryLoader.load(WolfTools.WOLF_LIB);

    // Listen for Doom events
    Natives.setListener(this);
    return true;
}

void MessageBox(String text) {
    WolfTools.MessageBox(this, getString(R.string.app_name), text);
}

void MessageBox(String title, String text) {
    WolfTools.MessageBox(this, title, text);
}
```

Creating Sound and Music Handlers

Good sound and background music are important for any computer game. They provide the realistic feeling for a great gaming experience. Listing 6-7 shows a section of the main activity that implements the sound callbacks, which are fired by the native interface class:

- OnStartSound: This callback fires whenever the native layer requests a sound to be played such as firing a gun. The argument is a sound number that maps to a file name within the project.

- OnStartMusic: This callback fires when background music is requested by the native interface class. Background music files are large and usually play once, as opposed to sounds that are small and play many times.

The singleton AudioManager handles all sound and music playing using the methods: startSound and startMusic. For more details, see the section "Sound Handler Classes."

Listing 6-7. *Audio Handlers from the Main Activity*

```
@Override
public void OnStartSound(int idx) {
```

```
        if (mSound && mAudioMgr == null)
            Log.e(TAG, "Bug: Audio Mgr is NULL but sound is enabled!");

        try {
            if (mSound && mAudioMgr != null)
                mAudioMgr.startSound(idx);

        } catch (Exception e) {
            Log.e(TAG, "OnStartSound: " + e.toString());
        }
    }

    public void OnStartMusic(int idx) {
        if (mSound && mAudioMgr == null)
            Log.e(TAG, "Bug: Audio Mgr is NULL but sound is enabled!");

        try {
            if (mSound && mAudioMgr != null)
                mAudioMgr.startMusic(this, idx);

        } catch (Exception e) {
            Log.e(TAG, "OnStartSound: " + e.toString());
        }
    }
```

Creating Movement Controller Handlers

Listing 6-8 shows the section of the main activity that handles the movement controller events. The movement controller is an SNES-style display (see Figure 6-4),which provides navigation capabilities for phones without a keyboard. The controller itself consists of a series of drawable resources and controller classes (see "Creating Movement Controller Classes"), which fire the following events whenever the user presses any of its buttons:

- ControllerDown(int btnCode): This event fires when the user presses any button in the controller. btnCode represents the Android key code defined in the KeyEvent class.

- ControllerUp(int btnCode): This event fires when the user releases a button in the controller. It will always fire after ControllerDown.

As Listing 6-8 shows, the controller buttons are mapped in the following way:

- *Y*: Strafe (or step) left

- *X*: Strafe right

- *B*: Fire

- *A*: Enable running

Also note that the Android key code must be mapped to a PC scan code and sent to the DSO using the native interface class: Natives.sendNativeKeyEvent (event, scan code). For more details on how the controller works see the "Creating the Movement Controller" section.

Listing 6-8. *Controller Events from the Main Activity*

```
@Override
public void ControllerDown(int btnCode) {
    switch (btnCode) {
    case KeyEvent.KEYCODE_Y:
        // strafe left
        Natives.sendNativeKeyEvent(Natives.EV_KEYDOWN,
                ScanCodes.sc_Alt);
        Natives.sendNativeKeyEvent(Natives.EV_KEYDOWN,
                ScanCodes.sc_LeftArrow);
        break;

    case KeyEvent.KEYCODE_X:
        // strafe right
        Natives.sendNativeKeyEvent(Natives.EV_KEYDOWN,
                ScanCodes.sc_Alt);
        Natives.sendNativeKeyEvent(Natives.EV_KEYDOWN,
                ScanCodes.sc_RightArrow);
        break;

    case KeyEvent.KEYCODE_B:
        // Fire
        Natives.sendNativeKeyEvent(Natives.EV_KEYDOWN,
                ScanCodes.sc_Control);
        break;

    case KeyEvent.KEYCODE_A:
        // Rshift (Run)
        Natives.sendNativeKeyEvent(Natives.EV_KEYDOWN,
                ScanCodes.sc_RShift);
        break;

    default:
        Natives.sendNativeKeyEvent(Natives.EV_KEYDOWN, ScanCodes
                .keySymToScancode(btnCode));
        break;
    }
}

@Override
public void ControllerUp(int btnCode) {
    switch (btnCode) {
    case KeyEvent.KEYCODE_Y:
        // strafe left
        Natives.sendNativeKeyEvent(Natives.EV_KEYUP,
                ScanCodes.sc_Alt);
```

```
                 Natives.sendNativeKeyEvent(Natives.EV_KEYUP,
                        ScanCodes.sc_LeftArrow);
                 break;

            case KeyEvent.KEYCODE_X:
                 // strafe right
                 Natives.sendNativeKeyEvent(Natives.EV_KEYUP,
                        ScanCodes.sc_Alt);
                 Natives.sendNativeKeyEvent(Natives.EV_KEYUP,
                        ScanCodes.sc_RightArrow);
                 break;

            case KeyEvent.KEYCODE_B:
                 // Fire
                 Natives.sendNativeKeyEvent(Natives.EV_KEYUP,
                        ScanCodes.sc_Control);
                 break;

            case KeyEvent.KEYCODE_A:
                 // shift (Run)
                 Natives.sendNativeKeyEvent(Natives.EV_KEYUP,
                        ScanCodes.sc_RShift);
                 break;

            default:
                 Natives.sendNativeKeyEvent(Natives.EV_KEYUP, ScanCodes
                        .keySymToScancode(btnCode));
                 break;
            }
        }
    }
```

Creating the Movement Controller

The movement controller is designed to provide navigation and other actions for phones with no keyboard. It is modeled after the popular SNES controller (see Figure 6-5), and provides the following buttons:

- *Navigation buttons*: For up, down, left, and right rotation

- *Selection buttons*: For the select and start actions

- *Extra buttons for miscellaneous actions*: In Wolf 3D, they are mapped as follows: Y to strafe left, X to strafe right, B to fire, and A to enable running.

Figure 6-5. *The game controller*

Controller Layout

The controller UI is defined by an absolute layout XML (see Listing 6-9) within the main layout file (wolf.xml). All buttons are placed on screen using absolute X and Y coordinates, where the upper left corner of the screen represents (0,0). For this reason, this controller will only work in portrait mode (it is too big for landscape at 480 ×320). Figure 6-4 shows the background image for the controller. On top of this image the following image buttons are placed:

- Arrows for up, down, left, and right buttons

- Select and start

- X, Y, A, and B buttons

Drawable resources are defined using the XML android:background="@drawable/IMAGE_NAME", where IMAGE_NAME must exist in the res folder within the project.

Listing 6-9. *Movement Controller Layout*

```
<AbsoluteLayout xmlns:android="http://schemas.android.com/apk/res/android"
    android:id="@+id/snes"
    android:orientation="vertical"
    android:layout_width="320px"
    android:layout_height="240px"
    android:background="@drawable/snes"
    android:layout_alignParentBottom="true"
    android:layout_alignParentLeft="true"
    android:focusable="false"
    android:focusableInTouchMode="false"
    android:visibility="gone"
    >

    <!-- Arrows -->
    <ImageButton android:id="@+id/btn_up"
        android:layout_width="wrap_content"
        android:layout_height="wrap_content"
```

```xml
    android:background="#00000000"
    android:layout_margin="0px"
    android:src="@drawable/snes_u0"
    android:layout_x="48px" android:layout_y="60px"/>

<ImageButton android:id="@+id/btn_down"
    android:layout_width="wrap_content"
    android:layout_height="wrap_content"
    android:background="#00000000"
    android:layout_margin="0px"
    android:src="@drawable/snes_d0"
    android:layout_x="45px" android:layout_y="128px"/>

<ImageButton android:id="@+id/btn_left"
    android:layout_width="wrap_content"
    android:layout_height="wrap_content"
    android:background="#00000000"
    android:layout_margin="0px"
    android:src="@drawable/snes_l0"
    android:layout_x="6px" android:layout_y="99px"/>

<ImageButton android:id="@+id/btn_right"
    android:layout_width="wrap_content"
    android:layout_height="wrap_content"
    android:background="#00000000"
    android:layout_margin="0px"
    android:src="@drawable/snes_r0"
    android:layout_y="99px" android:layout_x="80px"/>

<!-- Select/Start -->
<ImageButton android:id="@+id/btn_select"
    android:layout_width="wrap_content"
    android:layout_height="wrap_content"
    android:background="#00000000"
    android:layout_margin="0px"
    android:src="@drawable/snes_select0"
    android:layout_y="205px" android:layout_x="110px"/>

<ImageButton android:id="@+id/btn_start"
    android:layout_width="wrap_content"
    android:layout_height="wrap_content"
    android:background="#00000000"
    android:layout_margin="0px"
    android:src="@drawable/snes_start0"
    android:layout_y="205px" android:layout_x="160px"/>

<!-- X/Y -->
<ImageButton android:id="@+id/btn_X"
    android:layout_width="wrap_content"
    android:layout_height="wrap_content"
    android:background="#00000000"
```

```
    android:layout_margin="0px"
    android:src="@drawable/snes_x0"
    android:layout_y="63px" android:layout_x="223px"/>

<ImageButton android:id="@+id/btn_Y"
    android:layout_width="wrap_content"
    android:layout_height="wrap_content"
    android:background="#00000000"
    android:layout_margin="0px"
    android:src="@drawable/snes_y0"
    android:layout_x="174px" android:layout_y="99px"/>

<!-- A/B -->
<ImageButton android:id="@+id/btn_A"
    android:layout_width="wrap_content"
    android:layout_height="wrap_content"
    android:background="#00000000"
    android:layout_margin="0px"
    android:src="@drawable/snes_a0"
    android:layout_y="99px" android:layout_x="267px"/>

<ImageButton android:id="@+id/btn_B"
    android:layout_width="wrap_content"
    android:layout_height="wrap_content"
    android:background="#00000000"
    android:layout_margin="0px"
    android:src="@drawable/snes_b0"
    android:layout_x="223px" android:layout_y="141px"/>

</AbsoluteLayout>
```

Controller Class

The controller is constructed by the class SNESController (see Listing 6-10). Some of the key aspects of this class follow:

- *Constructor*: The class requires an Android context that contains the layout XML for the controller and is used for initialization.

- *Initialization*: In this step, touch events for the buttons are set up by querying the main activity for a button ID and setting a touch listener:

```
mView.findViewById(BUTTON_ID).setOnTouchListener(
    new View.OnTouchListener() {
        public boolean onTouch(View v, MotionEvent evt) {
        }
}
```

- *Key presses*: Depending on the action type, DOWN or UP, a key is sent to the listener using sendEvent(EVENT_TYPE, ANDROID_KEY).

- *Event listener:* Any class that wishes to receive controller events must implement the ControllerListener interface. This interface provides the callbacks to handle button presses:

```
public interface ControllerListener {
    public void ControllerUp(int btnCode);
    public void ControllerDown(int btnCode);
}
```

Listing 6-10. *The Controller Class SNESController.java.*

```
package game.controller;

// ...

public class SNESController {

    private Activity mView;

    private ControllerListener mListener;

    public SNESController(Context context) {
        mView = (Activity) context;
        init();
    }

    public SNESController(Context context, AttributeSet attrs) {
        mView = (Activity) context;
        init();
    }

    public SNESController(Context context, AttributeSet attrs, int style) {
        mView = (Activity) context;
        init();
    }

    public void setListener(ControllerListener l) {
        mListener = l;
    }

    private void init() {
        setupControls();
    }

    private void setupControls() {
        // up
        mView.findViewById(R.id.btn_up).setOnTouchListener(
            new View.OnTouchListener() {
                @Override
                public boolean onTouch(View v, MotionEvent evt) {
                    final ImageButton b = (ImageButton) v;
```

```java
            int action = evt.getAction();

            if (action == MotionEvent.ACTION_DOWN) {
                b.setImageResource(R.drawable.snes_u1);
                sendEvent(MotionEvent.ACTION_DOWN,
                        KeyEvent.KEYCODE_DPAD_UP);
            } else if (action == MotionEvent.ACTION_UP) {
                b.setImageResource(R.drawable.snes_u0);
                sendEvent(MotionEvent.ACTION_UP,
                        KeyEvent.KEYCODE_DPAD_UP);
            }
            return true;
        }
    });

// down
mView.findViewById(R.id.btn_down).setOnTouchListener(
    new View.OnTouchListener() {
        @Override
        public boolean onTouch(View v, MotionEvent evt) {
            final ImageButton b = (ImageButton) v;
            int action = evt.getAction();

            if (action == MotionEvent.ACTION_DOWN) {
                b.setImageResource(R.drawable.snes_d1);
                sendEvent(MotionEvent.ACTION_DOWN,
                        KeyEvent.KEYCODE_DPAD_DOWN);
            } else if (action == MotionEvent.ACTION_UP) {
                b.setImageResource(R.drawable.snes_d0);
                sendEvent(MotionEvent.ACTION_UP,
                        KeyEvent.KEYCODE_DPAD_DOWN);
            }
            return true;
        }
    });
// left
mView.findViewById(R.id.btn_left).setOnTouchListener(
    new View.OnTouchListener() {
        @Override
        public boolean onTouch(View v, MotionEvent evt) {
            int action = evt.getAction();
            final ImageButton b = (ImageButton) v;

            if (action == MotionEvent.ACTION_DOWN) {
                b.setImageResource(R.drawable.snes_l1);
                sendEvent(MotionEvent.ACTION_DOWN,
                        KeyEvent.KEYCODE_DPAD_LEFT);
            } else if (action == MotionEvent.ACTION_UP) {
                b.setImageResource(R.drawable.snes_l0);
                sendEvent(MotionEvent.ACTION_UP,
                        KeyEvent.KEYCODE_DPAD_LEFT);
```

187

```
                }
                return true;
            }
        });
    // Right
    mView.findViewById(R.id.btn_right).setOnTouchListener(
        new View.OnTouchListener() {
            @Override
            public boolean onTouch(View v, MotionEvent evt) {
                int action = evt.getAction();
                final ImageButton b = (ImageButton) v;

                if (action == MotionEvent.ACTION_DOWN) {
                    b.setImageResource(R.drawable.snes_r1);
                    sendEvent(MotionEvent.ACTION_DOWN,
                        KeyEvent.KEYCODE_DPAD_RIGHT);
                } else if (action == MotionEvent.ACTION_UP) {
                    b.setImageResource(R.drawable.snes_r0);
                    sendEvent(MotionEvent.ACTION_UP,
                        KeyEvent.KEYCODE_DPAD_RIGHT);
                }
                return true;
            }
        });

    // Events for the SELECT, START, X, Y, A, B buttons
    // have been removed for simplicity. See the class SNESController.java
    // for details

    /**
     * Send an event to the {@link ControllerListener}
     * @param state Up (MotionEvent.ACTION_UP) or
     *   down (MotionEvent.ACTION_DOWN)
     * @param btnAndroid{@link KeyEvent}
     */
    private void sendEvent(int state, int btn) {
        if (mListener != null) {
            if (state == MotionEvent.ACTION_UP)
                mListener.ControllerUp(btn);
            else
                mListener.ControllerDown(btn);
        }
    }
}
```

Listing 6-10 defines touch events for the buttons: UP, DOWN, LEFT, RIFGHT, START, SELECT, X, Y, A, and B. Let's take a closer look at how the controller reacts to user events. The next fragment shows how the select button in the controller is initialized:

```
    // Controller select button
    mView.findViewById(R.id.btn_select).setOnTouchListener(
```

```
new View.OnTouchListener() {
    @Override
    public boolean onTouch(View v, MotionEvent evt) {
        int action = evt.getAction();
        final ImageButton b = (ImageButton) v;

        // button down
        if (action == MotionEvent.ACTION_DOWN) {
            // change button image
            b.setImageResource(R.drawable.snes_select1);

            // Send key to native layer
            sendEvent(MotionEvent.ACTION_DOWN,
                    KeyEvent.KEYCODE_ENTER);
        }
        // Button up
        else if (action == MotionEvent.ACTION_UP) {
            // switch image
            b.setImageResource(R.drawable.snes_select0);

            sendEvent(MotionEvent.ACTION_UP,
                    KeyEvent.KEYCODE_ENTER);
        }
        return true;
    }
});
```

First, the button is extracted from the game layout using its ID by calling `mView.findViewById(R.id.btn_select)`, where `btn_select` is the ID of the select button described in the game layout XML (`wolf.xml`). Next, it listens for touch events by calling `setOnTouchListener` and implementing the touch listener interface. Whenever the user touches a button, the controller will send the Android key code to the listener (by calling onTouch). The listener, in turn, will process the key code and react appropriately. Note that when the user presses the controller, it will receive a `MotionEvent.ACTION_DOWN` event. When this happens the corresponding button image will be swapped with a pressed image using `button.setImageResource(BUTTON_DOWN_IMAGE_RESID)`. The same goes for the `ACTION_UP` event. This helps with the lack of sensitivity when using touch interfaces as opposed to a keyboard. Many users complain about this fact. Figure 6-6 shows the image resources used by the controller to implement this mechanism.

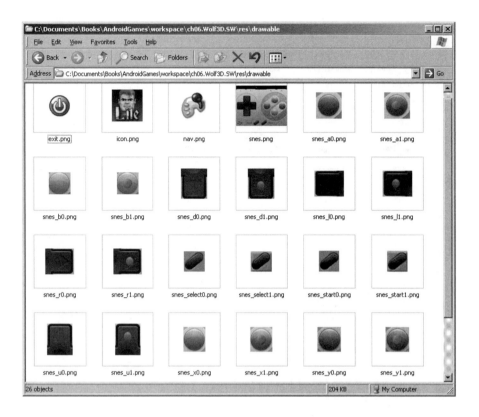

Figure 6-6. *Image resources used to define the controller key press and release events*

Sound Classes

In a perfect world, Wolf3D will use native sound for increased performance. Unfortunately Android uses a non standard sound library SoniVox EAS (Enhanced Audio System) whereas Wolf3D uses the Linux OSS (Operating System Sound). To make things worse, Google provides no documentation or sample code in the subject. This is a caveat as other smart phones such as the iPhone support a multitude of open sound libraries. Anyway to bypass the limitation, the sound track has been extracted from the original game files and stored in the res/raw folder under the main project. Figure 6-7 shows a snapshot of these files.

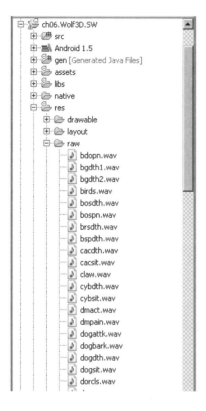

Figure 6-7. *Snapshot of the Wolf 3D sound tracks*

The sound architecture can be resumed in the following key steps:

1. When the native game loop requests a sound, a JNI callback will fire calling the method `wolf.jni.Natives.OnStartSound(idx)`, where `idx` represents an index or sound ID.

2. `wolf.jni.Natives` will delegate the sound request to the listener `WolfLauncher` which is the main activity of the application.

3. The main activity will use the classes `AudioManager` and `AudioClip` to play the sound by mapping the sound ID to the corresponding raw resource (`WAVE` file).

4. The mappings of native sound IDs to Android raw (`WAVE`) files are defined in the class `wolf.audio.SoundNames`.

Mapping Sound Names to Raw Sound Resources

The name mapping class SoundNames is the critical component that maps a native sound IDs to an Android raw resource IDs. Wolf 3D uses 86 sounds, which are defined using an array of integers where the array index represents the native sound ID and the array value represents the Android raw resource ID (see Listing 6-11). This class is used by the AudioManager. The native sound IDs were extracted from the native header file audiowl6.h within the native/gp2xwolf3d folder (see the chapter source code for details).

Listing 6-11. *Native Sound Name Mappings*

```
public class SoundNames {

    public static final int [] Sounds = new int[86];

    /* Native Sound
    typedef enum {
        HITWALLSNDWL6,                  // 0
        SELECTWPNSNDWL6,                // 1
        SELECTITEMSNDWL6,               // 2
        HEARTBEATSNDWL6,                // 3
        MOVEGUN2SNDWL6,                 // 4
        *** SEE SOUND NAMES CLASS ***
        MISSILEFIRESNDWL6,              // 85
        MISSILEHITSNDWL6,               // 86
        LASTSOUNDWL6
          }
    */

    static {
        //Sounds[0] = R.raw.noway;  // hit wall
        Sounds[1] = R.raw.wpnup;    // sel wpn
        Sounds[2] = R.raw.itemup;   // hit wall
        Sounds[4] = R.raw.wpnup;     // Move gun(weapon up)

        // *** SEE SOUND NAMES CLASS ***

        Sounds[76] = R.raw.podth2;
        Sounds[77] = R.raw.podth3;
        Sounds[78] = R.raw.bgdth2;

    }

    /* Music Indexes
    typedef enum {
        CORNER_MUS,                 // 0
        DUNGEON_MUSWL6,             // 1
        WARMARCH_MUS,               // 2
```

```
        // *** SEE SOUND NAMES CLASS ***

        } musicnamesWL6;
    */

    public static final int [] Music = new int[27];

    static {
        Music[0] = R.raw.mus_emnycrnr;
        Music[1] = R.raw.mus_emnycrnr;
        Music[2] = R.raw.mus_marchwar;
        Music[3] = R.raw.mus_getthem;

        // *** SEE SOUND NAMES CLASS ***

        Music[26] = R.raw.pacman;
    }
}
```

Besides sounds, Wolf 3D implements background music, which is processed in the same exact way. The difference being that background music is big and plays once, whereas sounds are tiny and can play multiple times during the game. Wolf 3D uses 27 music files defined in the C header audiowl6.h in the native/gp2xwolf3d folder (see the chapter source code for details). With the mappings in place, the AudioManager can do its work.

Creating the Audio Manager

AudioManager is a singleton helper class that manages all audio and performs the following tasks:

- It starts a sound given its native ID.

- It starts background music given its native ID.

- It cashes commonly used sounds for better performance.

AudioManager uses a HashMap for clip caching:

```
HashMap<String, AudioClip> mSounds = new HashMap<String, AudioClip>();
```

When a sound request comes along, the method void startSound(int sidx) will be invoked where sidx is the ID of the native sound. Next, the Android resource ID will be extracted using the SoundNames class:

```
int id = SoundNames.Sounds[sidx];
```

Finally, the cache table will be queried. If the table contains the sound, it will be played from cache. Otherwise, the sound will be loaded from disk and cached for the next event:

```
if (mSounds.containsKey(key)) {
```

```
  // Play from cache
  mSounds.get(key).play();
}
else {
  // load clip from disk
  AudioClip clip = new AudioClip(mContext, id);
  clip.play();

  // cache sound
  mSounds.put(key, clip);
  mClipCount++;
}
```

Listing 6-12 shows how it is done. Furthermore, AudioManager also implements several methods. First, getInstance() is a singleton method used to provide only one instance of AudioManager.

preloadSounds(Context ctx) preloads commonly used sounds. An application context is required for the inner AudioClip class, which is used to wrap the Android media player. The next fragment shows how this method uses the resource IDs of the most common sounds to load them into memory. The goal of this method is to improve performance by keeping these sounds in memory at all times:

```
public void preloadSounds(Context ctx) {
    int[] IDS = new int[] { R.raw.doropn, R.raw.dorcls,
            R.raw.pistol, R.raw.wpnup };

    // Preload sound WAVs using their IDs
    Resources res = mContext.getResources();

    for (int i = 0; i < IDS.length; i++) {
        final int id = IDS[i];
        final String key = res.getResourceName(id);

        Log.d(TAG, "PreLoading sound " + key + " ID " + id);
        mSounds.put(key, new AudioClip(ctx, id));
    }
}
```

Next, startMusic(Context ctx, int midx) starts the background music given a native music ID. Note that there is only one audio clip for music. This means only one music track can be played at a time. An Android context is required for the AudioClip:

```
public void startMusic(Context ctx, int midx) {
    // Obtain a the raw music ID from the SoundNames mapping class
    int id = SoundNames.Music[midx];

    if (id == 0)
        return;

    try {
        // Check if the RESOURCE exists on disk
        mContext.getResources().getResourceName(id);
```

```
        } catch (NotFoundException e) {
            System.err.println("Music resID for idx " + midx
                    + " no found");
            return;
        }

        // Stop any playing music
        if (music != null) {
            music.stop();
            music.release();
        }

        Log.d(TAG, "Starting music " + id);

        // Play it
        music = new AudioClip(ctx, id);
        music.play();
    }
```

Finally, the instance variable music is used to start playback. Note that music is an instance variable of type AudioClip.

Listing 6-12. *The Audio Manager for Wolf 3D*

```
package wolf.audio;

/**
 * Audio manager. Plays and caches sounds for Woldf 3D
 */
public class AudioManager {
    static final String TAG = "AudioMgr";

    static private AudioManager am;

    // Game sound (WAVs) cache table
    private volatile HashMap<String, AudioClip> mSounds
        = new HashMap<String, AudioClip>();

    private int MAX_CLIPS = 20;
    private int mClipCount = 0;
    private Context mContext;

    // BG music
    private AudioClip music;

    /**
     * AudioManager singleton getInstance
     */
    static public AudioManager getInstance(Context ctx) {
        if (am == null)
            return new AudioManager(ctx);
```

```
        return am;
    }

    private AudioManager(Context ctx) {
        mContext = ctx;
        preloadSounds(ctx);
    }

    /**
     * Start a sound by name & volume
     * @param idx Sound idx (see SoundNames for mappings)
     */
    public synchronized void startSound(int sidx) {
        if (sidx == 0)
            return;

        if (sidx < 0 || sidx > SoundNames.Sounds.length) {
            return;
        }

        // The sound key
        int id = SoundNames.Sounds[sidx];
        String key;

        if (id == 0)
            return;

        try {
            key = mContext.getResources().getResourceName(id);
        } catch (NotFoundException e) {
            return;
        }

        if (mSounds.containsKey(key)) {
            // Play from cache
            mSounds.get(key).play();
        } else {
            // load clip from disk
            // If the sound table is full last entry
            if (mClipCount > MAX_CLIPS) {
                // Remove a last key
                int idx = mSounds.size() - 1;

                String k = (String) mSounds.keySet().toArray()[idx];
                AudioClip clip = mSounds.remove(k);
                clip.release();
                clip = null;
                mClipCount--;
            }

            AudioClip clip = new AudioClip(mContext, id);
```

```
        clip.play();

        mSounds.put(key, clip);
        mClipCount++;
    }
}

/**
 * PreLoad the most used sounds into a hash map
 *
 * @param ctx App context
 * @return
 */
// public void preloadSounds(Context ctx) removed for simplicity

/**
 * Start background music
 * @param ctx
 * @param midx Music index, See SoundNames for mappings
 */
// public void startMusic(Context ctx, int midx) Removed for simplicity

}
```

Creating the Audio Clip

This is the final piece of the puzzle. AudioClip wraps the Android media player and provides methods for
(see Listing 6-13):

- Creating a clip using a resource ID or URI

- Playing or looping a sound

- Stopping a sound

- Setting the volume

AudioClip deals with the nasty idiosyncrasies of the media player such as illegal state exceptions
when the resources are not prepared, played, or stopped in the right sequence.

Listing 6-13. The Audio Clip Class for Wolf 3D.

```
package wolf.audio;

import android.content.Context;
import android.media.MediaPlayer;
import android.net.Uri;

public class AudioClip {
    static final String TAG = "AudioClip";
```

```java
    private MediaPlayer mPlayer;
    private String name;

    private boolean mPlaying = false;
    private boolean mLoop = false;

    public AudioClip(Context ctx, int resID) {
        name = ctx.getResources().getResourceName(resID);

        mPlayer = MediaPlayer.create(ctx, resID);
        mPlayer.setOnCompletionListener(
                new MediaPlayer.OnCompletionListener() {
                    @Override
                    public void onCompletion(MediaPlayer mp) {
                        mPlaying = false;
                        if (mLoop) {
                            mp.start();
                        }
                    }

                });
    }

    public AudioClip(Context ctx, Uri uri) {
        name = uri.toString();

        mPlayer = MediaPlayer.create(ctx, uri);
        mPlayer.setOnCompletionListener(
                new MediaPlayer.OnCompletionListener() {
                    @Override
                    public void onCompletion(MediaPlayer mp) {
                        mPlaying = false;
                        if (mLoop) {
                            mp.start();
                        }
                    }

                });
    }

    public synchronized void play() {
        if (mPlaying)
            return;

        if (mPlayer != null) {
            mPlaying = true;
            mPlayer.start();
        }
    }

    public synchronized void play(int vol) {
        if (mPlaying)
```

```
            return;

        if (mPlayer != null) {
            mPlaying = true;
            mPlayer.setVolume((float) Math.log10(vol)
                    , (float) Math.log(vol));
            mPlayer.start();
        }
    }

    public synchronized void stop() {
        try {
            mLoop = false;
            if (mPlaying) {
                mPlaying = false;
                mPlayer.pause();
            }

        } catch (Exception e) {
            System.err.println("AduioClip::stop " + name + " "
                    + e.toString());
        }
    }

    public synchronized void loop() {
        mLoop = true;
        mPlaying = true;
        mPlayer.start();
    }

    public void release() {
        if (mPlayer != null) {
            mPlayer.release();
            mPlayer = null;
        }
    }

    public String getName() {
        return name;
    }

    /**
     * Set volume
     * @param vol integer between 1-100
     */
    public void setVolume(int vol) {
        if (mPlayer != null) {
            mPlayer.setVolume((float) Math.log10(vol)
                    , (float) Math.log10(vol));
        }
    }
}
```

Native Interface Class

The native interface class (Natives.java) acts as the glue between the Java and the C code (see Listing 6-14). In Wolf 3D, this class is a two-way pipeline that handles all native access:

- It describes native methods that will be called from Java code.

- It implements Java callbacks, that is, java methods that will be called from C.

This class declares the following native methods implemented in C:

- native int WolfMain(String[] argv): This method starts the main game loop. argv represents an array of arguments that will be sent to the native layer.

- native int keyPress(int key): This method can be used to send a key pressed event to the native layer. The argument key represents a PC scan code.

- native int keyRelease(int key): This method can be used to send a key release event where key represents PC scan code.

■ **Tip** Note that PC scan codes are not the same as Android key codes. The utility class wolf.util.ScanCodes is used to convert these codes.

Listing 6-14. *Native Interface Class Natives.java.*

```
package wolf.jni;

import android.util.Log;

public class Natives {
    public static final String TAG = "Natives";

    public static final int EV_KEYDOWN = 0;
    public static final int EV_KEYUP = 1;
    public static final int EV_MOUSE = 2;

    private static EventListener listener;

    /**
     * Native event listener interface
     */
    public static interface EventListener {
        void OnMessage(String text);
        void OnInitGraphics(int w, int h);
        void OnImageUpdate(int[] pixels, int x, int y, int w, int h);
        void OnSysError(String text);
        void OnStartSound(int idx);
        void OnStartMusic(int idx);
```

```java
}

public static void setListener(EventListener l) {
    listener = l;
}

// Native Main game sub (takes an array of arguments)
public static native int WolfMain(String[] argv);

// Native Key press. It sends a pc scan code
public static native int keyPress(int key);

 // Native Key release. It sends a  pc scan  code
public static native int keyRelease(int key);


/***********************************************************
 * C - Callbacks
 **********************************************************/
 // This fires on messages from the C layer
private static void OnMessage(String text) {
    if (listener != null)
        listener.OnMessage(text);
}

 // Fires on init graphics: receives the width and height of the video
private static void OnInitGraphics(int w, int h) {
    if (listener != null)
        listener.OnInitGraphics(w, h);
}

// Fires on image update: receives the video RGBA pixels plus x,y
// coordinates and width and height of the image
private static void OnImageUpdate(int[] pixels, int x, int y,
        int w, int h) {
    if (listener != null)
        listener.OnImageUpdate(pixels, x, y, w, h);

}

// Fires when the C lib calls exit()
private static void OnSysError(String message) {
    if (listener != null)
        listener.OnSysError(message
                + " - Please report this error.");
}

 // Fires when a sound is requested in the C layer.
 // Receives a sound index
private static void OnStartSound(int idx) {
    if (listener != null)
```

```
            listener.OnStartSound(idx);
    }

    // Fires when music is played in the C layer.
    private static void OnStartMusic(int idx) {
        if (listener != null)
            listener.OnStartMusic(idx);
    }

     //  Sends a key event to the native layer
     // type : one of Natives.EV_KEYDOWN or Natives.EV_KEYUP
     // sym: PC scan code
    public static void sendNativeKeyEvent(int type, int sym) {
        try {
            if (type == Natives.EV_KEYDOWN)
                Natives.keyPress(sym);
            else
                Natives.keyRelease(sym);
        } catch (UnsatisfiedLinkError e) {
            Log.e(TAG, e.toString());
        }
    }
}
```

In order for the game activity (WolfLauncher) to receive native callbacks, such as when a video update occurs or a sound must be played, it must implement the interface Natives.EventListener. This interface provides the critical notifications at the core of the game:

- OnMessage(String text): This event sends a message from the native layer for information purposes.

- OnInitGraphics(int w, int h): This event gets called when the video graphics gets initialized. It returns the width and height of the video buffer.

- OnImageUpdate(int[] pixels, int x, int y, int w, int h): This is perhaps the most important method out there. It gets called when a video update occurs and returns an Android ARGB packed array of pixels to be displayed on the device. It also returns the X and Y coordinates of the top left pixel and the width and height of the video buffer.

- OnSysError(String text): This event fires when a fatal error occurs. The client should display the incoming message and terminate; otherwise, the application will certainly crash.

- OnStartSound(int idx): This event fires when a sound must be played. idx represents the native sound ID.

- OnStartMusic(int idx): This event fires when background music must be played. idx represents the native music ID.

Now, let's look at some of the native code where all the magic occurs.

Coding the Native Layer

Even though Wolf3D is an old game written in the 1980s, it is still big for a mobile device. The C code is roughly 30,000 lines of C code that's very hard to understand. This section will take a look at some tiny changes made to the core to add JNI functionality. You should look at the source code of the chapter when going through this section.

The changes made to the original game for JNI can be summarized as follows:

- New files:

  - jni_wolf.c: This file contains all JNI native method implementations plus C to Java callbacks

  - jni_wolf.h and wolf_jni_Natives.h. These are the C headers that support jni_wolf.c.

- Updated files:

  - sd_null.c: This file will be updated to cascade sound and music requests back to Java.

  - vi_null.c: This file will be updated to cascade video buffer events back to Java.

Let's take a look at sections of jni_wolf.c. This is the most important file and must be understood completely. Table 6-1 shows the name mappings of the native Java methods to their corresponding C counterparts:

Table 6-1. *Native Methods and Their C Names for Wolf 3D.*

Java	C
public static native int wolf.jni.Natives.WolfMain(String[] argv)	JNIEXPORT jint JNICALL Java_wolf_jni_Natives_WolfMain (JNIEnv * env, jclass cls, jobjectArray jargv)
public static native int wolf.jni.Natives.keyPress(int key)	JNIEXPORT jint JNICALL Java_wolf_jni_Natives_keyPress (JNIEnv * env, jclass cls, jint scanCode)
public static native int wolf.jni.Natives.keyRelease(int key)	JNIEXPORT jint JNICALL Java_wolf_jni_Natives_ keyRelease (JNIEnv * env, jclass cls, jint scanCode)

Consider the native wolf.jni.Natives.WolfMain. Internally, it gets translated to Java_wolf_jni_Natives_WolfMain. This must be done using the javah command (see the section "Compiling the DSO" for details). This function starts the main game loop.

Initializing the Game Loop

This is the most important function in this file. It starts the native game loop and will block execution. For this reason, this function should be called within a Java thread. The critical steps shown in Listing 6-15 follow:

1. Save a reference to the Java VM is using (*env)->GetJavaVM(env, &g_VM). This reference will be later used within the C to Java callbacks.

2. Convert the Java string array (jargv) to a C array (char **). The C array will be send to the native game loop. The key aspects of converting a Java string array to a C array follow:

   • Get the length of the java array with (*env)->GetArrayLength(env, jarray).

   • Get the value of the Nth row of the Java array as a Java string with jstring jrow = (jstring)(*env)->GetObjectArrayElement(env, jargv, i).

   • Convert the Java string above (jrow) to a C string: const char *row = (*env)->GetStringUTFChars(env, jrow, 0).

   • Allocate space for the C array for that specific row: args[i] = malloc(strlen(row) + 1).

   • Copy the new C string to the C array: strcpy (args[i], row).

   • Release the java string row: (*env)->ReleaseStringUTFChars(env, jrow, row).

   • Repeat the same process for each element in the Java array.

3. Load the native interface class wolf.jni.Natives.java: jNativesCls = (*env)->FindClass(env, "wolf/jni/Natives"). This class will be used by the C to Java native callbacks.

4. Load the video update callback using its name and signature: jSendImageMethod = (*env)->GetStaticMethodID(env, jNativesCls, "OnImageUpdate", "([IIIII)V").

5. Load the sound update callback: jStartSoundMethod = (*env)->GetStaticMethodID(env, jNativesCls, "OnStartSound", "(I)V").

6. Invoke the native game loop sending the C array created previously: wolf_main (clen, args).

At this point, execution will block, and the native video buffer should fill up; plus native events should start coming up. These events must be glued to the Android activity using the C to Java callbacks.

Listing 6-15. *The Main Game Loop from wolf_jni.c*

```
// Global Java VM
static JavaVM *g_VM;

// Java Native interface class
```

```
jclass jNativesCls;
// Video buffer java callback
jmethodID jSendImageMethod;

// Sound callback
jmethodID jStartSoundMethod;

// Java image pixels: int ARGB
jintArray jImage;
int iSize;

// Native game loop
extern int wolf_main(int argc, char **argv);

JNIEXPORT jint JNICALL Java_wolf_jni_Natives_WolfMain
  (JNIEnv * env, jclass cls, jobjectArray jargv)
{
    (*env)->GetJavaVM(env, &g_VM);

    // Extract char ** args from Java array
    jsize clen =  getArrayLen(env, jargv);

    // convert Java String[] arguments to C char **
    char * args[(int)clen];

    int i;
    jstring jrow;
    for (i = 0; i < clen; i++)
    {
        jrow = (jstring)(*env)->GetObjectArrayElement(env, jargv, i);
        const char *row  = (*env)->GetStringUTFChars(env, jrow, 0);

        args[i] = malloc( strlen(row) + 1);
        strcpy (args[i], row);

        // free java string jrow
        (*env)->ReleaseStringUTFChars(env, jrow, row);
    }

    /*
     * Load the Java native interface class wolf.jni.natives
     */
    jNativesCls = (*env)->FindClass(env, "wolf/jni/Natives");

    if ( jNativesCls == 0 ) {
        printf("Unable to find class: wolf/jni/Natives");
            return -1;
    }

    // Load wolf.jni.Natives.OnImageUpdate(int[] video, int x, int y, int w, int h)
    jSendImageMethod = (*env)->GetStaticMethodID(env, jNativesCls
```

205

```
                , "OnImageUpdate"
                , "([IIIII)V");

        if ( jSendImageMethod == 0 ) {
            jni_printf("Unable to find method wolf.jni.OnImageUpdate(byte[])");
            return -1;
        }

        // Load OnStartSound(int id)
        jStartSoundMethod = (*env)->GetStaticMethodID(env, jNativesCls
                , "OnStartSound"
                , "(I)V");

        if ( jStartSoundMethod == 0 ) {
            jni_printf("Unable to find method wolf.jni.OnStartSound sig: ([BI)V");
            return -1;
        }
        // Print args
        for (i = 0; i < clen; i++) {
            jni_printf("WolfMain args[%d]=%s", clen, args[i]);
        }

        // Invoke Quake's main sub. This will loop forever
        wolf_main (clen, args);
        return 0;
}
```

Cascading Messages with C to Java Callbacks

C to Java callbacks are used to cascade native events such as video and sound events back to the Java activity. The callbacks require a JNI implementation plus some tiny changes to the original C files. There are three types of callbacks in Wolf 3D:

- *Graphics initialization*: It is the very first callback that should fire to notify the main activity of the size (width and height) of the video buffer. The main activity will in turn use this information to create a bitmap to be displayed on the device.

- *Video buffer update*: This callback must fire after graphics initialization and send an Android packed ARGB bitmap back to the main activity for display.

- *Sound and music requests*: These are used to tell the main activity that a sound or background music must be played.

Initializing Graphics

Listing 6-15 shows the way graphics are initialized in the game. There are two functions in two different files: jni_init_graphics (int width, int height) in jni_wolf.c and VL_Startup() in vi_null.c.

jni_init_graphics implements the C to Java callback that tells the main activity that graphics are ready. It sends the width and height of the video buffer, and they are used to create a Java bitmap that will be used to display the video on the device. Note that this callback fires outside of the current JNI thread. When the callback fires, you cannot touch the JNI environment directly (JNIEnv *env), or you will cause an invalid thread access error that will crash the application. Instead, you must attach to the current thread with the following call:

```
(*g_VM)->AttachCurrentThread (g_VM, (void **) &env, NULL)
```

where env will get a reference to the current thread JNI environment. Furthermore to do this, you must save a global reference to the Java virtual machine (usually from the very first native call):

```
(*env)->GetJavaVM(env, &g_VM);
```

Once you have attached to the current thread, you can load the wolf.jni.Natives.OnInitGraphics(width, height) using the method name and signature and execute it with the width and height of the video buffer:

```
jmethodID mid = (*env)->GetStaticMethodID(
        env, jNativesCls, "OnInitGraphics", "(II)V");
(*env)->CallStaticVoidMethod(env, jNativesCls, mid, width, height);
```

The second part of the listing (a section of the file vi_null.c) shows where jni_init_graphics is called from VL_Startup(). This is the native video startup callback of the game (see Listing 6-16).

***Listing 6-16.** Graphics Initialization from wolf_jni.c and vi_null.c.*

```
// This function is new code for Android and lives in wolf_ini.c
void jni_init_graphics(int width, int height)
{
    JNIEnv *env;

    if ( !g_VM) {
        ERRORO("I_JNI: jni_init_graphics No JNI VM available.\n");
        return;
    }

    (*g_VM)->AttachCurrentThread (g_VM, (void **) &env, NULL);


    iSize = width * height;

    // Create a new int[] used by jni_send_pixels
    jImage = (*env)-> NewIntArray(env, iSize);

    // call doom.util.Natives.OnInitGraphics(w, h);
    jmethodID mid = (*env)->GetStaticMethodID(env, jNativesCls
        , "OnInitGraphics"
        , "(II)V");

    if (mid) {
        (*env)->CallStaticVoidMethod(env, jNativesCls
```

```
                  , mid
                  , width, height);
        }
}

// This function lives in vi_null.c
// byte* gfxbuf is the global graphics buffer
void VL_Startup()
{
    // Original code
    vwidth = 320;
    vheight = 200;

    if (MS_CheckParm("x2")) {
        vwidth *= 2;
        vheight *= 2;
    } else if (MS_CheckParm("x3")) {
        vwidth *= 3;
        vheight *= 3;
    }

    if (gfxbuf == NULL)
        gfxbuf = malloc(vwidth * vheight * 1);

    // New code for Android
    jni_printf("VL_Startup %dx%d. Calling init graphics.",vwidth, vheight);
    jni_init_graphics(vwidth, vheight);
}
```

The function VL_Startup is the video startup function called by the Wolf native engine. Look closer, and you can see that it initializes the size of the screen to a resolution of 320 ×200 pixels. It also checks for the argument x2 or x3 (which tell the Wolf engine to double or triple the screen resolution). It also allocates space for the video buffer. Finally, the last two lines display a debugging message and, most importantly, tell the Java layer that the graphics have been initialized. These two lines are critical for the game to work in Android.

Cascading Video Buffers

After the graphics are initialized, we can start sending video buffer updates to the main activity. To do so, we use the C to Java callback jni_send_pixels in jni_wolf.c and VW_UpdateScreen() in vi_null.c.

jni_send_pixels is almost identical to the callback in the previous section. The main difference being that this callback will fire many times per second and must be as quick and nimble as possible.

- To achieve maximum performance, the method ID for wolf.jni.Natives.OnImageUpdate is loaded by the native WolfMain implementation.

- To speed thing up even more, the array buffer used to send the pixels to Java (jImage) is created on jni_init_graphics using the width and height of the buffer.

- With these two variables, the array region is set by calling: `(*env)->SetIntArrayRegion(env, jImage, 0, iSize, (jint *) data)`, where data is an array of 32 bit integers packed in Android format (ARGB).

In the second file of Listing 6-17, two important functions are called:

- `VL_SetPalette (const byte *palette)`: This is the function that sets the palette that will be used to pack the pixels in Android format. Wolf 3D uses a 256-color palette of sequential red, green, and blue (RGB) bytes, (256×3 for a total of 768 bytes).

- `VW_UpdateScreen()`: With the palette in place, this game callback will fire every time there is a video update. Here, we simply make a palette lookup using the global graphics buffer (gfxbuf), and the video width and height (vwidth and vheight) for each byte in gfxbuf. Note that gfxbuf is an array of bytes that represent color indexes in the palette:

```
int size = vwidth * vheight;
int pixels[size], i;

for ( i = 0 ; i < size ; i ++) {
   byte colIdx = gfxbuf[i];
   pixels[i] = (0xFF << 24)
       | (pal[colIdx].red << 16)
       | (pal[colIdx].green << 8)
       | (pal[colIdx].blue);
}
```

Finally, the array of pixels is sent to Java along with the video width and height:

```
jni_send_pixels(pixels,0,0, vwidth, vheight).
```

Listing 6-17. *Cascading the Video Buffer*

```
// In jni_wolf.c
// g_VM is the global Java VM
void jni_send_pixels(int * data, int x, int y, int w, int h)
{
    JNIEnv *env;

    if ( !g_VM) {
        return;
    }

    (*g_VM)->AttachCurrentThread (g_VM, (void **) &env, NULL);

    // Send img back to java.
    if (jSendImageMethod) {
        (*env)->SetIntArrayRegion(env, jImage, 0, iSize, (jint *) data);

        // Call Java method
```

```c
        (*env)->CallStaticVoidMethod(env, jNativesCls
            , jSendImageMethod
            , jImage
            , (jint)x, (jint)y, (jint)w, (jint)h);
    }
}

// In file vi_null.c
/************************************************
 * Class XColor
 ************************************************/
typedef struct Color XColor;

struct Color
{
    int red;
    int green;
    int blue;
    //int pixel;
};

// Pallete
XColor pal[256];

void VL_SetPalette(const byte *palette)
{
    int i;

    VL_WaitVBL(1);

    for (i = 0; i < 256; i++)
    {
        pal[i].red = palette[i*3+0] << 2;
        pal[i].green = palette[i*3+1] << 2;
        pal[i].blue = palette[i*3+2] << 2;
    }
}

void VW_UpdateScreen()
{
    // screen size
    int size = vwidth * vheight;

    // ARGB pixels
    int pixels[size], i;

    for ( i = 0 ; i < size ; i ++) {
        byte colIdx      = gfxbuf[i];
        pixels[i]    = (0xFF << 24)
            | (pal[colIdx].red << 16)
            | (pal[colIdx].green << 8)
```

```
                | (pal[colIdx].blue);

    }
    // send thru JNI here
    jni_send_pixels(pixels,0,0, vwidth, vheight);

}
```

Cascading Sound and Music Requests

Sound and music requests are cascaded by two C to Java callbacks and changes to the native file
sd_null.c:

- jni_start_sound (int idx): This callback calls the Java method
  wolf.jni.Natives.OnStartSound(int idx), where idx is the native sound ID.

- jni_start_music (int idx): This callback calls the Java method
  wolf.jni.Natives.OnStartMusic(int idx), where idx is the native music ID.

Listing 6-18 shows the implementation of these callbacks. Remember that you must attach to the
current thread to prevent a JNI invalid thread access with

```
(*g_VM)->AttachCurrentThread (g_VM, (void **) &env, NULL)
```

Once the thread is attached, you can call the Java method using its ID plus the argument (the sound
ID in this case):

```
(*env)->CallStaticVoidMethod(env, jNativesCls, jStartSoundMethod, (jint) idx);
```

Note that the method IDs for sound and music, jStartSoundMethod and jStartMusicMethod
respectively, were loaded at startup for increased performance.

Listing 6-18. *Cascading Sound and Music Requests*

```
// In jni_wolf.c
void jni_start_sound (int idx)
{
    /*
     * Attach to the curr thread otherwise we get JNI WARNING:
     * threadid=3 using env from threadid=15 which aborts the VM
     */
    JNIEnv *env;

    if ( !g_VM) {
        return;
    }

    (*g_VM)->AttachCurrentThread (g_VM, (void **) &env, NULL);

    if ( jStartSoundMethod == 0 ) {
```

```
            jni_printf("BUG: Invalid JNI method method OnStartSound (I)V");
                return ;
        }

        // Call Java method wolf.jni.OnStartSound(int idx)
        (*env)->CallStaticVoidMethod(env, jNativesCls
                , jStartSoundMethod
                , (jint) idx);

}

void jni_start_music (int idx)
{
    /*
     * Attach to the curr thread otherwise we get JNI WARNING:
     * threadid=3 using env from threadid=15 which aborts the VM
     */
    JNIEnv *env;

    if ( !g_VM) {
        return;
    }

    if ( !jNativesCls ) {
        printf("JNIStartMusic: No JNI interface\n");
        return;
    }

    (*g_VM)->AttachCurrentThread (g_VM, (void **) &env, NULL);

    jmethodID mid = (*env)->GetStaticMethodID(env, jNativesCls
        , "OnStartMusic"
        , "(I)V");

    if (mid) {
        (*env)->CallStaticVoidMethod(env, jNativesCls
                , mid
                , (jint) idx);
    }
}

// In sd_null.c
extern void jni_start_sound (int idx);
extern void jni_start_music (int idx);

boolean SD_PlaySoundWL6(soundnamesWL6 sound)
{
    // New code for Android
    jni_start_sound (sound);
    return true;
}
```

```
boolean SD_PlaySoundSOD(soundnamesSOD sound)
{
    // New code for Android
    jni_start_sound (sound);
    return true;
}
```

Listing 6-18 also shows the changes required to the native sound handlers (in sd_null.c) to call the C to Java callbacks:

- SD_PlaySoundWL6 (soundnamesWL6 sound): This is the handler for the Wolf 3D chapter of the game. soundnamesWL6 s a C enumeration described in audiowl6.h, which defines the IDs for sounds and music.

- SD_PlaySoundSOD (soundnamesSOD sound): This is the handler for the Spear of Destiny (SOD) chapter of the game. soundnamesSOD s a C enumeration described in audiosod.h which defines the IDs for sounds and music.

Finally, you are ready to compile the code and see how it works on the device. Here is how.

Compiling the Native Library

The native library (or Dynamic Shared Object - DSO) contains all the native code and interacts with the Java side of Wolf 3D. Before we can test the game in the emulator, this library must be compiled. Here are the steps required to do this:

1. Write a Makefile to compile the native code.

2. Generate the JNI headers required by the JNI interface.

3. Compile the native code into the dynamic shared library (DSO): libwolf_jni.so.

4. Place the DSO under the libs/armeabi folder of the main project.

5. Start the project in the emulator.

Writing the Makefile

The Makefile for Wolf 3D uses the agcc and ald scripts for compiling and linking defined in Chapter 1. Some interesting features of this file are described in Listing 6-19:

- *Compilation*: We use –wall to display all warnings and -O2 to define a level of optimization.

- *Linking*: The linking step is performed by the script: ald -shared -o libwolf_jni.so $(OBJS), where –shared tells the compiler to build a shared library and -o defines the name of the output library (libwolf_jni.so).

- • *JNI Headers*: The make target jni is defined to create the headers required by the JNI interface using the javah command: javah -jni -classpath ../../bin -d include wolf.jni.Natives. The class path must point to the location of the compiled wolf.jni.Natives class, -d defines the directory where the output headers will be stored, and wolf.jni.Natives is the Java class that contains the native methods.

Listing 6-19. *The Makefile for Wolf 3D*

```
CC = agcc

# All warning + Optimizations
CFLAGS = -Wall -O2

# Object files
OBJS = objs.o misc.o id_ca.o id_vh.o id_us.o \
   wl_act1.o wl_act2.o wl_act3.o wl_agent.o wl_game.o \
   wl_inter.o wl_menu.o wl_play.o wl_state.o wl_text.o wl_main.o \
   wl_debug.o vi_comm.o sd_comm.o sd_null.o wl_draw.o

# JNI files
JNIOBJS = jni_wolf.o vi_null.o

OBJS += $(JNIOBJS)

# Main target
all: lib

# Library
lib: $(OBJS) j
        ald  -shared -o libwolf_jni.so $(OBJS)

.c.o:
        @echo
        $(CC) -fpic -c $(CFLAGS) $(INCLUDES) $<

# Create JNI headers
jni:
        @echo "Creating JNI C headers..."
        javah -jni -classpath ../../bin -d include wolf.jni.Natives

clean:
        rm -rf *.o
```

Generating JNI Headers

We must generate the headers for the JNI interface before we compile the DSO. Use the Makefile to do so:

```
$make jni
```

Note that this command must be run within the native/gp2xwolf3d folder of the chapter source. With the JNI headers in place, we can compile the DSO as follows:

```
$ make
```

If you make changes to the native code, you might wish to test for missing symbols in the DSO by compiling a simple test program against the library (see Listing 6-20). This is a small program that calls the game loop. It is not meant to be run but to detect linker errors (missing symbols) in the Wolf 3D native library.

Listing 6-20. *Wolf 3D Test Program Used to Detect Linker Errors*

```
#include <stdio.h>

void _start(int argc, char **argv) {
  int i;
  int myargc = 4;

  // wolf, wolfsw, sodemo, sod, sodm2, sodm3
  char * myargv[] = {"wolf3d", "wolfsw", "basedir" , "/data/wolf/"};

  for ( i = 0 ; i < myargc; i++ )
    printf("argv[%d]=%s\n", i, myargv[i]);

  wolf_main(myargc, myargv);
  exit(0);
}

$ agcc -c test.c
$ ald -o testwolf -L. -lwolf_jni
```

Testing Wolf 3D in the Emulator

Let's play Wolf 3D in the emulator. Make sure to do this sanity check first: the native library is critical and must be placed in the libs/armeabi folder of the main project (as shown in Figure 6-8). At runtime, the library will be loaded and cached to the right location in the device.

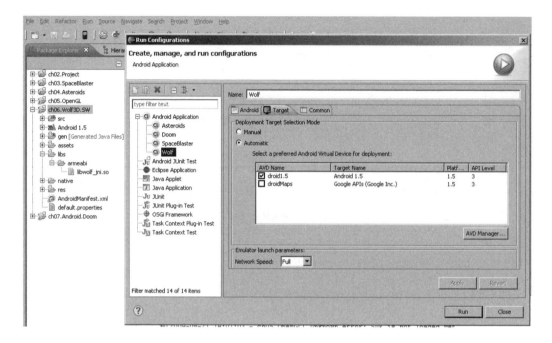

Figure 6-8. *Launch properties for Wolf 3D*

■ **Tip** If the library is not placed properly, the Java system call `System.loadLibrary()` will fail with an `UnsatisfiedLinkError`.

To create a launch configuration for Wolf 3D:

1. Click Run ➤ Run Configuration.

2. Right-click the Android Application on the left menu, and click New.

3. Enter a name: **Wolf**. Select the corresponding project: **ch06.Wolf3D.SW**. Click Run.

Take a look at the log messages from the device to make sure everything works (see Listing 6-21). This can be seen from the LogCat view of the Eclipse IDE.

Listing 6-21. *Log Messages from Wolf 3D*

```
08-21 18:12:50.823: DEBUG/WolfTools(710): Installing game wolfsw.zip in ↵
/data/data/game.wolfsw/files
08-21 18:12:53.653: DEBUG/Wolf3D(710): Start game base dir: /data/data/game.wolfsw/files/↵
 game=wolfsw port:true
08-21 18:12:53.663: DEBUG/Wolf3D(710): Loading JNI librray from wolf_jni
08-21 18:12:53.697: DEBUG/LibLoader(710): Trying to load library wolf_jni from LD_PATH:↵
 /system/lib
08-21 18:12:53.704: DEBUG/dalvikvm(710): Trying to load lib /data/data/game.wolfsw/lib/↵
libwolf_jni.so 0x43596e78
08-21 18:12:54.034: DEBUG/dalvikvm(710): Added shared lib /data/data/game.wolfsw/lib/↵
libwolf_jni.so 0x43596e78
08-21 18:12:55.305: INFO/System.out(710): ** Wolf Message: WolfMain args[4]=wolf3d
08-21 18:12:55.305: INFO/System.out(710): ** Wolf Message: WolfMain args[4]=wolfsw
08-21 18:12:55.314: INFO/System.out(710): ** Wolf Message: WolfMain args[4]=basedir
08-21 18:12:55.354: INFO/System.out(710): ** Wolf Message: WolfMain args[4]=/data/data/↵
game.wolfsw/files/
08-21 18:12:55.465: INFO/System.out(710): ** Wolf Message: Now Loading Wolfenstein 3D Plus↵
 basedir /data/data/game.wolfsw/files/
08-21 18:12:55.515: INFO/System.out(710): ** Wolf Message: You Chose Shareware Wolf3D
08-21 18:12:55.766: INFO/ActivityManager(580): Displayed activity game.wolfsw/↵
.WolfLauncher: 8499 ms
08-21 18:12:56.463: INFO/System.out(710): ** Wolf Message: VL_Startup 320x200. Calling↵
 init graphics.
08-21 18:12:56.514: DEBUG/Wolf3D(710): OnInitGraphics creating Bitmap of 320 by 200
```

The first line shows the game files being installed in /data/data/game.wolfsw/files. Note that without these data files the game will crash. The next lines show the native library being successfully loaded by the Java VM:

```
Trying to load lib /data/data/game.wolfsw/lib/libwolf_jni.so 0x43596e78
Added shared lib /data/data/game.wolfsw/lib/libwolf_jni.so 0x43596e78
```

At this point, the game should start successfully, and you should be able to use the controller buttons (or the keyboard if you wish) to play Wolfenstein 3D in your Android device (see Figure 6-9). Enjoy!

217

Figure 6-9. *Wolf 3D in action on the emulator*

What's Next?

Who would have thought that the PC version of Wolf 3D could ever be run on a mobile device? In this chapter, you have learned how this can be accomplished by embracing the power of two great languages: Java and C. Specifically, we covered the basic game architecture and how the following Java and C components—the main activity, audio, JNI interface, and native code—fit together. Next, we looked at the Java layer that controls the interaction with the device including:

- *The game launcher activity*: It contains the UI layout and the device event listeners for keyboard or touch events.

- *Game loop*: It contains the user-defined thread that loads the native library and starts the native game loop.

- *Sound and music handlers*: They receive notifications from the native layer when sound or background music should be started.

- *Movement controller handlers*: They control movement events using a UI-based game pad useful for phones that have no keyboard.

- *Sound classes*: They work in concert with the sound and music handlers to provide high quality sound to the game.

- *Native interface class*: It contains the native method implementations that allow the Java code to talk to the C code, plus C-to-Java callbacks for communication in the opposite direction.

Next, we looked at the native code where we made simple changes to the original C code to insert C to Java callbacks. These callbacks are used as part of the JNI layer to cascade graphics information, video buffers, and sound/music requests back to Java. Finally, we looked at compilation and testing. Here, we covered the Makefile required for building the DSO as well as how to set up the game project file system for testing on the emulator.

In the next chapter, we continue with 3D shooters by looking at the next great PC shooter, Doom. That chapter will show you how easy it is to bring this complex game for the PC to Android in record time with minimal changes.

CHAPTER 7

■■■

3D Shooters Episode II: Doom for Android

This chapter looks at another great game for the PC: Doom. Doom came along shortly after Wolfenstein 3D and put id Software at the lead of the pack in 3D graphics gaming for the PC. In this chapter, you'll learn how to bring the open source Doom engine (PrBoom) to the Android platform.

The chapter starts with fun facts about Doom itself, which will help you understand the breadth of this project. Bringing a PC game to a mobile device with little change to the original code is a difficult task. As you can probably tell from reading the previous chapters, I embrace the Java/C power combo for maximum performance.

Next, we dig into the game itself, which is divided into two big layers: Java and native. This makes sense, as the game is a mix of original C wrapped in Java code. In the Java layer are classes for the main activity, audio, and JNI interface (what I call the native interface class). The native layer has the native method implementations (using JNI) plus changes to the original C code. The latter is required to glue both layers together and requires less then 50 lines of new code (I consider this to be the most difficult to follow, as there are close to 80,000 lines of original C code, but I will explain the new C code as clearly as possible.)

Finally, we get to compilation, deployment, and playing Doom in the emulator! You will learn awesome tips for native library compilation—a subject that is obscure to the average Java developer.

This is a long a complex chapter, and I have tried my best to make it as simple and clean as possible. For the sake of simplicity, I have omitted some of the lengthier code. Even so, there are some big listings throughout this chapter and a lot of things to cover. To make the most of this chapter, you should grab the chapter source distributed with this book. The project has been built with Eclipse Galileo and can be imported into your workspace. The source will help you to understand the layout of the resources as you read through the chapter.

The Sky Is the Limit with the Java/C Power Combo

The goal here is not to try to explain how the game itself works (that would take a complete book), but to show the kinds of things that can be accomplished by combining the elegant object-oriented features of Java with the raw power of C. Most Java developers dismiss procedural languages like C, failing to see what can be accomplished when this duo coexists harmoniously. The trick is to find the right balance that combines the best of both worlds to solve a complex task with minimal time and effort. Here, you will learn how a task that would take a team of Java developers possibly months to complete can be done in a matter of days by someone who understands that object-oriented and procedural languages are not enemies, but simply pieces of the same puzzle.

221

Consider Tables 7-1 and 7-2. They show the total number of lines of new Java code, plus the number of lines inserted in the existing C code in Doom for Android.

Table 7-1. *Estimated Number of Lines for Java Files of Doom for Android*

File	Description	Lines of Code
DoomClient.java	Main game activity	700
DialogTool.java	Methods to create help dialogs	300
DoomTools.java	Miscellaneous helper subs	450
GameFileDownloader.java	A class to install game files to the SD card	180
WebDownload.java	Web download tool	200
AudioManager.java	Singleton for audio management	200
AudioClip.java	Wrapper for Android MediaPlayer to play sounds	110

Table 7-2. *Estimated Number of Lines Changed from the Original Doom C Code*

File	Description	Lines of Code
jni_doom.c (new)	Implementation of the JNI native methods plus C to Java callbacks	450
i_sound.c	C to Java callbacks to send sound events to Java	3
s_sound.c	C to Java callbacks to send sound events to Java	6
i_video.c	C to Java callbacks to send video events to Java	10

Here's the rundown of the estimated totals:

- Total number of lines of new Java Code = 2140
- Total number of lines of original C code = 80,000
- Total number of lines of new C code = 469

The bottom line? One developer has managed to reuse about 80,000 lines of C code, thus bringing a PC game to Android with a few thousand lines of new code in a couple of days. Imagine the potential savings in development costs and time. Now compare this to a team of three developers trying to port the 80,000 lines of raw C to pure Java. It would probably take them months of head-pounding work with no financial gain (as the code is open sourced). This simply makes no sense. I hope that at this point you understand why this chapter is my personal favorite and a must-read for the aspiring Android game developer. So get the source code for the chapter, and let's get started.

Bringing Doom to a Mobile Device

After working on Wolfenstein 3D for Android, I was so excited that I decided my next challenge would be to bring the great game Doom to the platform. But I had my doubts that this could even be achieved once I looked at the complexity and the amount of original C code. Listing 7-1 shows a portion of the total number of lines of C code of the popular Doom engine PrBoom (available from http://prboom.sourceforge.net/).

I knew I had two choices for this project:

- Port the C code line by line to Java. I even started porting a few files to Java. Believe me when I say that this is not a good idea. The amount of time that it would take to do this makes the project unfeasible, especially considering that the hard work must be done *pro bono*.

- Find a way to pack the game as a dynamic shared object (DSO) and call it from Java using JNI. This option seems to be simpler and quicker, but requires expert knowledge of C and JNI, as well as changes to the original game to glue both languages together.

Given these two options, the latter is the best approach to the problem, so I decided to build a DSO and glue it to Java with JNI.

Listing 7-1. *Portion of Code for the PrBoom Doom Engine (Approximately 90,000 Lines in Total)*

```
$ wc -l *.c
   1585 am_map.c
    554 d_client.c
   3093 d_deh.c
    140 d_items.c
   1744 d_main.c
    759 d_server.c
     48 doomdef.c
    108 doomstat.c
     85 dstrings.c
    668 f_finale.c
    202 f_wipe.c
   2979 g_game.c
   2717 gl_main.c
    957 gl_texture.c
    767 hu_lib.c
   1593 hu_stuff.c
    866 mmus2mid.c
    467 p_ceilng.c
// …
    450 r_fps.c
    649 r_main.c
    788 r_patch.c
    468 r_plane.c
    854 r_segs.c
     56 r_sky.c
   1077 r_things.c
    714 s_sound.c
```

```
    245 sounds.c
    374 st_lib.c
   1160 st_stuff.c
    128 tables.c
   1037 v_video.c
     38 version.c
    166 w_memcache.c
    335 w_mmap.c
    476 w_wad.c
   1968 wi_stuff.c
    123 z_bmalloc.c
    705 z_zone.c
  73176 total

$ wc -l *.h
    111 am_map.h
    209 config.h
   1118 d_deh.h
    707 d_englsh.h
    125 d_event.h
     59 d_items.h
     82 d_main.h
    214 d_net.h
    234 d_player.h
     94 d_think.h
     59 d_ticcmd.h
    204 doomdata.h
// …
     64 r_bsp.h
    109 r_data.h
    428 r_defs.h
     45 r_demo.h
    163 r_draw.h
    174 r_filter.h
    100 s_sound.h
    305 sounds.h
    209 st_lib.h
    102 st_stuff.h
     93 tables.h
    207 v_video.h
     40 version.h
    146 w_wad.h
     64 wi_stuff.h
     52 z_bmalloc.h
    131 z_zone.h
  13460 total
```

As I've noted, I chose to use the PrBoom Doom engine. Even though the game was created by id Software and released under the GNU license in 1993 (see http://en.wikipedia.org/wiki/Doom_(video_game)), there are many Doom engines out there. I did try a few engines before settling on PrBoom.

The first engine I tried was the original code from id Software—after all, it is the original creator. But I had a lot of trouble with id Software's Linux implementation of the game, due to two main issues:

- *Color palette*: The Linux flavor supports an 8-bit color palette, which looks pretty bad on 32-bit machines. This code was written for old machines (it has not been updated for a long time). There should be a more modern implementation out there.

- *Sine and cosine tables*: These are used for ray casting. I had many compiler idiosyncrasies (using the CodeSourcery GCC 4.3.*x* compiler) where these tables, which have hard-coded values, were not filled in correctly, making sprites go through walls or move in the wrong way and creating many other display problems.

PrBoom is a modern Doom engine. It is highly portable, although it is much bigger than the original game. I found it to be the best choice due to the plethora of platforms it has been ported to and the powerful support available for it from the developer community.

Game Architecture for Doom

Doom's game architecture is a bit similar to the architecture of Wolfenstein 3D. When the user starts the game, the main activity org.doom.DoomClient will start (see Figure 7-1). This activity is bound to the other pieces in the following manner:

- The main activity is bound to the device UI through an XML layout (doom.xml). This layout defines an image buffer used to display the graphics and a set of controller buttons for navigation (see the "Game Layout" section for details).

- The Doom engine is written in C and compiled as a DSO (libdoom_jni.so). All communication with the DSO goes through the JNI layer (or native interface class Natives.java). Events are cascaded back to the main activity, which dispatches them to their respective handler. Game files are read from the SD card by the DSO, which handles all game aspects except sound.

- Sound requests are delegated by the native library to the native interface class to the main activity, and finally to the sound classes, which play them using the Android MediaPlayer.

- Video buffers (pixels) are cascaded by the native library to the native interface class to the main activity, which renders them into the ImageView of the layout XML.

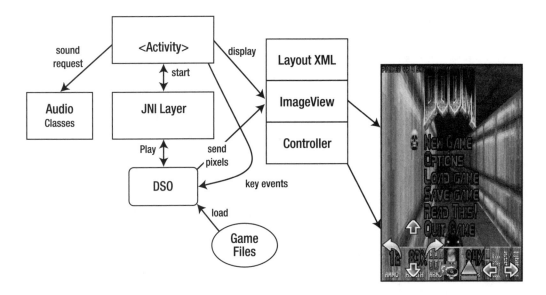

Figure 7-1. *Doom for Android architecture*

This process continues in an endless loop, where key and touch events are dispatched back to the DSO, which updates the game accordingly.

The game is composed of the following Java packages:

- `org.doom`: This is the main game package and contains the main activity `DoomClient.java`. This class controls the application life cycle and the key and touch events, dispatches sound and music requests to the audio classes, and dispatches user events to the DSO through the native interface class.

- `doom.audio`: This package contains the audio classes `AudioManager` and `AudioClip`.

  - `AudioManager`: This class is in charge of playing sounds and background music using `AudioClip`. It also caches sounds for better performance.

  - `AudioClip.java`: This class is capable of playing, stopping, and looping a sound using the Android `MediaPlayer`. Sound files use the WAVE format.

- `doom.jni`: This JNI package contains the native interface class `Natives.java`. This class is a two-way pipe for all access with the DSO. This includes native Java methods and C to Java callbacks.

- `doom.util`: This package contains the following utility classes:

  - `DialogTool.java`: This class contains miscellaneous dialogs to start the game and install shareware game files, message boxes, and other items.

  - `DoomTools.java`: This class contains basic game constants and commonly used subroutines.

- GameFileDownloader.java: This class is capable of downloading shareware game files from the Internet into the SD card.

- LibraryLoader.java: This class loads the DSO, which is required before the native methods can be invoked.

- WebDownload.java: This is a web download tool used by the GameFileDownloader class.

Again, before we look at these components in more detail, make sure you have the chapter code at hand; most of the listings have been stripped down for simplicity.

Java Main Activity

The main activity class is invoked when the user starts the game and controls the life cycle of the application. In Doom, this life cycle is handled by the following:

- *Creation handler*: This handler is implemented by onCreate and it is called when the activity is first created. It sets the UI layout XML (doom.xml) and initializes the game.

- *Menu handlers*: Here, we have onCreateOptionsMenu and onOptionsItemSelected. The first method creates the game menu, and the latter processes the menu when the user selects an option.

- *Key and touch handlers*: These methods receive key and touch events and dispatch them to the right JNI component.

- *Native callback handlers*: These methods receive video and sound updates from the native interface and dispatch them.

- *Controller toolbar*: The controller toolbar is a set of image buttons displayed at the bottom of the screen for navigation. It is helpful for devices that do not have a keyboard.

Creation Handler

The creation handler is defined by onCreate (see Listing 7-2). For Doom, this method performs the following steps:

- Sets the display to full screen and hides the title

- Sets the content view layout to R.layout.doom, which maps to doom.xml

- Gets a reference to the video buffer (R.id.doom_iv), which will be used to display the pixels sent by the DSO

- Sets the navigation controls

Listing 7-2. *Main Activity Life Cycle*

```
public void onCreate(Bundle savedInstanceState) {
    super.onCreate(savedInstanceState);

    // Full screen
    getWindow().setFlags(WindowManager.LayoutParams.FLAG_FULLSCREEN,
            WindowManager.LayoutParams.FLAG_FULLSCREEN);

    // No title
    requestWindowFeature(Window.FEATURE_NO_TITLE);

    setContentView(R.layout.doom);

    mView = (ImageView)findViewById(R.id.doom_iv);

    if (mGameStarted) {
        setGameUI();
        setupPanControls();
        return;
    }

    // Pan controls
    setupPanControls();

}
```

onCreate is the very first function called when the game starts, and it is called only once while the application is in memory. Next, let's look at the game layout loaded by this function.

Game Layout

GUIs in Android are defined by XML layouts, where visual components are placed in a variety of layout schemes. Doom's layout (doom.xml) is a relative layout, which has widgets placed relative to each other (meaning they can overlap depending on the widget size). The master layout contains an image view and two table layouts.

In Android, an image view encapsulates an array of pixels representing an image. The great thing about image views is that they have efficient automatic resize capabilities. This will allow the game to be resized on the fly!

The two table layouts are for the navigation controls (see Figure 7-2). The first table layout defines a three-row table that contains image buttons for up, down, left, and right navigation. The second table layout is a one-row table that contains buttons for the level map, object pick up, and strafing left and right.

Figure 7-2. *Doom displaying the game layout*

Listing 7-3 shows Doom's relative layout XML. The most important attributes are explained in Table 7-3.

Table 7-3. *Main Attributes of doom.xml*

Attribute	Meaning
android:id="@+id/doom_iv"	Defines the ID of the widget, which can be used for programmatic access. The format must be @+id/NAME.
android:layout_width="fill_parent"	Defines the width of the widget. The values can be fill_parent or wrap_content.
android:focusableInTouchMode="true"	Specifies that the widget should be focusable and receive touch events from the main activity.
android:focusable="true"	Specifies that the widget should be focusable and receive key events from the main activity.

Table 7-3. *Main Attributes of doom.xml (continued)*

Attribute	Meaning
`android:src="@drawable/up"`	Defines the bitmap source of the widget (applies to image view only). The format is @drawable/NAME, where NAME is the bitmap filename saved under the res/drawable folder of the project.
`android:layout_alignParentBottom="true"`	Tells the relative layout to align the widget to the bottom of the parent, possibly overlapping other widgets.
`android:layout_alignParentLeft="true"`	Tells the relative layout to align the widget to the left of the parent, possibly overlapping other widgets.
`android:visibility="gone"`	Sets the visibility of the widget. Possible values are visible or gone (indicates the widget occupies no space).

Listing 7-3. *Doom Game UI layout doom.xml*

```xml
<?xml version="1.0" encoding="utf-8"?>
<RelativeLayout
    xmlns:android="http://schemas.android.com/apk/res/android"
    android:layout_width="fill_parent"
    android:layout_height="fill_parent"
    >

    <!-- GAME IMAGE -->
    <ImageView android:id="@+id/doom_iv"
        android:layout_width="fill_parent"
        android:layout_height="fill_parent"
        android:adjustViewBounds="true"
        android:visibility="visible"
        android:background="@drawable/doom"
        android:focusableInTouchMode="true"
        android:focusable="true"/>

    <!-- Nav Controls -->
    <TableLayout android:id="@+id/pan_ctls"
            android:layout_width="wrap_content"
            android:layout_height="wrap_content"
            android:layout_alignParentBottom="true"
            android:layout_alignParentLeft="true"
            android:visibility="gone"
            android:focusable="false"
            android:focusableInTouchMode="false">

        <TableRow>
        <ImageButton android:id="@+id/btn_upleft"
```

```
        android:layout_width="wrap_content"
        android:layout_height="wrap_content"
        android:background="#00000000"
        android:layout_margin="0px"
        android:src="@drawable/blank"
          />
    <ImageButton android:id="@+id/btn_up"
        android:layout_width="wrap_content"
        android:layout_height="wrap_content"
        android:src="@drawable/up"
        android:background="#00000000"
        android:layout_margin="0px"
          />
    <ImageButton android:id="@+id/btn_upright"
        android:layout_width="wrap_content"
        android:layout_height="wrap_content"
        android:src="@drawable/blank"
        android:background="#00000000"
        android:layout_margin="0px"
          />
    </TableRow>
</TableLayout>

<!-- Other controls: Map, Open, strafe -->
 <!--  This XML has been removed for simplicity →
 <!-- See the file doom.xml for details -->
</RelativeLayout>
```

Once the GUI is all set, the next step is to provide a menu and handlers for the application.

Menu and Selection Handlers

The application menu can be easily defined by overriding the following methods:

- onCreateOptionsMenu(Menu menu): Override this method to add items to the menu. To do this, use menu.add(groupId, itemId, order, Menu Label), where groupId is the ID of the group for this item. This can be used to define groups of items for batch state changes. itemId is the unique item ID. order is the order for the item.

- onOptionsItemSelected(MenuItem item): Override this method to process menu selections. The item selected can be obtained with item.getItemId().

The following menus are defined for Doom (see Listing 7-4):

- Start, to run the native game loop

- Install Game, to download and install game files

- Navigation, to switch the navigation controls between the keyboard and touch screen

- Exit, to quit the application

Listing 7-4. *Game Menu and Selection*

```
public boolean onCreateOptionsMenu(Menu menu) {
    super.onCreateOptionsMenu(menu);
    menu.add(0, 0, 0, "Start").setIcon(R.drawable.icon);
    menu.add(0, 2, 2, "Install Game").setIcon(R.drawable.install);
    menu.add(0, 3, 3, "Navigation").setIcon(R.drawable.nav);
    menu.add(0, 6, 6, "Exit").setIcon(R.drawable.exit);
    return true;
}

/**
 * Menu selection
 */
public boolean onOptionsItemSelected(MenuItem item) {
    super.onOptionsItemSelected(item);
    switch (item.getItemId()) {
    case 0:
        if ( mGameStarted) {
            MessageBox("Game already in progress.");
            return true;
        }
        mMultiPlayer = false;
        showLauncherDialog(this, mMultiPlayer);

        return true;
    case 2:
        if ( mGameStarted) {
            MessageBox("Can't install while game in progress.");
            return true;
        }

        // SD card required
        if ( ! DoomTools.checkSDCard(this) ) return true;

        // Download Game file
        DialogTool.showDownloadDialog(this);
        return true;

    case 3:
        DialogTool.showNavMethodDialog(this);
        return true;

    case 6:
        // Exit
        DoomTools.hardExit(0);
        return true;

    }
    return false;
}
```

Key and Touch Event Handlers

Key and touch handlers can be overridden to process key and touch events. Doom handles key and touch events as follows (see Listing 7-5):

- The Android keyCode is first translated to an ASCII key symbol by calling int sym = DoomTools.keyCodeToKeySym(keyCode).

- The ASCII symbol is the sent to the DSO through the native interface class Natives.keyEvent(EVENT_TYPE, SYMBOL), where the event type must be either Natives.EV_KEYUP or Natives.EV_KEYDOWN. Note that any errors in the native side (such as a missing symbol or invalid signature) will throw an UnsatisfiedLinkError.

Listing 7-5. *Key and Touch Handlers*

```
public boolean onKeyUp(int keyCode, KeyEvent event) {
    //
    if (keyCode == KeyEvent.KEYCODE_MENU) {
        return false;
    }

    int sym = DoomTools.keyCodeToKeySym(keyCode);

    try {
        Natives.keyEvent(Natives.EV_KEYUP, sym);

    } catch (UnsatisfiedLinkError e) {
        // Should not happen
        Log.e(TAG, e.toString());
    }
    return false;
}

public boolean onKeyDown(int keyCode, KeyEvent event) {
    // Ignore menu key
    if (keyCode == KeyEvent.KEYCODE_MENU) {
        return false;
    }

    int sym = DoomTools.keyCodeToKeySym(keyCode);

    try {
        Natives.keyEvent(Natives.EV_KEYDOWN, sym);
    }
    catch (UnsatisfiedLinkError e) {
        // Should not happen
        Log.e(TAG, e.toString());
    }
    return false;
}
```

233

```java
public boolean onTouchEvent(MotionEvent event)
{

    try {
        if ( event.getAction() == MotionEvent.ACTION_DOWN) {
            // Fire on tap R-CTL
            Natives.keyEvent(Natives.EV_KEYDOWN, DoomTools.KEY_RCTL);
        }
        else if ( event.getAction() == MotionEvent.ACTION_UP) {
            Natives.keyEvent(Natives.EV_KEYUP, DoomTools.KEY_RCTL);
        }
        else if ( event.getAction() == MotionEvent.ACTION_MOVE) {
            // Motion event
        }
        return true;
    }
    catch (UnsatisfiedLinkError e) {
        // Should not happen!
        Log.e(TAG, e.toString());
        return false;
    }
}
```

For touch events, Android provides three actions: ACTION_DOWN, ACTION_UP, and ACTION_MOVE, when the user is pressing, releasing, and dragging fingers in the device screen, respectively. When a finger press or release occurs, Doom will send a right control (KEY_RCTL) to the native layer, which will result in the weapon being fired.

Native Callback Handlers

The native callback handlers are implemented by the main activity (DoomClient.java) via the Natives.EventListener interface. This allows the activity to listen for native callbacks. The handlers are divided in the following categories:

- *Graphics initialization*: This handler receives information when the native graphics have been initialized. It receives the width and height of the video buffer.

- *Image update*: This handler receives video buffer updates and fires multiple times per second.

- *Message update*: This handler receives string messages from the native rendering engine.

- *Fatal errors*: This handler will fire whenever an unrecoverable error occurs.

- *Sound and music requests*: A series of handlers handle audio.

Graphics Initialization Handler

The graphics initialization handler is critical and must be the first to fire before the game can start. It receives the width and height of the video buffer, which are used to create the Android bitmap that renders the video on the device (see Listing 7-6). To create a 32-bit ARGB bitmap in Android, you use the following call:

```
Bitmap.createBitmap(width, height, Config.ARGB_8888)
```

Config.ARGB_8888 tells the system you wish to use a 4-byte (32-bit) ARGB bitmap. You will use this bitmap to set pixels for the video in later sections. Note that this callback fires only once during the lifetime of the game. To set the width and height of the video buffer ImageView, use a call to ImageView.getLayoutParams().

Listing 7-6. *Graphics Initialization*

```
public void OnInitGraphics(int w, int h) {
    Log.d(TAG, "OnInitGraphics creating Bitmap of " + w + " by " + h);
    mBitmap = Bitmap.createBitmap(w, h, Config.ARGB_8888);
    LayoutParams lp =  mView.getLayoutParams();
    mWidth = w;
    mHeight = h;
    lp.width = w;
    lp.height = h;
}
```

Image Update Handler

The image update handler receives an array of ARGB packed pixels representing a color (see Listing 7-7). It fires multiple times per second, and its job is to replace pixels in the bitmap with the colors in the array by calling the following method:

```
mBitmap.setPixels(pixels, offset, stride, x, y, width, height)
```

Here, the arguments are as follows:

- pixels is the colors to write to the bitmap.

- offset is the index of the first color to read from pixels[].

- stride is the number of colors in pixels[] to skip between rows (normally, this value will be the same as the width of the bitmap.

- x is the x coordinate of the first pixel to write to in the bitmap.

- y is the y coordinate of the first pixel to write to in the bitmap.

- width is the number of colors to copy from pixels[] per row.

- height is the number of rows to write to the bitmap.

Listing 7-7. *Image Update Handler*

```
public void OnImageUpdate(int[] pixels) {
    mBitmap.setPixels(pixels, 0, mWidth, 0, 0, mWidth, mHeight);
```

```
    mHandler.post(new Runnable() {
        public void run() {
            mView.setImageBitmap( mBitmap);
        }
    });
}
```

Note that because this handler fires from a non-UI thread, you cannot set the pixels directly into the ImageView, but must use an `android.os.Handler` to post a Runnable to the message queue:

```
Handler.post(new Runnable() {
    public void run() {
        // Code that updates the UI goes here
    }
});
```

■ **Note** A handler allows you to send and process message and runnable objects associated with a thread's message queue. Each handler instance is associated with a single thread and that thread's message queue. When you create a new handler, it is bound to the thread and message queue of the thread that is creating it. Always use a handler when updating UI widgets from a non-UI thread!

Message Updates

The message updates handler receives native messages, which are very helpful for debugging. Listing 7-8 shows this handler, which logs the text to the Android console.

Listing 7-8. *Message Update Handler*

```
/**
 * Fires on DSO message
 */
public void OnMessage(String text, int level) {
    Log.d(TAG, "**Doom Message: " + text);
}
```

Fatal Error Handler

The fatal error handler deals with unrecoverable errors. This means displaying a message to the user and exiting gracefully. There are many things that can cause unrecoverable errors, such as code bugs, corrupted game files, I/O errors, and network failures.

Listing 7-9 shows the way Doom deals with this situation. It uses a message handler to display a message box to the user (remember that this method fires from a non-UI thread, where all UI widget access must go through an OS handler). It then waits for a while so the user can read the message, and finally exits gracefully.

Listing 7-9. *Fatal Error Handler*

```
public void OnFatalError(final String text) {
    mHandler.post(new Runnable() {
        public void run() {
            MessageBox("Fatal Error",
                    text + " - Please report this error.");
        }
    });

    // Wait for the user to read the box
    try {
        Thread.sleep(8000);
    } catch (InterruptedException e) {

    }
    // Must quit here or the LIB will crash
    DoomTools.hardExit(-1);
}
```

Audio Request Handlers

The native Doom engine cannot access the sound device directly. This is due to the nonstandard audio library used by Android (Enhanced Audio System, EAS, by SoniVOX). To overcome this very serious limitation, audio requests are cascaded back to these handlers, which start sound events at a given volume, start and stop background music events, and set the background music.

Listing 7-10 shows the audio handlers for Doom. Note that all requests are delegated to the doom.audio.AudioManager class, which deals with the Android audio system.

Listing 7-10. *Sound and Music Handlers*

```
public void OnStartSound(String name, int vol)
{
    if ( mSound && mAudioMgr == null)
        Log.e(TAG, "Bug: Audio Mgr is NULL but sound is enabled!");

    try {
        if ( mSound && mAudioMgr != null)
            mAudioMgr.startSound( name, vol);

    } catch (Exception e) {
        Log.e(TAG, "OnStartSound: " + e.toString());
    }
}

/**
 * Fires on background music
 */
public void OnStartMusic(String name, int loop) {
    if ( mSound && mAudioMgr != null)
```

```
        mAudioMgr.startMusic(DoomClient.this, name, loop);
}

/**
 * Stop bg music
 */
public void OnStopMusic(String name) {
    if ( mSound &&  mAudioMgr != null)
        mAudioMgr.stopMusic( name);
}

public void OnSetMusicVolume(int volume) {
    if ( mSound &&  mAudioMgr != null)
        mAudioMgr.setMusicVolume(volume);
}
```

■ **Note** Even though cascading audio in this way will make the game slower, it will provide high-quality sound to the game. I believe it is a mistake by Google not to support open audio standards, such as the Advanced Linux Sound Architecture (ALSA). After all, Android itself is built on open source foundations. This will hamper porting efforts of thousands of native games out there.

Navigation Controls

Android devices feature a trackball, which is cumbersome for mobile games. In fact, most gaming devices, such as PlayStation Portable (PSP) and Game Boy, feature multiple keypad arrows, which are great for navigation. On the plus side, the QWERTY keyboard is helpful for PC games. But the latest Android devices have neither a keyboard nor a trackball. Here is where the navigation controls can help. Figure 7-3 shows the navigation controls in action during a game.

Figure 7-3. *Navigation controls for Doom*

The controls themselves are implemented as image buttons within the game layout (see the "Game Layout" section). The RelativeLayout of the game allows the controls to overlap the video ImageView, as shown in Figure 7-3. To set up events for the buttons, simply load the button widget using its ID and set a touch listener:

```
findViewById(R.id.BUTTON_ID).setOnTouchListener(new View.OnTouchListener(){
  public boolean onTouch(View v, MotionEvent evt) {
      // ACTION_DOWN or ACTION_UP
      int action = evt.getAction();
      // …
  }
});
```

Depending on the touch event action, ACTION_DOWN or ACTION_UP, you simply send a key event to the native layer with the following code:

```
public static void sendNativeKeyEvent (int type, int sym) {
    try {
        Natives.keyEvent(type, sym);
    } catch (UnsatisfiedLinkError e) {
        Log.e(TAG, e.toString());
    }
}
```

Listing 7-11 shows the setupPanControls function for the up, down, left, and right buttons of the Doom controller.

Listing 7-11. *Controller Event Setup*

```
private void setupPanControls() {
    // Up
    findViewById(R.id.btn_up).setOnTouchListener(
            new View.OnTouchListener(){
        public boolean onTouch(View v, MotionEvent evt) {
            int action = evt.getAction();
            if ( action == MotionEvent.ACTION_DOWN) {
                Natives.sendNativeKeyEvent(Natives.EV_KEYDOWN
                        , DoomTools.KEY_UPARROW);
             }
            else if ( action == MotionEvent.ACTION_UP) {
                Natives.sendNativeKeyEvent(Natives.EV_KEYUP
                        , DoomTools.KEY_UPARROW);
            }
            return true;
        }
    });

    // Down
    findViewById(R.id.btn_down).setOnTouchListener(
            new View.OnTouchListener(){
        public boolean onTouch(View v, MotionEvent evt) {
```

```java
            int action = evt.getAction();
            if ( action == MotionEvent.ACTION_DOWN) {
                Natives.sendNativeKeyEvent(Natives.EV_KEYDOWN
                        , DoomTools.KEY_DOWNARROW);
            }
            else if ( action == MotionEvent.ACTION_UP) {
                Natives.sendNativeKeyEvent(Natives.EV_KEYUP
                        , DoomTools.KEY_DOWNARROW);
            }
            return true;
        }
});

    // Right
    findViewById(R.id.btn_right).setOnTouchListener(
            new View.OnTouchListener(){
        public boolean onTouch(View v, MotionEvent evt) {
            int action = evt.getAction();
            if ( action == MotionEvent.ACTION_DOWN) {
                Natives.sendNativeKeyEvent(Natives.EV_KEYDOWN
                        , DoomTools.KEY_RIGHTARROW);
            }
            else if ( action == MotionEvent.ACTION_UP) {
                Natives.sendNativeKeyEvent(Natives.EV_KEYUP
                        , DoomTools.KEY_RIGHTARROW);
            }
            return true;
        }
});

    // More ...
}
```

Audio Classes

The audio classes are implemented in the package doom.audio and consist of two files: AudioManager and AudioClip.

AudioManager is a singleton class very similar to the AudioManager class presented in the previous chapter. Some of the method signatures are different to accommodate the Doom engine:

- preloadSounds(): This method preloads the most common Doom sounds to improve performance. Sounds are encoded in WAVE format.

- startSound(String name, int vol): This method starts the sound given by a name key at volume vol. The key does not include the file extension, and the volume ranges from 0 to 100.

- startMusic (Context ctx, String key, int loop): This method starts a background music file given by key and loops if loop is set to anything other than 0. An Android context is required by the background AudioClip.

- stopMusic (String key): This method stops the background music given by key.

- setMusicVolume (int vol): This method sets the background music volume. vol ranges from 0 to 100.

The AudioClip class is the same as Wolfenstein 3D's AudioClip (shown in the previous chapter). The only difference is that the package has been renamed.

Because the audio files (including background music) can occupy more than 5MB, files have been packed in a zip archive and installed at runtime into the SD card. This will save precious disk space in the main file system. The zip archive lives in the assets folder of the Doom project.

■ **Tip** Android features an automated media scanner service that searches for audio files within the file system. This can be really annoying, as your media player will suddenly display a few hundred unwanted Doom sounds and music. You can fix the problem by adding an empty file called .nomedia to the sound folder. This will tell the media scanner to bypass this directory.

Native Interface Class

The native interface class is the two-way pipe that sends messages from Java to the Doom engine through native methods, and from the engine to Java using C to Java callbacks (see Listing 7-12). This class consists of three parts: callback listener, native methods, and C to Java callbacks.

Callback Listener

The callback listener is implemented by the interface EventListener. It must be implemented by clients that wish to receive C to Java callbacks (in this case, by the main activity DoomClient.java). The C to Java callbacks are as follows:

- OnMessage(String text, int level): This is mostly a debug callback that sends messages to let Java know what is happening on the native side.

- OnInitGraphics(int w, int h): This is the very first callback and fires only once after graphics initialization. It tells Java the width and height of the video buffer.

- OnImageUpdate(int[] pixels): This fires many times per second and sends an Android packed video buffer to Java, which will use it to render the game bitmap.

- OnFatalError(String text): This callback fires when there is an unrecoverable error in the engine. The receiver should display the message and terminate.

- OnQuit(int code): This callback fires when the user exits the game. It sends a return code back to the receiver.

- OnStartSound(String name, int vol): This fires when the native engine starts a sound. It delegates to the receiver.

241

- `OnStartMusic(String name, int loop)`: This fires on background music. It delegates to the receiver.

- `OnStopMusic(String name)`: This fires on stop music background. It delegates to the receiver.

- `OnSetMusicVolume(int volume)`: This fires when the user sets the music volume. It delegates to the receiver.

Native Methods

The native methods invoke the native Doom engine. There are three basic native methods:

- `static native int DoomMain(String[] argv)`: This method invokes the main game loop of the Doom engine.

- `static native int keyEvent(int type, int key)`: This method sends a key event to the engine. The event type is either EV_KEYDOWN or EV_KEYUP. The argument key must be an ASCII symbol, not an Android key code. This means the key code must be translated before being sent to the engine.

- `static native int motionEvent(int b, int x, int y)`: This method sends a motion event to the engine (such as when the user drags a finger on the display). The first argument is a mouse button (always zero in this case), plus the x and y coordinates of the event itself.

`static native int DoomMain(String[] argv)` requires a list or arguments and blocks execution, so it must be run within a thread. The following are the most important arguments:

- `width` defines the width of the video buffer.

- `height` defines the height of the video buffer.

- `iwad` defines the game to be played. The following game files are supported by the engine:

  - `doom1.wad`: This is the shareware episode of Doom.

  - `doom.wad`: This is the retail episode.

  - `doom2.wad`: This is the second episode in the Doom series.

  - `plutonia.wad`: This is the Plutonia Experiment episode, part of the Ultimate Doom series.

  - `tnt.wad`: This is an episode dubbed Evilution, also part of the ultimate Doom series.

- `file` defines extra game files to be used by the engine.

For example, to play Doom shareware in landscape mode, the list arguments that must be sent to DoomMain (as a `String` array) would be `doom -width 480 -height 320 -iwad doom1.wad`.

C to Java Callbacks

C to Java callbacks are used to delegate engine messages to the listener activity. To do so, the native interface class uses a private listener and a static setter method:

```
private static EventListener listener;
public static void setListener(EventListener l) {
        listener = l;
}
```

Note that there can be only one listener. When the Doom engine sends a message (such as have some text), the native interface class simply delegates to the listener, which deals with the event:

```
private static void OnMessage(String text, int level) {
        if (listener != null)
            listener.OnMessage(text, level);
}
```

In the preceding example, the engine is saying "have some text," along with an integer log level. The rest of callbacks are shown in Listing 7-12.

Listing 7-12. *Native Interface Class (Natives.java)*

```
package doom.jni;

import android.util.Log;

public class Natives {
    public static final String TAG = "Natives";

    private static EventListener listener;

    public static final int EV_KEYDOWN = 0;
    public static final int EV_KEYUP = 1;
    public static final int EV_MOUSE = 2;

    public static interface EventListener {
        void OnMessage(String text, int level);
        void OnInitGraphics(int w, int h);
        void OnImageUpdate(int[] pixels);
        void OnFatalError(String text);
        void OnQuit(int code);
        void OnStartSound(String name, int vol);
        void OnStartMusic(String name, int loop);
        void OnStopMusic(String name);
        void OnSetMusicVolume(int volume);
    }

    public static void setListener(EventListener l) {
        listener = l;
    }
```

```java
/**
 * Send a key event to the native layer
 *
 * @param type : key up down or mouse
 * @param sym: ASCII symbol
 */
public static void sendNativeKeyEvent(int type, int sym) {
    try {
        Natives.keyEvent(type, sym);
    } catch (UnsatisfiedLinkError e) {
        Log.e(TAG, e.toString());
    }
}

 // Native Main Doom Loop: @param argv: program arguments
public static native int DoomMain(String[] argv);

/**
 * Send a Key Event
 * @param type: event type: UP/DOWN
 * @param key: ASCII symbol
 */
public static native int keyEvent(int type, int key);


/*********************************************************
 * C to Java - Callbacks
 *********************************************************/

/**
 * This fires on messages from the C layer
 */
private static void OnMessage(String text, int level) {
    if (listener != null)
        listener.OnMessage(text, level);
}

private static void OnInitGraphics(int w, int h) {
    if (listener != null)
        listener.OnInitGraphics(w, h);
}

private static void OnImageUpdate(int[] pixels) {
    if (listener != null)
        listener.OnImageUpdate(pixels);

}

private static void OnFatalError(String message) {
    if (listener != null)
        listener.OnFatalError(message);
}
```

```
    private static void OnQuit(int code) {
        if (listener != null)
            listener.OnQuit(code);
    }
    /**
     * Fires when a sound is played in the C layer.
     */
    private static void OnStartSound(byte[] name, int vol) {
        if (listener != null)
            listener.OnStartSound(new String(name), vol);
    }

    /**
     * Start background music callback
     */
    private static void OnStartMusic(String name, int loop) {
        if (listener != null)
            listener.OnStartMusic(name, loop);
    }

    /**
     * Stop background music
     * @param name
     */
    private static void OnStopMusic(String name) {
        if (listener != null)
            listener.OnStopMusic(name);
    }

    /**
     * Set background music volume
     * @param volume Range: (0-255)
     */
    private static void OnSetMusicVolume(int volume) {
        if (listener != null)
            listener.OnSetMusicVolume((int) (volume * 100.0 / 15.0));
    }
}
```

Native Layer

The native layer glues the Java and C code together by defining three types of tasks to be performed:

- *Native method implementations*: These are the C implementations of the native Java methods defined by the native interface class. This code lives in the file jni_doom.c.

- *Original game changes*: The original Doom engine needs to be modified slightly to accommodate the JNI glue. This consists of inserting calls to the C to Java callbacks in the correct files.

- *Removal of invalid dependencies*: Invalid dependencies in the original code must be removed. For example, the original Simple DirectMedia Layer (SDL) dependency used by the PC code must be deleted.

Let's look a these tasks in more detail.

Native Method Implementations

Table 7-4 shows the Java native signatures and their C counterparts in jni_doom.c.

Table 7-4. *Java Native Methods and Their Native Counterparts*

Java Method	C Method
static native int DoomMain(String[] argv)	JNIEXPORT jint JNICALL Java_doom_jni_Natives_DoomMain(JNIEnv * env, jclass class, jobjectArray jargv)
static native int keyEvent(int type, int key)	JNIEXPORT jint JNICALL Java_doom_jni_Natives_keyEvent(JNIEnv * env, jclass cls, jint type, jint key)
static native int motionEvent(int btn, int x, int y)	JNIEXPORT jint JNICALL Java_doom_jni_Natives_motionEvent(JNIEnv * env, jclass cls, jint btn, jint x, jint y)

Before you can proceed with the implementation, the javah command must be used to generate the required header files and signatures:

```
javah -jni -classpath PATH_TO_PROJECT_FOLDER/bin -d include doom.jni.Natives
```

Note that a class path to the bin folder is required for javah to find the doom.jni.Natives class. The output file doom_jni_Natives.h will be dumped in the include folder by using -d. The header file is then used by jni_doom.c, as shown in this fragment:

```
#include <stdio.h>
#include "include/doom_jni_Natives.h"
#include "include/jni_doom.h"
#include "doomdef.h"
#include "d_event.h"
```

The code will use Doom code, thus the inclusion of doomdef.h and d_event.h. The header jni_doom.h defines prototypes for the C to Java callbacks and miscellaneous constants.

You also need a static reference to the JVM used by the C to Java callbacks, as in the next fragment:

```
// Global  Java VM  reference
static JavaVM *g_VM;
```

For improved performance, static references to the Java native interface class (doom.jni.Natives) are kept in jNativesCls. References to the Java methods to send the video image (jSendImageMethod) and sound file (jStartSoundMethod) are also kept. This is because these methods will be invoked multiple times, and looking up this names every time can slow things.

```
static jclass jNativesCls;
static jmethodID jSendImageMethod;
static jmethodID jStartSoundMethod;
```

Also, since you may send a pixel buffer (image) multiple times per second, you should keep a reference to the Java array and its size, as in the next fragment:

```
static jintArray jImage;
static int iSize;
extern int doom_main(int argc, char **argv);
```

The line extern int doom_main defines the main engine function and tells the compiler it is defined somewhere else in the library. The header jni_doom.h included up front defines the constants and method signatures required to invoke the C to Java callbacks. For example, the next fragment of the header defines constants for the Java native interface class (doom/jni/Natives), and the method names and signatures for the callbacks OnImageUpdate and OnStartSound (see the "C to Java Callbacks" section for more details).

```
#define CB_CLASS "doom/jni/Natives"
#define CB_CLASS_IU_CB  "OnImageUpdate"
#define CB_CLASS_IU_SIG  "([I)V"

#define CB_CLASS_SS_CB  "OnStartSound"
#define CB_CLASS_SS_SIG  "([BI)V"
```

Let's take a look at the actual implementations. They are divided in three groups:

- *Native game loop*: This invokes the engine loop doom_main.

- *Key and motion events*: These post key and motion events to the engine.

- *C to Java callbacks*: These callbacks are critical for the Java code to receive information from the Doom engine.

Native Game Loop

The native game loop's job is to extract the arguments sent as a jobjectArray into a C char ** array and invoke the main Doom engine function (doom_main). This function performs additional steps:

- Obtain a reference to the JVM using (*env)->GetJavaVM(env, &g_VM). This reference will be used by the C to Java callbacks.

- Load the doom.jni.Natives class, also used by the C to Java callbacks: jNativesCls = (*env)->FindClass(env, "doom/jni/Natives").

- Load the doom.jni.Natives.OnImageUpdate and doom.jni.natives.OnStartSound Java methods. This is done for performance reasons, as these methods are called many times.

Listing 7-13 shows the native game loop.

Listing 7-13. *JNI Call to the Main Game Loop*

```
/*
 * Class:     doom_jni_Natives
 * Method:    DoomMain
 * Signature: ([Ljava/lang/String;)V
 */
JNIEXPORT jint JNICALL Java_doom_jni_Natives_DoomMain
  (JNIEnv * env, jclass class, jobjectArray jargv)
{
    // Obtain a global ref to the Java VM
    (*env)->GetJavaVM(env, &g_VM);

    // Extract char ** args from Java array
    jsize clen =  getArrayLen(env, jargv);

    char * args[(int)clen];

    int i;
    jstring jrow;
    for (i = 0; i < clen; i++)
    {
        jrow = (jstring)(*env)->GetObjectArrayElement(env, jargv, i);
        const char *row  = (*env)->GetStringUTFChars(env, jrow, 0);

        args[i] = malloc( strlen(row) + 1);
        strcpy (args[i], row);

        jni_printf("Main argv[%d]=%s", i, args[i]);

        // Free Java string jrow
        (*env)->ReleaseStringUTFChars(env, jrow, row);
    }

    /*
     * Load the Image update class (called many times)
     */
    jNativesCls = (*env)->FindClass(env, CB_CLASS);

    if ( jNativesCls == 0 ) {
        jni_printf("Unable to find class: %s", CB_CLASS);
        return -1;
    }
```

```
    // Load doom.util.Natives.OnImageUpdate(char[])
    jSendImageMethod = (*env)->GetStaticMethodID(env, jNativesCls
            , CB_CLASS_IU_CB
            , CB_CLASS_IU_SIG);

    if ( jSendImageMethod == 0 ) {
        jni_printf("Unable to find method OnImageUpdate(): %s"
                , CB_CLASS);
        return -1;
    }

    // Load OnStartSound(String name, int vol)
    jStartSoundMethod = (*env)->GetStaticMethodID(env, jNativesCls
            , CB_CLASS_SS_CB
            , CB_CLASS_SS_SIG);

    if ( jStartSoundMethod == 0 ) {
        jni_printf("Unable to find method OnStartSound signature: %s "
                , CB_CLASS_SS_SIG);
        return -1;
    }

    // Invoke Doom's main sub. This will loop forever
    doom_main (clen, args);

    return 0;
}
```

Key and Motion Events

Key and motion events are posted via the extern symbol D_PostEvent, as shown in Listing 7-14. The event type (event_t) is defined by the engine and consists of the following:

- A type (0 for key down, 1 for key up, and 2 for mouse events)

- An ASCII key stored in event.data1 for key events

- A mouse button and x and y coordinates for mouse events, stored as event. data1 = MOUSE BUTTON, event.data2 = x, and event.data3 = y. Mouse buttons can be 1 for left, 2 for middle, or 3 for right.

Listing 7-14. *Posting Key and Motion Events with JNI*

```
/*
 * Class:     doom_util_Natives
 * Method:    keyEvent
 * Signature: (II)V
 */
extern void D_PostEvent (event_t* ev);

JNIEXPORT jint JNICALL Java_doom_jni_Natives_keyEvent
```

```
  (JNIEnv * env, jclass cls, jint type, jint key)
{
    event_t event;
    event.type = (int)type;
    event.data1 = (int)key;
    D_PostEvent(&event);

    return type + key;
}
/*
 * Class:     doom_util_Natives
 * Method:    motionEvent
 * Signature: (II)I
 */
JNIEXPORT jint JNICALL Java_doom_jni_Natives_motionEvent
  (JNIEnv * env, jclass cls, jint x, jint y, jint z)
{
    event_t event;
    event.type = ev_mouse;
    event.data1 = x;
    event.data2 = y;
    event.data3 = z;
    D_PostEvent(&event);
    return 0;
}
```

C to Java Callbacks

Table 7-5 shows the callbacks on the left side and the Java methods they invoke on the right. The callbacks can be divided into the following types:

- Graphics initialization (jni_init_graphics)

- Video buffer (jni_send_pixels)

- Sound and music (jni_start_sound, jni_start_music, jni_stop_music and jni_set_music_volume)

- Fatal errors (jni_fatal_error)

Table 7-5. C to Java Callbacks in jni_doom.c

C Method	Invoked Java Method
void jni_init_graphics(int width, int height)	static void OnInitGraphics(int w, int h)
void jni_send_pixels(int * data)	static void OnImageUpdate(int[] pixels)

Table 7-5. *C to Java Callbacks in jni_doom.c (continued)*

C Method	Invoked Java Method
void jni_start_sound (const char * name, int vol)	static void OnStartSound(byte[] name, int vol)
void jni_start_music (const char * name, int loop)	static void OnStartMusic(String name, int loop)
void jni_stop_music (const char * name)	static void OnStopMusic(String name)
void jni_set_music_volume (int vol)	static void OnSetMusicVolume(int volume)
void jni_fatal_error(const char * text)	static void OnFatalError(String message)

The callbacks must be inserted in the C code as explained in the next sections.

Graphics Initialization

Constants for the graphics initialization callback are defined in jni_doom.h, as shown in Listing 7-15. CB_CLASS_IG_CB indicates the Java method name OnInitGraphics. CB_CLASS_IG_SIG "(II)V" defines the signature: two integer parameters and a void return type, as shown in the next fragment:

```
#define CB_CLASS_IG_CB   "OnInitGraphics"
#define CB_CLASS_IG_SIG  "(II)V"
```

This callback also performs some critical steps:

- It attaches to the current thread with (*g_VM)->AttachCurrentThread (g_VM, &env, NULL). Here is where the global JVM reference comes into play. Furthermore, the JNI environment (env) will be used to invoke the callback.

- It allocates space for the Java pixel array (video buffer) used by jni_send_pixels using the width and height of the display: jImage = (*env)-> NewIntArray(env, width * height).

- It invokes the static void method doom.util.Natives.OnInitGraphics(width, height) using its method ID: (*env)->CallStaticVoidMethod(env, jNativesCls, METHOD_ID, ARGUMENTS), where ARGUMENTS are the width and height of the display. Note that the arguments must match the arguments in the Java method!

Listing 7-15. *Graphics Initialization*

```
/**
 * Fires when Doom graphics are initialized.
 * params: img width, height
 */
void jni_init_graphics(int width, int height)
```

251

```
{
    JNIEnv *env;

    if ( !g_VM) {
        printf("No JNI VM available.\n");
        return;
    }

    (*g_VM)->AttachCurrentThread (g_VM, (void **) &env, NULL);


    iSize = width * height;

    // Create a new int[] used by jni_send_pixels
    jImage = (*env)-> NewIntArray(env, iSize);

    // Call doom.util.Natives.OnInitGraphics(w, h);
    jmethodID mid = (*env)->GetStaticMethodID(env, jNativesCls
            , CB_CLASS_IG_CB
            , CB_CLASS_IG_SIG);

    if (mid) {
        (*env)->CallStaticVoidMethod(env, jNativesCls
                , mid
                , width, height);
    }
}
```

Video Buffer Callback

The video buffer callback is critical, and it must be lean and mean. It gets called continuously and must not create any objects (see Listing 7-16). Like the previous callback, it attaches to the current thread. It also calls the static void method doom.jni.Natives.OnImageUpdate(int[] pixels). But before calling this method, it must set the pixels into the Java array (jImage):

```
(*env)->SetIntArrayRegion(env, jImage, 0, iSize, (jint *) data)
```

data is an array of integers already formatted as 32-bit ARGB pixels, as required by Android, and iSize is the size of the display calculated in the previous callback.

Listing 7-16. *Sending Video Pixels*

```
/**
 * Image update Java callback. Gets called many times per sec.
 * It must not look up JNI classes/methods or create any objects; otherwise
 * the local JNI ref table will overflow & the app will crash
 */
void jni_send_pixels(int * data)
{
    JNIEnv *env;
```

```
    if ( !g_VM) {
        return;
    }

    (*g_VM)->AttachCurrentThread (g_VM, (void **) &env, NULL);

    // Send img back to Java.
    if (jSendImageMethod) {
        (*env)->SetIntArrayRegion(env, jImage, 0, iSize, (jint *) data);

        // Call Java method
        (*env)->CallStaticVoidMethod(env, jNativesCls
                , jSendImageMethod
                , jImage);
    }

}
```

Sound and Music Callbacks

The sound and music callbacks fire from the engine when a sound or background music must be played. In a perfect world, sound would be handled in the native layer; however, due to the lack of documentation and support for open audio standards in Android, requests are cascaded back to Java for processing.

There are four sound and music callbacks in Doom, with their names and signatures defined in the header jni_doom.h:

```
// doom.jni.Natives.OnStartSound(byte[] name, int volume)
#define CB_CLASS_SS_CB  "OnStartSound"
#define CB_CLASS_SS_SIG  "([BI)V"

// doom.jni.Natives.OnStartMusic (String name , int loop)
#define CB_CLASS_SM_CB  "OnStartMusic"
#define CB_CLASS_SM_SIG  "(Ljava/lang/String;I)V"

// doom.jni.Natives.OnStopMusic (String name )
#define CB_CLASS_STOPM_CB  "OnStopMusic"
#define CB_CLASS_STOPM_SIG  "(Ljava/lang/String;)V"

//   doom.jni.Natives.OnSetMusicVolume (int volume)
#define CB_CLASS_SETMV_CB  "OnSetMusicVolume"
#define CB_CLASS_SETMV_SIG  "(I)V"
```

Note the method signature for OnStartSound with ([BI)V, where [B represents an array of bytes (the name of the sound), I represents an integer (volume), and V is the return type of the method (void). Another interesting signature is OnStartMusic with (Ljava/lang/String;I)V, where Ljava/lang/String; means the class java.lang.String (enclosed in L;).

Listing 7-17 shows the implementation of these callbacks. They are pretty similar in nature, in that they all must attach to the current thread using the global JVM (g_VM). The following are some of the key aspects of the code:

- To create a Java byte array, you can use jbyteArray ARRAY = (*env)->
  NewByteArray(env, SIZE), where the words byte/Byte can be replaced with
  boolean/Boolean, int/Int, object/Object, and other primitive types, depending on
  your needs.

- To insert data into the array, use (*env)->SetByteArrayRegion(env, ARRAY,
  START, SIZE, (jbyte *) C_ARRAY), where Byte can be replaced with any Java
  primitive type.

- To call a static void method, use (*env)->CallStaticVoidMethod(env, CLASS,
  METHOD_ID, ARG1, ARG2,…).

- To release resources for an array, use (*env)->DeleteLocalRef(env, ARRAY).

Listing 7-17. *Cascading Sound and Music Requests Back to Java*

```
/**
 * Fires multiple times when a sound is played
 * @param name Sound name
 * @param volume
 */
void jni_start_sound (const char * name, int vol)
{
    /*
     * Attach to the curr thread; otherwise we get JNI WARNING:
     * threadid=3 using env from threadid=15 which aborts the VM
     */
    JNIEnv *env;

    if ( !g_VM) {
        return;
    }

    (*g_VM)->AttachCurrentThread (g_VM, (void **) &env, NULL);

    if ( jStartSoundMethod == 0 ) {
        jni_printf("BUG: Invalid Doom JNI method OnStartSound %s"
          , CB_CLASS_SS_SIG);
        return ;
    }

    // Create a new char[] used by jni_send_pixels
    // Used to prevent JNI ref table overflows
    int iSize = strlen(name);
    jbyteArray jSound = (*env)-> NewByteArray(env, iSize);

    (*env)->SetByteArrayRegion(env, jSound, 0, iSize, (jbyte *) name);

    // Call Java method
    (*env)->CallStaticVoidMethod(env, jNativesCls
            , jStartSoundMethod
            , jSound //(*env)->NewStringUTF(env, name)
```

```c
        , (jint) vol);

    (*env)->DeleteLocalRef(env,jSound);
}

/**
 * Fires when a background song is requested
 */
void jni_start_music (const char * name, int loop)
{
    /*
     * Attach to the curr thread; otherwise we get JNI WARNING:
     * threadid=3 using env from threadid=15 which aborts the VM
     */
    JNIEnv *env;

    if ( !g_VM) {
        return;
    }

    (*g_VM)->AttachCurrentThread (g_VM, (void **) &env, NULL);

    jmethodID mid = (*env)->GetStaticMethodID(env, jNativesCls
        , CB_CLASS_SM_CB
        , CB_CLASS_SM_SIG);

    if (mid) {
        (*env)->CallStaticVoidMethod(env, jNativesCls
                , mid
                , (*env)->NewStringUTF(env, name)
                , (jint) loop );

    }
}

/**
 * Fires when a background song is stopped
 */
void jni_stop_music (const char * name)
{
    /*
     * Attach to the curr thread; otherwise we get JNI WARNING:
     * threadid=3 using env from threadid=15 which aborts the VM
     */
    JNIEnv *env;

    if ( !g_VM) {
        return;
    }

    (*g_VM)->AttachCurrentThread (g_VM, (void **) &env, NULL);
```

```
    jmethodID mid = (*env)->GetStaticMethodID(env, jNativesCls
        , CB_CLASS_STOPM_CB
        , CB_CLASS_STOPM_SIG);

    if (mid) {
        (*env)->CallStaticVoidMethod(env, jNativesCls
                , mid
                , (*env)->NewStringUTF(env, name)
                );

    }
}

/**
 * Set bg msic vol callback
 */
void jni_set_music_volume (int vol) {
    JNIEnv *env;

    if ( !g_VM) {
        return;
    }

    (*g_VM)->AttachCurrentThread (g_VM, (void **) &env, NULL);

    jmethodID mid = (*env)->GetStaticMethodID(env, jNativesCls
        , CB_CLASS_SETMV_CB
        , CB_CLASS_SETMV_SIG);

    if (mid) {
        (*env)->CallStaticVoidMethod(env, jNativesCls
                , mid
                , (jint) vol
                );

    }

}
```

Fatal Errors

Fatal or unrecoverable errors occur in any type of software. In Doom, these errors are cascaded back to Java, where a message is presented to the user, and then the application aborts. The next fragment from jni_doom.h shows the callback name and signature for this task:

```
#define CB_CLASS_FATAL_CB  "OnFatalError"
#define CB_CLASS_FATAL_SIG  "(Ljava/lang/String;)V"
```

This callback is simple (see Listing 7-18). It works as follows:

- It attaches to the current thread, aborting if no JNI environment is available.

- It looks up the doom.jni.Natives Java class, aborting if not found.

- It looks up the doom.jni.Natives.OnFatalError(String) using the method name and signature.

- It calls the static void method.

Listing 7-18. *Cascading Fatal Errors*

```
/**
 * Called when a fatal error has occurred.
 * The receiver should terminate
 */
void jni_fatal_error(const char * text) {
    JNIEnv *env;

    if ( !g_VM) {
        printf("JNI FATAL: No JNI Environment available. %s\n", text);
        exit(-1);
    }

    (*g_VM)->AttachCurrentThread (g_VM, (void **) &env, NULL);

    if ( !env) {
        printf("JNI FATAL: Unable to attach to thread: %s.\n", text);
        exit(-1);
    }

    if ( !jNativesCls ) {
        jNativesCls = (*env)->FindClass(env, CB_CLASS);

        if ( jNativesCls == 0 ) {
                printf("JNI FATAL: Unable to find class: %s", CB_CLASS);
                exit(-1);
        }
    }
    jmethodID mid = (*env)->GetStaticMethodID(env, jNativesCls
        , CB_CLASS_FATAL_CB
        , CB_CLASS_FATAL_SIG);

    if (mid) {
        (*env)->CallStaticVoidMethod(env, jNativesCls
                , mid
                , (*env)->NewStringUTF(env, text) );
    }
    else {
        printf("JNI FATAL: Unable to find method: %s, signature: %s\n"
                , CB_CLASS_MSG_CB, CB_CLASS_MSG_SIG );
        exit (-1);
    }

}
```

Original Game Changes

In order for the JNI glue to work, changes are required to the original game engine. Some are simple, such as inserting calls to the C to Java callbacks; some are not so simple, such as removing invalid dependencies. Table 7-6 shows the original files and the changes required. Considering that the engine has a total of 90,000 lines of code, these changes are not that bad.

Table 7-6. *Changes Required to the Original Engine to Insert the JNI Glue*

File	Changes
i_main.c	Rename the main subroutine to doom_main.
i_system.c	In I_Error, insert jni_fatal_error.
i_sound.c	Comment SDL dependencies. In I_StartSound, insert start sound callback jni_start_sound.
s_sound.c	In S_SetMusicVolume, insert volume callback jni_set_music_volume.
i_video.c	Comment SDL dependencies. Insert code to build an Android ARBG pixel array from the video buffer. In I_SetRes, add JNI callback to initialize graphics. In I_FinishUpdate, send pixels to Java with jni_send_pixels.

These changes are explained in more detail in the next sections.

Renaming main

Let's start with the simplest change: renaming the main() subroutine in i_main.c so it can be invoked from the Java native Java_doom_jni_Natives_DoomMain, which will start the game from Java, as shown in the next fragment:

```
// In i_main.c
int main(int argc, char **argv)
int doom_main(int argc, char **argv)

// In jni_doom.c
extern int doom_main(int argc, char **argv);

JNIEXPORT jint JNICALL Java_doom_jni_Natives_DoomMain

  (JNIEnv * env, jclass class, jobjectArray jargv)

{
  ...
  doom_main (clen, args);
  ...
}
```

Once main is renamed to doom_main, simply add the extern symbol extern int doom_main(int argc, char **argv) to jni_doom.c and invoke it from the game starter function.

Inserting the Fatal Error Callback

Another simple change is to insert the C to Java callback jni_fatal_error whenever an unrecoverable error occurs. The changes occur in the I_Error function in the i_system.c file, as shown in Listing 7-19.

Listing 7-19. *Changes Required to i_system.c*

```
void I_Error (char *error, ...)
{
    va_list      argptr;
    static char  string[1024];

    // Message first.
    va_start (argptr,error);
    vsprintf (string, error ,argptr);
    va_end (argptr);

    // Shutdown. Here might be other errors.
    if (demorecording)
      G_CheckDemoStatus();

    D_QuitNetGame ();
    I_ShutdownGraphics();

    // Send the error back to JNI layer
    jni_fatal_error(string);

    // Something wrong has happened
    // OLD CODE -> exit(-1);
}
```

Commenting SDL Occurrences

The Doom engine is built on top of SDL, which is an open framework to access system resources such as sound and video hardware. Doom uses SDL to display video and play music. This is a relatively hard problem, as Android has no support for SDL. Thus, any SDL occurrence must be commented or removed and replaced by a JNI equivalent. This happens in two files: i_sound.c and i_video.c.

Changes to i_sound.c are simple and consist of commenting the sdl.h header file and inserting jni_doom.h instead, as shown in the next fragment:

```
#include <sdl.h>
#include "include/jni_doom.h"
```

Furthermore, any function that starts with SDL_ must be commented. Luckily, these functions do not affect the game flow itself, and thus they can be safely commented.

Sound System Changes

Other changes are required to i_sound.c to insert a call to jni_start_sound, as shown in Listing 7-20. The global variable S_sfx[id].name provides the sound name, which will be sent back to Java and loaded from the file system, along with its volume.

Listing 7-20. Changes Required to i_sound.c to Insert the jni_start_sound Callback

```c
int I_StartSound(int id, int channel, int vol, int sep, int pitch, int priority)
{
  const unsigned char* data;
  int lump;
  size_t len;

  // ...

  // The entries DSBSPWLK, DSBSPACT, DSSWTCHN
  // and DSSWTCHX are all zero-length sounds
  if (len<=8) return -1;

  /* Find padded length */
  len -= 8;
  // Do the lump caching outside the SDL_LockAudio/SDL_UnlockAudio pair
  // Use locking which makes sure the sound data is in a malloced area and
  // not in a memory mapped one
  data = W_LockLumpNum(lump);

  // JNI changes: Send a sound request to Java
  // id is the sound index, S_sfx[id].name (soundname)
  // vol = volume
  jni_start_sound(S_sfx[id].name , vol);

  // ...

  return channel;
}
```

Changes are also required to s_sound.c to insert a call to jni_set_music_volume (volume) to send the background music volume back to Java (see Listing 7-21). Note that this function is called within the game when the user changes the music volume from the options menu.

Listing 7-21. Changes Required to s_sound.c to Insert the Music JNI Callback

```c
void S_SetMusicVolume(int volume)
{
  // Return if music is not enabled
  if (!mus_card || nomusicparm)
    return;

  if (volume < 0 || volume > 15)
```

```
    I_Error("S_SetMusicVolume: Attempt to set music volume at %d", volume);

  // JNI Changes: Send a volume request to Java
  // volume = [0..100]
  jni_set_music_volume (volume);

  I_SetMusicVolume(volume);
  snd_MusicVolume = volume;
}
```

Video Buffer Changes

Here is where the toughest changes must be done. The file i_video.c is the one that renders the video buffer and uses SDL heavily. All SDL references must be removed and replaced with structures compatible with Android.

Down to the pipe, a video buffer is simply an array of packed colors, represented as either bytes indicating the index of a color in a color palette or integers specifying an RGB color. SDL uses a structure called SDL_Surface to encapsulate the video buffer as an array of bytes plus a palette used to map colors to the buffer. Consider the next fragment, which replaces the SDL screen with a similar structure called XImage (actually taken from the X11 structure of the same name).

```
static SDL_Surface *screen;     // OLD CODE
static XImage * image;          // NEW CODE
```

In Doom, SDL_Surface will be replaced with the equivalent XImage that holds the array of bytes for the video buffer. Note that the video buffer cannot be rendered directly to a display. Instead, it must be cascaded back to Java using the C to Java callbacks, where Android will take care of the actual rendering.

Because XImage doesn't exist, it must be written. This isn't difficult, as XImage is simply a C struct holding the width, height, and array of bytes for the video buffer, as shown in Listing 7-22.

Listing 7-22. *Video Buffer Image Object from i_video.c*

```
/********************************************************
 * Class XImage
 ********************************************************/
typedef struct Image XImage;

struct Image
{
  int width;
  int height;
  byte * data;
};

/**
 * Class Color
 */
typedef struct Color XColor;

struct Color
```

```
{
  int red;
  int green;
  int blue;
};

// The Image
XImage *              image;

/**
 * XImage Constructor
 */
XImage * XCreateImage(int width, int height)
{
    XImage * this = (XImage*) malloc(sizeof(XImage));

    // set width, height
    this->width = width;
    this->height = height;

    // allocate image buffer
    this->data = (byte *)malloc (width * height);

    return this;
}
/********************************************************
 * Class XImage
 ********************************************************/
```

In addition to XImage, you need a color palette used to map the bytes on XImage to ARGB colors used by Android. For this purpose, you use the struct XColor, which holds the red, green, and blue values of a color. You also need a function to allocate memory for the XImage given its width and height (XCreateImage). This function will allocate space for the image byte buffer. You must modify the palette upload function (I_UploadNewPalette) in i_video.c to use the new XColor structure, as shown in Listing 7-23.

Listing 7-23. *Setting the Color Palette in i_video.c*

```
// Color palette
static XColor * colours;

static void I_UploadNewPalette(int pal)
{
  // This is used to replace the current 256 colour cmap with a new one
  // Used by 256 colour PseudoColor modes

  static int cachedgamma;
  static size_t num_pals;

  if (V_GetMode() == VID_MODEGL)
    return;
```

```
  if ((colours == NULL) || (cachedgamma != usegamma)) {

    int pplump = W_GetNumForName("PLAYPAL");
    int gtlump = (W_CheckNumForName)("GAMMATBL",ns_prboom);

    register const byte * palette = W_CacheLumpNum(pplump);
    register const byte * const gtable = (const byte *)W_CacheLumpNum(gtlump)
     + 256*(cachedgamma = usegamma);

    register int i;

    num_pals = W_LumpLength(pplump) / (3*256);
    num_pals *= 256;

    if (!colours) {
      // First call - allocate and prepare colour array
      colours = malloc(sizeof(*colours)*num_pals);
    }

    // set the colormap entries
    for (i=0 ; (size_t)i<num_pals ; i++) {
      colours[i].red    = gtable[palette[0]];
      colours[i].green = gtable[palette[1]];
      colours[i].blue   = gtable[palette[2]];
      palette += 3;
    }

    W_UnlockLumpNum(pplump);
    W_UnlockLumpNum(gtlump);
    num_pals/=256;
  }
}
```

In Listing 7-23, the original SDL palette has been replaced by XColor * colours. Note that the Doom engine uses a 768-color palette (256 colors for each one of red, green, and blue). The palette is read from the game file, along with a gamma table (used to apply a brightness factor to each color). With this information, the palette is filled and kept in memory for later use.

The final change to i_video.c is the function that does the actual rendering, I_FinishUpdate (see Listing 7-24). This function uses the width and height of the screen to create an array of pixels (each one representing an Android packed ARGB color). It then loops through the array and uses the byte value from the screen buffer to look up the color from the palette:

```
byte b = screens[0].data[i];  // Video buffer byte
XColor color = colours[b];  // Palette color for that byte
```

It then constructs a 32-bit pixel using the RGB values of color:

```
pixels[i] = (0xFF << 24) | (color.red << 16) | (color.green << 8) | color.blue
```

Note that 0xFF << 24 represents the alpha (opacity) value of the pixel—fully visible in this case.

Finally, the array is sent back using the callback jni_send_pixels(pixels), where Android will do the rendering.

Listing 7-24. *Video Buffer Renderer Function from i_video.c*

```
void I_FinishUpdate (void)
{
  if (I_SkipFrame()) return;

  // Screen size
  int size = SCREENWIDTH * SCREENHEIGHT;

  // ARGB pixels
  int pixels[size], i;

  for ( i = 0 ; i < size ; i ++) {
      byte b = screens[0].data[i];

      XColor color = colours[b];

      pixels[i] = (0xFF << 24)
          | (color.red << 16)
          | (color.green << 8)
          | color.blue;
  }

  // Send pixels to Java
  jni_send_pixels(pixels);

}
```

At this point, the Doom engine is all set and ready for compilation.

Doom Library (DSO) Compilation

Listing 7-25 shows the Makefile for the DSO. It uses the compiler and linker helper scripts agcc and ald, created in Chapter 1. The default optimization level is set to 2. Other compilation flags include the following:

- -ffast-math: Use fast math.

- -Wall: Display all warnings.

- -nostdinc: Do not include standard header files.

The build targets are as follows:

- lib builds the DSO libdoom_jni.so.

- jni creates the JNI headers for doom.jni.Natives.java and places them in the include folder.

- deploy-lib deploys the DSO to the device using the SDK adb tool.

- clean cleans up the object files.

Listing 7-25. *Makefile for the Doom Engine DSO*

```
##############################################
# Android Makefile for Doom
##############################################
CC      = agcc
MACROS  = -DNORMALUNIX -DLINUX -DHAVE_NET -DUSE_SDL_NET -DHAVE_CONFIG_H
FLAGS   = -O2 -ffast-math -Wall -nostdinc

LINKER  = ald
LFLAGS  =
LIBS    =

MAIN_OBJS   = \
 am_map.o     m_cheat.o     p_lights.o  p_user.o    sounds.o \
 hu_lib.o     md5.o         p_map.o     r_bsp.o     s_sound.o \
 d_deh.o      hu_stuff.o    m_menu.o     p_maputl.o r_data.o  st_lib.o \
 d_items.o    i_main.o      m_misc.o     p_mobj.o    r_demo.o  st_stuff.o \
 d_main.o     info.o        p_plats.o   r_draw.o    tables.o \
 doomdef.o    i_sound.o     m_random.o   p_pspr.o    r_filter.o version.o \
 doomstat.o   i_system.o    p_ceilng.o   p_saveg.o   r_fps.o    v_video.o \
 p_checksum.o p_setup.o     r_main.o    wi_stuff.o \
 dstrings.o   p_doors.o     p_sight.o   r_patch.o   w_memcache.o \
 f_finale.o   jni_doom.o    p_enemy.o    p_spec.o    r_plane.o  w_mmap.o \
 f_wipe.o     lprintf.o     p_floor.o    p_switch.o r_segs.o   w_wad.o \
 g_game.o     m_argv.o      p_genlin.o   p_telept.o r_sky.o    z_bmalloc.o \
 m_bbox.o     p_inter.o     p_tick.o    r_things.o  z_zone.o \
 d_client.o  i_video.o i_network.o d_server.o

LIB    = ../bin/libdoom_jni.so
DYN    = ../bin/doom-cli

all: lib

jni:
    @echo "Creating JNI C headers..."
    javah -jni -classpath ../../bin -d include doom.jni.Natives
```

```
# DSO
lib:  $(MAIN_OBJS)
    @echo
    $(LINKER) -shared $(LFLAGS) $(LIB_PATHS) $(LIBS) -o $(LIB) \
        $(MAIN_OBJS) $(LIBRARIES)
    @echo
    @echo Done. Out file is $(LIB)
    @echo

.c.o:
    @echo
    $(CC) -fpic -c $(FLAGS) $(MACROS) $(INCLUDES) $<

# Deploy lib
deploy-lib: lib
    adb push $(LIB) /data/data/org.doom/files

clean:
    rm -f *.o $(EXE)
```

Testing Doom for Android in the Emulator

To test the game in the emulator, create a launch configuration within your Eclipse IDE, as follows:

1. From the main menu, select Run ➤ Run Configurations.

2. Enter a name for the configuration (Doom) and select the project
    ch07.Android.Doom.

3. Set the Launch Action as Launch Default Activity. Figure 7-4 shows the
    completed Run Configurations dialog box for this example.

4. Click Run.

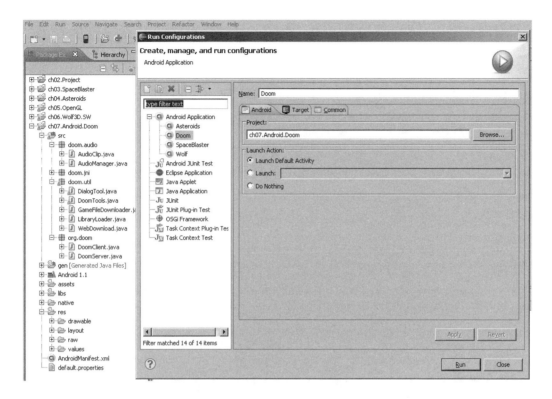

Figure 7-4. *Android run configuration for Doom*

Now let's play some Doom. From the emulator, click Menu ➤ Start and monitor the log view to make sure everything works. Consider the log fragment in Listing 7-26.

Listing 7-26. *Log Fragment from a Doom Run*

```
DEBUG/DoomClient(23981): Loading JNI librray from doom_jni
DEBUG/LibLoader(23981): Trying to load library doom_jni from LD_PATH: /system/lib
DEBUG/dalvikvm(23981): Trying to load lib /data/data/org.doom/lib/libdoom_jni.so 0x43733de8
DEBUG/dalvikvm(23981): Added shared lib /data/data/org.doom/lib/libdoom_jni.so 0x43733de8
DEBUG/dalvikvm(23981): No JNI_OnLoad found in /data/data/org.doom/lib/libdoom_jni.so↩
 0x43733de8
DEBUG/DoomTools(23981): Sound folder: /sdcard/doom/sound
DEBUG/DoomClient(23981): Starting doom thread with wad doom1.wad sound enabled? true↩
 Orientation:1
DEBUG/DoomClient(23981): **Doom Message: Main argv[0]=doom
DEBUG/DoomClient(23981): **Doom Message: Main argv[1]=-width
DEBUG/DoomClient(23981): **Doom Message: Main argv[2]=480
DEBUG/DoomClient(23981): **Doom Message: Main argv[3]=-height
DEBUG/DoomClient(23981): **Doom Message: Main argv[4]=320
DEBUG/DoomClient(23981): **Doom Message: Main argv[5]=-iwad
```

```
DEBUG/DoomClient(23981): **Doom Message: Main argv[6]=doom1.wad
DEBUG/DoomClient(23981): **Doom Message: I_UpdateVideoMode: 480x320 (fullscreen)↵
 default VM=8
DEBUG/DoomClient(23981): **Doom Message: I_SetRes: Creating 480x320 image.
```

The next two lines show the native library is loaded successfully by the JVM:

```
Trying to load lib /data/data/org.doom/lib/libdoom_jni.so
Added shared lib /data/data/org.doom/lib/libdoom_jni.so
```

So far, so good. Next, the game arguments are displayed:

```
**Doom Message: Main argv[0]=doom
**Doom Message: Main argv[1]=-width
**Doom Message: Main argv[2]=480
**Doom Message: Main argv[3]=-height
**Doom Message: Main argv[4]=320
**Doom Message: Main argv[5]=-iwad
**Doom Message: Main argv[6]=doom1.wad
```

This tells us the size of the display, 480-by-20 (landscape mode), plus the name of the game file, doom1.wad. At this point, the game has successfully loaded and is ready for action (see Figure 7-5).

Figure 7-5. *Doom running in the Android emulator*

You Have Done It

Congratulations! You have seen how easy it is to bring one of the first PC shooters to Android using a mix of Java and the original C engine. We have looked at the complexity of the game and the best way to implement it. We covered the following topics:

- The game architecture, where Java activities and UI XML layouts are glued with C subroutines using JNI native methods and C to Java callbacks

- The main activity, which is the Java class that controls the life cycle of the application, along with a UI layout

- User interface handlers, such as menus and key and touch event handlers, and native callback handlers for graphics initialization, video buffer updates, fatal errors, and audio requests

We have also looked at custom touch screen controls for phones that do not have a keyboard. You saw that the native interface class has callback listeners for clients that wish to receive C to Java callbacks, native methods invoked through JNI to start the game loop and send key and motion event information to the Native library, and C to Java callbacks used to delegate engine messages to the listener activity.

We have looked at the native layer that glues the Java and C code together and provides the native method implementations. Changes to the original code are also required to remove invalid dependencies and insert the C to Java callbacks. Finally, you saw the Makefile required to compile the Native library and the IDE launch configuration to test the game in the emulator.

Using the Java/C power combo, we have brought one of the great PC games, Doom, to the platform. Even though Google is pushing for Java-only development and provides little or no support for native development, Java alone is not the best choice when it comes to advanced mobile gaming. Java-only code works fine for the regular mobile app, but it is not enough for high-performance graphics.

I hope that the material in this book has opened a new frontier for you to explore, and you're excited about the possibility of bringing thousands of PC games to Android with minimal time and effort.

Deployment and Compilation Tips

In this appendix, we explore some helpful tips to deploy your application, NDK 1.5, and OpenGL tricks as well as compiling the native code in chapters 6 and 7 using the NDK for extra time savings. Specifically, this section includes tips for the following:

- Creating a key store for signature of you application package

- Signing you application using the workbench

- Compiling the project from Chapter 6 (Wolf 3D for Android) using NDK 1.5

- Adding custom support for OpenGL to the NDK 1.5.

- Compiling the project from Chapter 7 (Doom for Android) with NDK 1.6

Let's get started!

Signing Your Application

Before your application can be installed in any Android device, it must be signed using a Java key store. This section describes the steps you must follow to accomplish this task. You can find more details in the Android Developer Guide.

■ **Note** Android developers, more information about signing your applications is available at
`http://developer.android.com/guide/publishing/app-signing.html#setup`.

Creating a Key Store

A key store is a password-protected file that contains public/private key pairs used for JAR signatures. You can create a key store with the following command:

```
$ keytool -genkey -v -keystore my-release-key.keystore -alias alias_name -keyalg RSA↵
  -validity 10000 -storepass <password1> -keypass <password2>
```

Table A-1 lists the possible arguments for the keytool command.

Table A-1. *Arguments for the Keytool Command*

Argument	Description
-genkey	Generate a public and private key pair.
-v	Use verbose output.
-keystore	Specify the name of the key store.
-alias <alias_name>	Add an alias for the key pair.
-validity <valdays>	Specify the validity period in days.
-storepass <password>	Add a password for the key store.
-keypass <password>	Add a password for the key.

■ **Tip** When you run your applications in the emulator, the Eclipse workbench automatically signs the application using a debug key store. This key store can be found in %USERPROFILE%\debug.keystore (in Windows) and $HOME/.android/debug.keystore (in Linux). The debug key store password is "android", and the key alias and password are androiddebugkey/android.

Signing the Application

Prior to the Android SDK 1.5, the application signature had to be done manually using the Java SDK jarsigner command (see Listing A-1).

Listing A-1. *Windows Batch Script to Sign the Wolf3D Application Package (APK)*

```
@echo off
set JAVA_HOME=c:\Program Files\Java\jdk1.6.0_07
set PKG=c:\tmp\APK\Wolf3D.apk

rem To sign
"%JAVA_HOME%\bin\jarsigner" -verbose -keystore ar-release-key.keystore %PKG% android_radio

rem To verify that your .apk is signed, you can use a command like this
"%JAVA_HOME%\bin\jarsigner" -verbose -verify %PKG%
```

Listing A-1 uses the Java SDK `jarsigner` command and the key store created in the previous section to sign the packed application as follows:

```
jarsigner -verbose -keystore ar-release-key.keystore Wolfd3D.apk android_radio
```

The arguments are as follows:

- verbose displays information about the files being signed.

- keystore defines the location of the Java key store created in the previous section.

- Wolfd3D.apk is the application package to sign.

- android_radio is the alias that represents the public/private key pair used for signature.

■ **Caution** The `keytool` and `jarsigner` commands are part of the Java SDK, not the JRE. You will have to install a Java SDK and set up the paths in your system to be able to create a key store and sign your applications with `jarsigner`.

With the Android SDK 1.5 or later, signing your package is much easier, provided you already have a key store; you don't need the `jarsigner` command in this instance. To sign your package with the Eclipse workbench, follow these steps:

1. Right-click the project to be signed, and select Android Tools ➤ Export Signed Application Package (see Figure A-1).

2. In the "Keystore selection" dialog shown in Figure A-2, select "Use existing keystore," and navigate to the key store created previously. Type the password for the key store.

3. Select the alias that represents the key pair to be used for signature, and enter the corresponding password (see Figure A-3).

4. Enter the destination of the package as shown in Figure A-4. Click Finish.

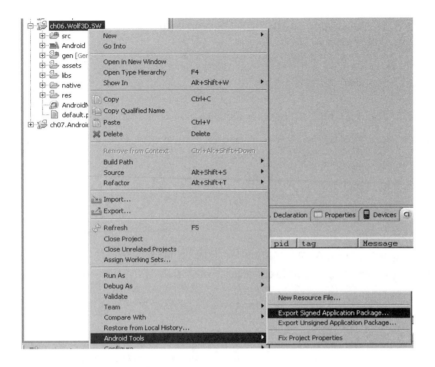

Figure A-1. *Exporting the application menu*

Figure A-2. *The "Keystore selection" dialog*

Figure A-3. The "Key alias selection" dialog

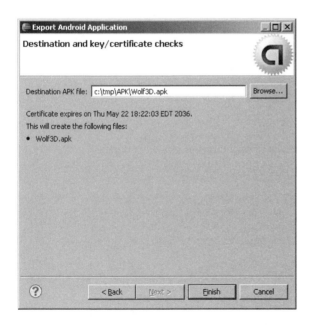

Figure A-4. Choosing the destination folder for the application package

Using the Android NDK to Compile Libraries from Chapters 6 and 7

In this section, we will compile the library from Chapter 6 (Wolf3D) using the NDK 1.5 as well as the Chapter 7 library (Doom for Android) using the NDK 1.6. Knowing how to use the NDK is important for you and can be a time saver if you have a slow system (such as a laptop/VMware combination). When I started writing the games in Chapters 6 and 7, the NDK didn't yet exist. That was the reason I used the CodeSourcery G++ toolkit; then along came the NDK 1.5. All in all, I don't advocate the use of the NDK 1.5, particularly at this early stage. The reasons I don't like to use the NDK 1.5 are simple:

- *Limited support for the C runtime*: The NDK includes only bare bones support for the stable portions of the C runtime (the portions that are very unlikely to change in the future). This limitation is stressed by Google in the documentation. The components supported are the C runtime (libc.so), Math library (libm.so), and Compression library (libz.so), and there's minimal support for C++. This level of C support is fine for a game like Wolf3D or Doom but is not enough for the advanced graphics, like OpenGL, that are required for more advanced games such as Quake. If you find yourself in the latter situation, you are forced to either translate all code to Java or hack the NDK to add support for OpenGL as explained in the section "Adding OpenGL Support."

- *Poor integration with the Eclipse workbench*: The NDK is a cumbersome and difficult tool to use at this point. For example, the output folder, where the library is compiled, is independent from your Eclipse workspace, and this disconnect forces you to copy the file every time you make changes. Although the output folder includes space for your Android project, this will force you to switch the workspace to every location instead of centralizing the workspace as we are used to with eclipse. The bottom line is that this tool needs to be integrated within the workbench so you can add native libraries and compile them on the fly along with the Java code, similar to the way the C Development Tools (CDT) work with the workbench.

- *Limited firmware support*: According to Google, the NDK supports only versions 1.5 or later of the firmware. This can be a problem if you wish to support other firmware versions, because 1.5 is fairly new and not supported in every device. Although Google claims that the NDK only supports firmware 1.5, I have been able to run native libraries in firmware 1.2 and 1.1 on the emulator.

- *No support for the media player, logging, and OpenGL*: Google has omitted the libraries that are likely to change in future releases. This omission makes sense but leaves many users in the dark when needing support for an advanced graphics, audio, or logging mechanism. If you're in this boat, you will have to install the header files and libraries manually.

Despite these caveats, the NDK is a very useful tool for working with native code that is worth using:

- It provides a fast compilation environment for Windows users that rely on VMware for compilation. This feature is very important, and the NDK is more than enough to replace your slow VMware Linux image (especially if you run it in a laptop) with the fast NDK, Cygwin, and Windows combination.

- It helps in debugging. In some cases, differences in the C compiler can cause runtime crashes and many issues that are difficult to debug. For example, the CodeSourcery G++ compiler used in this book is at version 4.3.x, while the NDK compiler is at 4.2.x. This difference can have a significant impact in the way programs run. As a matter of fact, I had crashes on libraries compiled with CodeSourcery that work just fine using the NDK. The NDK will ensure your library is on par with the C runtime running in the device.

All in all, the NDK is a good tool that can be a time saver once you get used to it. Plus, you can add manual library support to satisfy custom needs. In the next section, you'll learn how to use this tool to compile Wolf 3D from source.

Installing the Android NDK and Cygwin

Installing the Android NDK is simple. Just download the zip archive and uncompress it somewhere in your file system. You can get it at `http://developer.android.com/sdk/ndk/1.6_r1/index.html`.

If you are using a Windows system, you will also need Cygwin, the Linux-like environment for Windows. Cygwin installation can be a little time consuming but isn't difficult. Simply download the installer, and follow the easy instructions (make sure you select `GNU make` under development tools in the package selection page of the install). You can get the Cygwin installer at `http://www.cygwin.com/`.

■ **Tip** If using Cygwin, you must install `GNU make`. This tool is not enabled by default in the Cygwin installation wizard, and it is required by the Android NDK. Please read the NDK installation instructions under `NDK_HOME/docs/INSTALL.TXT` before your proceed!

Compiling Wolf 3D with the NDK 1.5

In this section, you will learn how to use the NDK to compile the native code in Chapter 6 in a Windows system running Cygwin. Take a look at the NDK folder structure. There are two folders that any application must use:

- app: This folder contains all the modules to be compiled.

- sources: This folder contains the code for every module in the app folder.

Let's compile the Wolf3D library using the NDK:

1. Create an application module folder in `NDK_HOME\apps\Wolf3D`.

2. Within the folder above you need to create the folder `NDK_HOME\apps\Wolf3D\ project\libs\armeabi`. This folder will contain the actual compiled library.

3. Create the application module descriptor file `NDK_HOME\apps\ Wolf3D\Application.mk`. This file describes the name of the module as follows:

```
APP_PROJECT_PATH := $(call my-dir)/project
APP_MODULES := wolf3d
```

In the preceding snippet, APP_MODULES is critical. It defines the name of the module and must match the application folder (Wolf3D). At the end of the process, the output library name will be named libwolf3d.so.

The next folder we need is an application source folder:

1. Create NDK_HOME\sources\Wolf3D. This folder will contain the native code.

2. Copy the contents from ch06.Wolf3D.SW/native/gp2xwolf3d into the Wolf3D folder created in step 1.

3. Create NDK_HOME\sources\Wolf3D\Android.mk. This is the Makefile used for compilation (see Listing A-2).

Listing A-2. *NDK Makefile for Wolf3D*

```
# Copyright (C) 2009 The Android Open Source Project
#
# Licensed under the Apache License, Version 2.0 (the "License");
# you may not use this file except in compliance with the License.
# You may obtain a copy of the License at
#
#       http://www.apache.org/licenses/LICENSE-2.0
#
# Unless required by applicable law or agreed to in writing, software
# distributed under the License is distributed on an "AS IS" BASIS,
# WITHOUT WARRANTIES OR CONDITIONS OF ANY KIND,
# See the License for the specific language governing permissions and
# limitations under the License.
#
LOCAL_PATH := $(call my-dir)

include $(CLEAR_VARS)

LOCAL_MODULE    := libwolf3d

LP := $(LOCAL_PATH)

INC := -Isources/Wolf3D/include

# optimization
OPTS := -O6 -ffast-math -fexpensive-optimizations -funroll-loops -fomit-frame-pointer

# compilation flags
LOCAL_CFLAGS := -DANDROID $(OPTS) $(INC)

LOCAL_LDLIBS :=
LOCAL_SHARED_LIBRARIES :=
```

```
FILES := objs.c misc.c id_ca.c id_vh.c id_us.c \
        wl_act1.c wl_act2.c wl_act3.c wl_agent.c wl_game.c \
        wl_inter.c wl_menu.c wl_play.c wl_state.c wl_text.c wl_main.c \
        wl_debug.c vi_comm.c sd_comm.c \
        wl_draw.c jni_wolf.c vi_null.c sd_null.c

LOCAL_SRC_FILES := $(FILES)

include $(BUILD_SHARED_LIBRARY)
```

Let's take a closer look to the variables defined in Listing A-2:

- LOCAL_PATH: This variable defines the local path of the module, NDK_HOME/sources/Wolf3D in this particular case.

- LOCAL_MODULE: This variable defines the name of the local module. It must match the module name (wolf3d) with the prefix lib, thus libwolf3d.

- LOCAL_CFLAGS: Here is where you can put the optimization flags of your choice and extra include directories (where C headers live). For Wolf 3D, I use

-Isources/Wolf3D/include

- LOCAL_SRC_FILES: These are the source files that compose the library.

The following actions will be executed during the make process:

- include $(CLEAR_VARS): This action clears previous values of the local variables used by the module.

- include $(BUILD_SHARED_LIBRARY): This action tells the compilation project to build a shared library.

Types of libraries in Linux

The types of libraries that can be compiled with the NDK can be confusing for the newcomer:

- *Shared libraries*: These are loaded dynamically by an executable at runtime. In Linux, they use the naming convention lib<SOME_NAME>.so. For example, libwolf3d.so is the shared library used by our project.

- *Static libraries*: These are binary code archives that will be included into a master shared library at compile time. They use the naming convention lib<SOME_NAME>.a.

Compiling the Shared Library

Finally, we are ready to go. Start the compilation process by typing the following within the NDK home folder (see Figure A-5):

```
$make APP=Wolf3D
```

■ **Tip** Make sure you type the previous command within the NDK `root` folder. Furthermore, if you use Windows, you must use the Cygwin console to do so, as shown in Figure A-5.

```
➤ /cygdrive/c/eclipse-SDK/android-ndk-1.5_r1                              _ □ x

Owner@TOSHIBA-USER /cygdrive/c/eclipse-SDK/android-ndk-1.5_r1
$ make APP=Wolf3D
Android NDK: Building for application 'Wolf3D'
Compile thumb   : wolf3d <= sources/Wolf3D/objs.c
Compile thumb   : wolf3d <= sources/Wolf3D/misc.c
Compile thumb   : wolf3d <= sources/Wolf3D/id_ca.c
Compile thumb   : wolf3d <= sources/Wolf3D/id_vh.c
Compile thumb   : wolf3d <= sources/Wolf3D/id_us.c
Compile thumb   : wolf3d <= sources/Wolf3D/wl_act1.c
Compile thumb   : wolf3d <= sources/Wolf3D/wl_act2.c
Compile thumb   : wolf3d <= sources/Wolf3D/wl_act3.c
Compile thumb   : wolf3d <= sources/Wolf3D/wl_agent.c
Compile thumb   : wolf3d <= sources/Wolf3D/wl_game.c
Compile thumb   : wolf3d <= sources/Wolf3D/wl_inter.c
Compile thumb   : wolf3d <= sources/Wolf3D/wl_menu.c
Compile thumb   : wolf3d <= sources/Wolf3D/wl_play.c
Compile thumb   : wolf3d <= sources/Wolf3D/wl_state.c
Compile thumb   : wolf3d <= sources/Wolf3D/wl_text.c
Compile thumb   : wolf3d <= sources/Wolf3D/wl_main.c
Compile thumb   : wolf3d <= sources/Wolf3D/wl_debug.c
Compile thumb   : wolf3d <= sources/Wolf3D/vi_comm.c
Compile thumb   : wolf3d <= sources/Wolf3D/sd_comm.c
Compile thumb   : wolf3d <= sources/Wolf3D/wl_draw.c
Compile thumb   : wolf3d <= sources/Wolf3D/jni_wolf.c
Compile thumb   : wolf3d <= sources/Wolf3D/vi_null.c
Compile thumb   : wolf3d <= sources/Wolf3D/sd_null.c
SharedLibrary   : libwolf3d.so
Install         : libwolf3d.so => apps/Wolf3D/project/libs/armeabi

Owner@TOSHIBA-USER /cygdrive/c/eclipse-SDK/android-ndk-1.5_r1
$
```

Figure A-5. Compiling Wolf3D using the NDK within the Cygwin console

The output library `libwolf3d.so` will be created in the application folder `NDK_HOME/apps/Wolf3D/project/libs/armeabi`. You can copy this file to your project workspace folder of the same name (`libs/armeabi`).

Adding Support for OpenGL to the NDK 1.5

One of the limitations of the NDK 1.5 is the lack of support for OpenGL. Although Google discourages the use of this native API due to its unstable nature, you can manually add support for it within the NDK by following two simple steps. In this section, you will learn how to add support for OpenGL to the NDK. This is a critical tool if you are bringing games to the platform that use native OpenGL calls. In my case, I used this technique to get the native code from the great game Quake to compile for the Android platform. I hope it will be as useful for you as it was for me.

You need to add support for two things to use custom APIs with the NDK:

- *Header files*: These are required for compilation. The problem is that they are not distributed with the NDK source, which means you will need to obtain them by other means (from the Android source, perhaps).

- *Native libraries*: The native libraries are required to link the final library.

In the case of OpenGL, the best bet is to download the Android source to obtain the header files. This can be a time consuming but necessary step (Chapter 1 shows how to do this). Next, assuming that you have downloaded the Android source to a Windows PC under `c:\tmp\mydroid`, follow the next steps to setup OpenGL

1. Copy the OpenGL header file folders `EGL` and `GLES` from the Android source (located in `c:\tmp\mydroid\frameworks\base\opengl\include`) to `NDK_HOME\build\platforms\android-1.5\arch-arm\usr\include` (see Figure A-6).

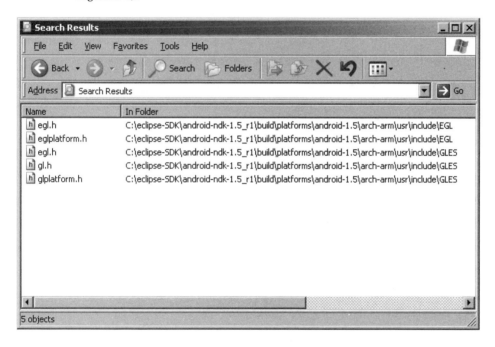

Figure A-6. *OpenGL header files within the NDK*

2. Next, you need to copy OpenGL libraries to `NDK_HOME\build\ platforms\android-1.5\arch-arm\usr\lib`, as shown in Figure A-7.

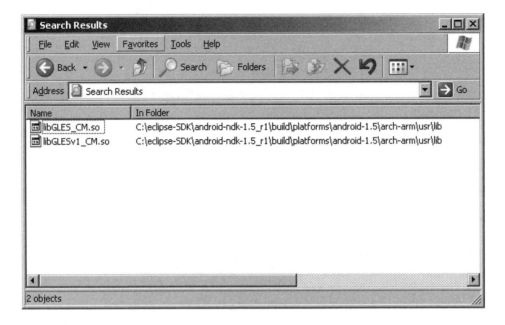

Figure A-7. *OpenGL libraries within the NDK*

You can extract the OpenGL library from the device using the console command:

```
adb pull /system/lib/libGLESv1_CM.so libGLESv1_CM.so
```

■ **Tip** Note that libGLESv1_CM.so is the name of the OpenGL library for firmware version 1.2 or later, and libGLES_CM.so is for firmware version 1.0. This means that libraries compiled for firmware 1.2 or later will not run in firmware 1.0.

Compiling Doom with NDK 1.6

If you read this book carefully, you'll get the sense that that I don't like the NDK 1.5 (when I started in this project the NDK didn't even exist). I think the NDK 1.5 is cumbersome to use, because of the lack of integration with the Eclipse workbench. Plus, version 1.5 has only the bare bones to compile a native library (that is, the C runtime, Compression library, and basic C++ support). Just when this book was being finished up, Google released the NDK 1.6, a nice improvement over 1.5. Here are the highlights of this new version:

- The sources folder from the NDK folder structure is gone (see the section on Wolf 3D and NDK 1.5). Now, all code (Java and native) lives in the apps folder. Within the apps folder, the project folder contains the Android Java project, and within project, the jni folder contains the native code and the Makefile Android.mk.

- NDK 1.6 adds support for OpenGL ES 2.0. This welcome addition will help many 3D games out there.

I would recommend the NDK over the CodeSourcery G++ compiler if you have a slow system such as a laptop or VMware combination or if your library crashes mysteriously, perhaps because of GNU compiler version issues, which can happen in programs that are not highly portable. Discrepancies in the GNU compiler version (for example, CodeSourcery uses GCC 4.3.x instead of Android's 4.2.x) can cause optimization errors and other types of runtime errors that ultimately crash the game.

All in all, NDK 1.6 is a good improvement but still has far to go to catch up with other powerful tools, such as Apple's iPhone Xcode platform. For example, the NDK will recompile the entire library if you change the Makefile, Android.mk (too add a new source file for example). This is really annoying when you have a big library with lots of source files. Other tools such as GNU make will detect the changes and recompile only the right files in the library. Anyway, for Doom, the folder structure for NDK 1.6 should look as follows:

- android-ndk-1.6_r1/apps/Doom/Application.mk: This file defines the module name to be built.

- android-ndk-1.6_r1/apps/Doom/project: This folder contains the actual Android project for the game.

- android-ndk-1.6_r1/apps/Doom/project/jni: This folder contains the native code and the Makefile, Android.mk.

Here is how you get Doom to compile with NDK 1.6:

1. Create android-ndk-1.6_r1/apps/Doom/Application.mk. This file contains the module (doom) that we are building:

```
APP_PROJECT_PATH := $(call my-dir)/project
APP_MODULES      := doom
```

2. Create the folder android-ndk-1.6_r1/apps/Doom/project. Copy the Android project from ch07.Android.Doom to this folder. You don't need to copy the native folder (this is the native code).

3. Create the folder android-ndk-1.6_r1/apps/Doom/project/jni, and copy the native code from ch07.Android.Doom/native/prboom.

4. Create a Makefile called Android.mk in android-ndk-1.6_r1/apps/Doom/project/jni. This make file should look as follows:

```
LOCAL_PATH := $(call my-dir)

# clear vars
include $(CLEAR_VARS)

# module name
LOCAL_MODULE := doom
```

```
LP := $(LOCAL_PATH)

# doom folder
DOOM := apps/Doom/project/jni

# includes
INC := -I$(DOOM) -I$(DOOM)/include

DOOM_FLAGS := -DNORMALUNIX -DLINUX -DHAVE_CONFIG_H

OPTS := -O3 -ffast-math  -fexpensive-optimizations
LOCAL_CFLAGS := $(DOOM_FLAGS)  $(OPTS) $(INC)

# sources
LOCAL_SRC_FILES           := \
am_map.c    m_cheat.c    p_lights.c p_user.c    sounds.c \
hu_lib.c      md5.c         p_map.c    r_bsp.c     s_sound.c \
d_deh.c    hu_stuff.c    m_menu.c    p_maputl.c r_data.c    st_lib.c \
d_items.c        m_misc.c      p_mobj.c    r_demo.c    st_stuff.c \
d_main.c   info.c          p_plats.c   r_draw.c    tables.c \
doomdef.c        m_random.c   p_pspr.c    r_filter.c version.c \
doomstat.c       p_ceilng.c   p_saveg.c   r_fps.c     v_video.c \
p_checksum.c p_setup.c   r_main.c    wi_stuff.c \
dstrings.c   p_doors.c    p_sight.c   r_patch.c   w_memcache.c \
f_finale.c       p_enemy.c    p_spec.c    r_plane.c   w_mmap.c \
f_wipe.c    lprintf.c    p_floor.c   p_switch.c r_segs.c    w_wad.c \
g_game.c    m_argv.c     p_genlin.c  p_telept.c r_sky.c     z_bmalloc.c \
m_bbox.c         p_inter.c    p_tick.c    r_things.c z_zone.c \
d_client.c   d_server.c \
droid/i_video.c droid/i_network.c droid/i_joy.c \
droid/i_system.c droid/i_main.c droid/i_sound.c \
droid/jni_doom.c

# Build libdoom.so
include $(BUILD_SHARED_LIBRARY)
```

5. Finally, run make APP=Doom from the NDK root folder android-ndk-1.6_r1. The output library libdoom.so will be stored in Doom/project//libs/armeabi and ready to use. Import Doom/project into your Eclipse workspace, and start the game.

Final Thoughts

I hope that you have enjoyed *Pro Android Games*. I wrote this book to show you the things that can be done with two powerful languages: Java and C. I have shown how one person can bring a complex PC game to Android with little effort in record time using these two great languages. I'd like to finish up with the things I liked and disliked about writing software for Android as opposed to other mobile platforms, such as the iPhone OS. You may not agree with my statements, but they could be useful in your game development career. These are the limitations in Android I have found writing the games for this book:

- *Lack of an open audio library*: I consider this to be a serious limitation. Audio is critical in gaming, and most vendors nowadays try to use open APIs such Open Audio Library (AL) or the standard Linux sound devices. Up to version 2.0, Android uses the SoniVox Enhanced Audio System (EAS).

- *Lack of streaming audio*: This is another serious issue. I found the lack of streaming audio to be the most frustrating thing about Android. I don't mind learning the EAS audio API, but the darn thing doesn't even support audio streaming? Audio streaming is critical and used extensively by Wolfenstein 3D and Doom in Chapters 6 and 7. To overcome this shortcoming, I was forced to cascade audio events to the Java layers, put the soundtracks in external files, and have the MediaPlayer handle them. In Android, you are boxed in by the MediaPlayer. Although I have heard that Google is planning support for OpenAL (audio library); this would be a good move.

- *Lack of support for native development*: I am happy to see that Google has realized how critical native development support will be if Android is to become a competitor in the mobile gaming arena. With the release of the Android NDK 1.6, things have improved greatly, but Android still lags behind the iPhone OS in this field.

- *Only basic OpenGL ES implementation*: As of version 1.5 of the SDK, Android implemented OpenGL ES 1.x. The iPhone OS has been supported OpenGL ES 2.0 for a long time now. Although I am happy to report that, with firmware 2.0, Android implements OpenGL ES 2.0, development in this area still lags behind the iPhone.

On the other hand, Android has some great features that make it a serious contender as a mobile development platform:

- *Open source*: An army of developers is out there ready to build code for this open platform, and new devices are popping out all the time.

- *Built on Linux*: I love Linux, and I am always ready to support development in this beautiful OS. It is a masterpiece of software engineering.

- *Multitasking*: multitasking as an advantage is in the eye of the beholder (I am not sure where to put this one). In one hand, there are some who say that multitasking is great for social networking applications, because you can have multiple background processes feeding you information, but detractors claim that it hogs the CPU resources and diminishes battery life. I have to go with the detractors on this one.

All in all, I am happy to see that, with the release of the NDK 1.6, Google is realizing the need for native development if Android is to be serious contender to the iPhone OS for gaming. Android has a way to go to catch up, but the platform development seems to run at a tremendous pace. Android versus the iPhone OS—I can't wait to see who wins. At the moment, my money is on the iPhone OS, but my heart is with Android.

Index

■X, Y, Z

You Need the Companion eBook

Your purchase of this book entitles you to buy the companion PDF-version eBook for only $10. Take the weightless companion with you anywhere.

We believe this Apress title will prove so indispensable that you'll want to carry it with you everywhere, which is why we are offering the companion eBook (in PDF format) for $10 to customers who purchase this book now. Convenient and fully searchable, the PDF version of any content-rich, page-heavy Apress book makes a valuable addition to your programming library. You can easily find and copy code—or perform examples by quickly toggling between instructions and the application. Even simultaneously tackling a donut, diet soda, and complex code becomes simplified with hands-free eBooks!

Once you purchase your book, getting the $10 companion eBook is simple:

❶ Visit **www.apress.com/promo/tendollars/**.

❷ Complete a basic registration form to receive a randomly generated question about this title.

❸ Answer the question correctly in 60 seconds, and you will receive a promotional code to redeem for the $10.00 eBook.

233 Spring Street, New York, NY 10013

Offer valid through 4/10.